MEDIA HOUSES

PETER LANG
New York • Washington, D.C./Baltimore • Bern
Frankfurt • Berlin • Brussels • Vienna • Oxford

MEDIA HOUSES

Architecture, Media, and the Production of Centrality

EDITED BY
STAFFAN ERICSON AND KRISTINA RIEGERT

PETER LANG
New York • Washington, D.C./Baltimore • Bern
Frankfurt • Berlin • Brussels • Vienna • Oxford

Library of Congress Cataloging-in-Publication Data
Media houses: architecture, media and the production of centrality /
edited by Staffan Ericson, Kristina Riegert.
p. cm.
Includes bibliographical references and index.
1. Architecture and society—History—20th century.
2. Architecture and society—History—21st century. 3. Mass media—
Social aspects—History—20th century. 4. Mass media—Social aspects—
History—21st century. 5. Space (Architecture)—History—20th century.
6. Space (Architecture)—History—21st century. I. Ericson, Staffan.
II. Riegert, Kristina. III. Title: Architecture, media and the production of centrality.
NA2543.S6M44   720.1'03—dc22   2009049019
ISBN 978-1-4331-0584-5 (hardcover)
ISBN 978-1-4331-0583-8 (paperback)

Bibliographic information published by **Die Deutsche Nationalbibliothek**.
Die Deutsche Nationalbibliothek lists this publication in the "Deutsche
Nationalbibliografie"; detailed bibliographic data is available
on the Internet at http://dnb.d-nb.de/.

Grateful acknowledgment for the research partnership with the project
"Tuning In:Diasporic Contact Zones at the BBC World Service,"
(Grant Award Reference:AH/ES58693/1)

Cover image: 1958 sketch of Ostankino Tower, from Leonid Batalov's archive,
printed with kind permission from Andrei Batalov

© 2010 Peter Lang Publishing, Inc., New York
29 Broadway, 18th floor, New York, NY 10006
www.peterlang.com

All rights reserved.
Reprint or reproduction, even partially, in all forms such as microfilm,
xerography, microfiche, microcard, and offset strictly prohibited.

Contents

Acknowledgements. vii
Chapter One: Introduction
    Staffan Ericson, Kristina Riegert, and Patrik Åker. 1
Chapter Two: The Interior of the Ubiquitous: Broadcasting House, London
    Staffan Ericson. 19
Chapter Three: The End of the Iconic Home of Empire: Pondering the Move
of the BBC World Service from Bush House
    Kristina Riegert. 59
Chapter Four: Ostankino TV Tower, Moscow: An Obsession with Space
    Patrik Åker. 81
Chapter Five: Googleplex and Informational Culture
    Peter Jakobsson and Fredrik Stiernstedt. 113
Chapter Six: Edge Blending: Light, Crystalline Fluidity, and the Materiality of
New Media at Gehry's IAC Headquarters
    Shannon Mattern. 137
Chapter Seven: Looping Ideology: The CCTV Center in Beijing
    Sven-Olov Wallenstein. 163
Chapter Eight: Real TV: Architecture as Social Media
    Helena Mattsson. 183

Contributors.. 205
Index... 209

Acknowledgements

This book is very much the result of a collaboration between the members of the Media Houses project, led by Staffan Ericson and Patrik Åker and financed by the Baltic Sea Foundation, with extra support from the research program Techno-Cult (www.technocult.se) and Södertörn University's Publications Committee. We are grateful for their continuing encouragement.

Mark Hines, formerly of MacCormac Jamieson Prichard Architects (MJP) and project architect for the renovation of Broadcasting House, generously provided his time and expertise for chapter two. The BBC Archives, MJP Architects, and The Architectural Review assisted with illustrations. We are grateful for the collaboration with "Tuning In: Diasporic Contact Zones at the BBC World Service," a project headed by Marie Gillespie at Open University, for the help with the design and implementation of the study in chapter three. In Moscow, Yassen Zassoursky, Lena Degtereva, Olga Korobeynikova, Ludmila Voronova and Anna Kozlova, all at Moscow State University, were instrumental in many capacities. Thanks also go to Natalia Arshavskaya (The Shukhov Tower Foundation) and Sergey Alexandrov (Ostankino TV tower), and all who helped us at the Moscow Museum of Architecture and at the Ostankino Television Center. We would like to especially thank Andrei Batalov (Moscow Kremlin Museums) for graciously allowing us to use the pictures from his father's archive (in chapter 4). The field work in Beijing was greatly facilitated by Håkan Lindhoff (JMK, Stockholm University), Lena

Rydholm (Uppsala University) and Leif Dahlberg (Royal Institute of Technology) on this end, and in Beijing Zengzhi Shi and Alfred Peng (both at Beijing University), Zhengrong Hu (University of China), Wu Jing (Beijing University), Liu Ning and Chen Yan (at CCTV). For the study in chapter six, we wish to thank Shannon Johnson at IAC and Emily Chapman at STUDIOS Architecture.

Earlier drafts of these articles have been discussed at various research conferences: among them IAMCR in Cairo 2006, ACSIS 2007 in Norrköping, ICA in Montreal 2008 and Chicago 2009, CRESC's 2006 conference on "Media and Social Change" in Oxford, Theory, Culture & Society's 2007 conference on "Ubiquitous Media" in Tokyo, and Texas A & M's conference on "New Media Worlds" in 2008. We collectively thank the organisers and participants. We are also grateful for the closer readings given by André Jansson, Amanda Lagerkvist, Göran Bolin, Nick Couldry at different stages of the project. Finally, we are indebted to our editor Mary Savigar and production editor Bernadette Shade at Peter Lang, whose continuous encouragement and enthusiasm for this project helped to bring this book to fruition.

CHAPTER ONE

Introduction

STAFFAN ERICSON, KRISTINA RIEGERT, PATRIK ÅKER

Do modern societies have a center? If so, where are they situated? During the twentieth century, social theory has tended to stress the role of the media in the framing of such centers: for instance, in representing a "public sphere" (Habermas 1961/1989) where common matters are debated, or in staging "media events" that produce social cohesion and cultural identity (Dayan & Katz 1992). Such "centers" are not necessarily conceived in terms of actual places or territories. In fact, the emergence of "non-localized" publics, of social interaction taking place within a "de-spatialized simultaneity," is widely regarded as one of the media's major influences on modern social life (cf. Thompson 1995). These very developments also invite the assumption that the media themselves are the occupiers of our social center. In the words of Michael Real, the media "serve as the central nervous system of modern society" (1989, p. 13)–since it is through them that we connect to our fellow human beings, become aware of other parts of the social whole, gain access to the most important realities of our world.

It is this figure of thought–vaguely expressed here, but surely familiar to most readers of media theory–that has been challenged by Nick Couldry (2003, 2004, 2006), in what he called "the myth of the mediated center." What must be challenged, according to Couldry, is (1) the idea that society *has* a center, and (2) the idea that we gain access to that center through the media.

> In reality, and whatever the competing pressures of social centralisation and (we should not forget) the rival pressures of decentralisation, there is no such social center that acts as a moral or cognitive foundation for society and its values, and therefore no natural role for the media as that "center´s" interpreter, but there are enormous pressures to believe in each. (Couldry 2003, p. 45)

Couldry is not denying the existence of various *claims* that place the media at the center of modern society—these are to be expected from institutions or people whose positions in different ways rely on the media. What he is arguing is that such claims are always to be regarded as "constructions" and never as expressions of some "deeper," more "natural" truth about modern society. Furthermore, that academic media studies have had the unfortunate tendency to subscribe to, even reproduce, such claims and constructions, ignoring the lack of empirical evidence in their support, preferring to direct our attention to the dominant media institutions, the most spectacular events, the largest audiences, framing these with theories that reinforce the integrating power of the media. Since these theories fail to challenge the media's own distribution of symbolic power, they also naturalize various hierarchies between those "inside" and those "outside" the media (Couldry claims many of these tendencies can be found in Dayan & Katz's seminal book *Media Events: The Live Broadcasting of History*.)

In several ways, Couldry's points are immediately sobering. Still, to discard the whole notion of a mediated center as "mythology" is a bold move that should evoke new questions: What would count as empirical evidence for or against this notion? What are the further implications of the denial of the "real" existence of the mediated center? To what extent is it even possible to distinguish between the "constructed" and the "real" in the case of, for instance, contemporary media events?

The project from which this book emanates did not, however, start out with such tricky questions, rather with the simple observation that the activity of modern media *has* produced "centers," which certainly appear real, spatial, tangible, material. In most capitals of the modern world, most citizens know where they stand: the headquarters of the national radio and television companies or the major newspapers. These buildings are often imposing, at times monumental. Under certain conditions, they are obviously perceived as fortresses of power (as in times of political crisis, when they are sites of demonstrations and/or military incidents). Their external authority, though, will often differ from the traditions of the church, the state, and the museum.

Unlike other features in a modern cityscape—the mall, the stadium, the movie theatre—these houses are not sites for collective experiences. Most of us will never see their interiors, as the boundary between "inside" and "outside" is upheld by electronic gates and security guards. Still, these buildings are presented to the public as civic centers: in most cases, they are surrounded by parks, or connected to squares, that appear to invite outsiders to come closer. Often, there will be guided pathways into the interiors: the observation decks of the towers, so that we may see what the outside looks like from the inside, the sets of the studios, so that the production going on inside is made transparent. Transparency is, in fact, often a dominant theme in the external organization of such buildings, as if the use of glass would erase the boundary between inside and outside. So, what sort of power is being represented here? What sort of centrality? And how are we to distinguish between what is mythical, constructed, real, in such representations?

In his countermove to the myth of the mediated center, Couldry suggests that "only by imagining mediation as something other than the 'necessary' expression of a social 'center' can we address the *depth* of the current crises of public communication" (2003, p. 141). This book is rather an attempt to think about *how* the notion of the media as a social center is expressed, through media houses that are built in different time periods and in different parts of the world. It deals with the ways this "myth" is given physical, architectural form, and how this process may be linked to real, historical power: How do these buildings communicate demarcations of "inside" and "outside" the media, or between the "private" and the "public"? To what extent do their architectural form and organization reflect different media technologies and ideologies? How are these influenced by relations between the nation and media institutions; between the state and architects and town planners, and indeed between these and the public at large?

Did This Kill That?

One should not expect the conceptual unification of the categories "media" and "architecture" to proceed smoothly. After all, the historical evolution of the former has often been described in terms of the dissolution of the latter. *Ceci tuera cela*—this will kill that—is the famous prophecy uttered by Frollo, the fifteenth-century arch-deacon in Victor Hugo's *The Hunchback of Notre Dame* (1831). "This," which kills, is Gutenberg's printing press, and "that," which is killed, is Frollo's cathedral. Hugo uses a separate chapter of the novel to explicate this prophecy in detail: Frollo's concern that "the book is about to kill the edifice" indicates a historical shift of power ("the press will kill the church"), but also, more importantly, a change in the dominant expression of human ideas ("printing will kill architecture"). According to Hugo, architecture had served as the "great book of humanity" from the beginning of time,

> . . . in that architecture was, down to the fifteenth century, the chief register of humanity; that in that interval not a thought which is in any degree complicated made its appearance in the world, which has not been worked into an edifice; that every popular idea, and every

religious law, has had its monumental records; that the human race has, in short, had no important thought which it has not written in stone. And why? Because every thought, either philosophical or religious, is interested in perpetuating itself; because the idea which has moved one generation wishes to move others also, and leave a trace. (Hugo 1831/2009)

Hugo notes some of the more obvious gains when recording human thought in books of paper, not stone, in terms of costs, production time, transportability. The true reason the invention of the printing press is to be regarded as the "greatest event in history," however, is the way the expression of human thought is transformed from "mass" into "ubiquity." With the change from architecture to printing, what was "solid" has "become alive," what was limited by "duration in time" may pass into "immortality":

> In its printed form, thought is more imperishable than ever; it is volatile, irresistible, indestructible. It is mingled with the air. In the days of architecture it made a mountain of itself, and took powerful possession of a century and a place. Now it converts itself into a flock of birds, scatters itself to the four winds, and occupies all points of air and space at once. (Ibid.)

A little more than a century later, the idea of human thought—and images and sounds—that "mingles with the air" will cut deeper into social experience, with the arrival of broadcast radio and television. The opening scenario of Joshua Meyrowitz's (1985) *No Sense of Place*, a study of how the electronic media have changed our sense of situational geography, suggests the collapse of a spatial structure:

> Perhaps the best analogy for the process of change described in this book is an architectural one. Imagine that many of the walls that separate rooms, offices, and houses in our society were suddenly moved or removed and that many once distinct situations were suddenly combined. Under such circumstances, the distinctions between our private and public selves and between the different selves we project in different situations might not entirely disappear, but they would certainly change. (Meyrowitz 1985, p. 6)

Meyrowitz's book is by now held to be a seminal text of the so-called "spatial turn" of media studies. This is a turn that demands that we focus our attention on the ways in which "media take place and claim space" (Löfgren 2006, p. 298). Or, with a different formulation, how we may "think media and space, communications theory and spatial theory, *together*" (Couldry & McCarthy 2004, p. 15; similar ambitions are present in anthologies like Rattenbury 2002, Jansson & Lagerkvist 2009).

At first glance, this looks like good news for anyone with an interest in the links between media and architecture. Or, more specifically, in the actual buildings of the major media institutions. After all, the relations between architecture land media as *representation* could be expected to be particularly intense in such objects, and their very materialization could be expected to reveal the *real* connections to societal power (state, politics, and commercial actors). No such investigations, however, were to be found in the first anthologies of the spatial turn. And maybe they were not to be expected, judging from the introductory maps of the field presented in some of these books. According to one (Jansson & Falkheimer 2006), the spatial turn was preceded by a "contextual turn," a "cultural turn," and an "ethnographic turn." And this series of re-navigations produces what looks like an exemplary type of study in which the preferred context is that of our contemporary everyday life: the familiar social space of our private homes (Morley 2000), cities (McQuire 2008), and/or public spaces of leisure, like the street or the shopping mall (Fornäs 2006; McCarthy 2001). The relevant material media objects are the screens, receivers, cables that are integrated in those spaces. The preferred methodology is that of ethnographical fieldwork, rather than textual interpretation. And its contemporary relevance is to be understood in terms of a specific historical context: the spatial turn is motivated by "the era of hyper-space biased communication," an era which makes "space itself a less reliable category," that proclaims the ephemerality of any text, context, geography of communication (Jansson & Falkheimer 2006). An era, it would seem, in which "all that is solid melts into air." Not an era to be represented by massive media houses, with centralistic claims. If anything, the era of their final disappearance—as predicted by William J. Mitchell (1995) in *City of Bits*:

> When the *Chicago Tribune* Tower was constructed, it stood as the proudly visible center of a vast collection and a distribution system and an emblem of the power of the press. Every day the news flowed in and the printed papers flowed out to the surrounding metropolis. But on the Infobahn, where every node is potentially both a publication and consumption point, such centralized concentrations of activity will be supplanted by millions of dispersed fragments. (Mitchell 1995, p. 53)

Here, the logic of Frollo's *ceci tuera cela* returns—though the medieval cathedral has been replaced by a media house from the 1920s and the book by the Infobahn. As indicated above, though, there might be a problem with this periodization: powerful media institutions (like the British Broadcasting Corporation [BBC] or the China Central Television [CCTV] in China) do not seem to agree. Enormous sums are currently being spent on the construction of new media headquarters, and architects of international stardom are currently in high demand for supplying "landmark" buildings with iconic values (Jencks 2005). The periodization suggested by Mitchell could draw our attention from such processes, and their underlying logic, as explained by Saskia Sassen:

> It is precisely because of the territorial dispersal facilitated by telecommunication advances that agglomeration of centralizing activities has expanded immensely. (Sassen 1999, p. 59)

Such periodizations may also work against the attempt to think architecture and media *together*, and to think about their links *historically*. To briefly illustrate the intricate nature of such links, one may begin with the example mentioned by Mitchell: the Chicago Tribune Tower.

Fig. 1. Chicago Tribune Tower, 2009. Photo by Amanda Lagerkvist.

The claim to fame of this building does not rest on its position in the centralized collection and distribution of news but on its intervention in *architectural* history. In 1922, the *Chicago Tribune*, a newspaper in need of future headquarters, announced an international competition for the design of "the ultimate in civic expression—the world's most beautiful office building." Since then, this competition has been regarded as a landmark in the transition from classical to modern architecture and in developing the esthetics of the skyscraper (Solomonson 2001). The competition drew over 260 entries, engaging many of the radical architects of the day: Adolf Loos, Walter Gropius, Eliel Saarinen. The final winner, though, was a group of New York architects, proposing a relatively safe tower in neo-Gothic style (supposedly influenced by a French medieval cathedral, i.e., Frollo's "book of humanity"). And in a way, this "landmark" was never made of stone: it was constructed from the total event of the competition, carefully orchestrated by the *Chicago Tribune*, covering every phase of the competition during its six months through pictorials, articles, letters to the editors, inviting its readers to evaluate the merits of civic monuments from other historical phases, openly displaying and debating the drawings and models of the entries, first in the pages of the *Chicago Tribune*, and then in a book (1923) and in a traveling exhibition. An early demonstration of the *medialization* of architecture—in which the relevant "site of construction" may not only be the local, physical one, but also the site of photography, publicity, exhibitions. But also, and simultaneously, a demonstration of a private media company that uses architecture to "take place and claim space" as a civic institution, cultural gatekeeper, guardian of democracy.

Two years later in Moscow, in 1924, the Vesnin brothers, leaders of the movement of Soviet constructivism, delivered a radical proposal for a new building for *Pravda*, the official organ of the communist party. Though the building never materialized, its conception has survived through countless reproductions in the literature on modern architecture.

Fig. 2. Proposal for Pravda building, 1924. Courtesy of Schusev State Museum of Architecture (MUAR).

It is basically a box of steel and glass, six stories high, held together by trusses (triangulated frameworks). The gaps between these frames are filled with either large glass sheets or communicating signs, mixing the media technologies available at the time: banners, posters, loudspeakers, clocks, projection screens. A façade that fulfils the definition of a house proposed by Le Corbusier (1930): "stages of floors ... all around them *walls of light.*"[1] In the case of the Vesnin brothers, this "wall" mixes natural and artificial light and fulfils two functions simultaneously: the wall of glass, opening up the interior of the building to the outside masses, and making that outside visible from the inside, and the wall of signs, supplying a vehicle of public address through media technology. Thus, the Vesnins' façade anticipates not only the currently intensified use of screen technology in architecture (Slaatta 2006)— light-emitting diode (LED) panels, video, computer graphics—but also the shift of attention from three-dimensional to two-dimensional signs, to an "architecture of persuasion" (Venturi et al. 1972/1998), where buildings are "decorated sheds," designed to communicate within urban cityscapes. As in Times Square, New York, where local legislation requires a minimum of signage and lighting on every building, to preserve the "sense of place" that once established this square as "the crossroads of the world," and, simultaneously, an architectural organization of the spectacle of television, "avant la lettre" (Traub 2004).

In 1931, just some blocks away from Times Square, another sort of "media center" was being erected: the Rockefeller Center, in its first phase consisting of 14 buildings, originally occupied by the Associated Press and the broadcasting studios of RCA (currently housing, among others, the studios of the television network NBC). This project immediately catches the interest of Sigfried Giedion, master historian of modern architecture. (And, simultaneously, an indirect contributor to the media theory of the twentieth century through his strong influence on Walter Benjamin [1999] in his *Passagen-Werk* and the young Marshall McLuhan [1951/2002] in *The Mechanical Bride.*) In Giedion´s seminal work on *Space, Time and Architecture* (1941), the Rockefeller Center is held to be the first major civic center that uses a complex, many-sided, modern constellation of space and time. Its site is not a traditional agora or square and its buildings are not conventional towers. In spatial terms, this complex is not a centralized unit. The arrangement of the buildings is rationally motivated, so that no building will shadow another and every room will get maximum light from the windows. But this form cannot be experienced from the street, nor from inside the buildings—it "cannot be grasped from any single position or embraced in any single view." In other words, the single, fixed point of view of the Renaissance has been abandoned. To graphically illustrate the organization of these buildings in printed form, Giedion switches to the techniques of the photomontage and stroboscophic photography.

Fig. 3. Illustration of Rockefeller Center in Giedion (1941), courtesy of Harvard University Press and Paul & Peter Fritz AG.

The example of Rockefeller Center, and the theme of decentralization, returns in a more recent study of American corporate architecture: Reinhold Martin's (2003) *The Organizational Complex—Architecture, Media, and Corporate Space.* The term in the title refers to the "aesthetic and technological extension" of the so-called military-industrial complex. After the Second World War, prominent modernist architects—Eero Saarinen, Skidmore, Owings & Merrill—were involved in the construction of huge office complexes for companies like IBM, General Motors, Bell Telephone, that developed the techniques of glass, curtain walls, and modular assembly. According to Martin, this architecture should not be reduced to a "corporate image"—it is part and parcel of the infrastructure of a flexible, systems-based network of computers, discourses, buildings, communication and transportation lines that "works actively to integrate spaces and subjects into naturalized organization."

In particular, Martin sees these buildings as the spatial articulations of the theory of cybernetics:

> Networked, feedback-driven, system-based—this organism, and the systems of power that it serves, sustains myths of dynamic deregulation, corporate benevolence, and dispersed, dehierarchisized interactivity. (Martin 2003, p. 8)

Such houses may belong to the prehistory of those dispersed nodes of information production/consumption that Mitchell predicts will follow the centralized activity of the Chicago Tribune Tower. Or, as several authors of this book argue, to a history where the materialization of the myth of the mediated center has evolved simultaneously with a myth of decentralized power.

As these examples demonstrate, the categories of modern architecture and modern media may certainly be connected, and the links may be metaphorical, analogical, theoretical, causal, and institutional. This does not imply that their histories should be systematically "thought together," nor the existence of some "necessary" connection between them. The latter claim, however, motivates the most ambitious study of the relations between media and architecture: Beatriz Colomina´s (1994) *Privacy and Publicity: Modern Architecture as Mass Media*. This book declares that the relation between inside and outside, private and public, has been drastically changed by the presence of the media. Its impact on modern architecture is measured in terms of the strategies developed by two canonical figures: Adolf Loos and Le Corbusier (particularly their construction of private houses). With Loos, the main response is to reinsert the boundaries of the interior, the inner space increasingly threatened by publicity and visibility. With Le Corbusier, it is to transgress the demarcations of inner and outer, through light and transparence, or the use of windows which transforms the home into a camera, directed towards outer forms of life (nature, urbanity). In both cases, architecture is "taking place" through and within the media:

> It is actually the emerging systems of communication that came to define 20th century culture—the mass media—that are the true site within which modern architecture is produced and with which it directly engages. In fact, one could argue (this is the main argument of the book) that modern architecture only becomes modern with its engagement with the media. (Colomina 1994, p. 14)

The structure of this argument may remind us of Couldry's critique of the "myth of the mediated center." For what sort of "true site" could be evoked by this reference to "the mass media"? Within the context of her book, more specific interpretations appear. First and foremost, Colomina's view is contrasted to the portrayal of modern architecture as high, autonomous art, defined by its distance to mass culture. Further, she demonstrates how the architecture of an icon like Le Corbusier is not only produced for the media (that is, for symbolic, immaterial reproduction, rather than construction on a specific site) but also by the media (since it is heavily influenced by the surrounding media culture, by ads, newspaper clippings, films). But there is also a more fundamental connection at stake:

> The building should be understood in the same terms as drawings, photographs, writing, films, and advertisements; not only because these are the media in which more often we encounter it, but because the building is a mechanism of representation in its own right. (Colomina 1994, p. 13)

In other words, the book's deepest concern is properly announced in the subtitle: the possibility of thinking modern architecture as mass media. Even those inclined for tolerance in the uses of media definitions, may find this idea—that a modern building, for instance, the private houses of Le Corbusier or Loos, is a mass medium—hard to swallow. Why so? Probably because our use of the category "mass media" does not stop at designating a "mechanism of representation," but involves additional signals. Among these, at least, the possibility to communicate beyond the limits of space and the social organization of this communication through powerful institutions (cf. Thompson 1995). These are, of course, the very signals that have been necessary for constructing the notion of the mediated center. But they are not necessary, nor easily applied, to the construction of buildings. In fact, the category of "architecture" will evoke its own signals, some of which—the articulating of local place and the construction of volume and mass—will counter the dissolution or compression of time, space, and power, attributed to modern media. This may be the reason that architecture, though heavily influenced by all the pressures, of media society—mechanization, standardization, abstraction, placelessness, ephemerality—still may be understood as a strategy of *resistance* against such pressures through its insistence on the tactile, tectonic, topographic, territorial, place-formed, site-oriented (as argued by Frampton 1983). This also points to the continued relevance of Harold Innis' classic distinction between time-biased and space-biased media of communication:

> A medium of communication has an important influence on the dissemination of knowledge over space and over time and it becomes necessary to study its characteristics in order to appraise its influence in its cultural settings. According to its characteristics it may be better suited to the dissemination of knowledge over time than over space, particularly if the medium is heavy and durable and not suited to transportation, or to the dissemination of knowledge over space than over time, particularly if the medium is light and easily transported. (Innis 1951/2006, p. 33)

Historically, Frollo's cathedral certainly would count as a time-biased medium. While the book, and to an even greater extent radio and television, would be space-biased media. With modern architecture, however, things might get more complicated. For one of the aspirations of such architecture might precisely be to lose weight and solidity, to "mingle with the air," in Hugo's words. At least according to Siegfried Giedion, writing about Le Corbusier in the 1920s:

> Corbusier's houses are neither spatial nor plastic: *air* flows through them! Air becomes a constituent factor! Neither space nor plastic form counts, only RELATION and INTER-PENETRATION! There is only a *single*, indivisible space. . . . There arises—as with certain lighting conditions in snowy landscapes—that *dematerialization* of solid demarcation that distinguishes neither rise nor fall and that gradually produces the feeling of walking in clouds. (Giedion 1928/1995, p. 169)

And it could get even more complicated, with buildings that represent the activity of major media institutions. According to one interpretation of Innis (Blondheim 2003), his time/space polarity meant to express the dialectics of an "inverted determinism"; once a culture is dominated by space-biased forms of communication (like broadcasting), it is also threatened by the discontinuity of time. To compensate, it may develop strongly time-biased concerns (like the building of broadcasting temples). Such a site will intensify intriguing paradoxes—the solidification of that which "mingles with the air," the centralization of that which is ubiquitous.

According to Ole Scheeren, the project leader for the Office for Metropolitan Architecture (OMA), the idea behind Rem Koolhaas' design for CCTV in Beijing is to present a building that will "reverse the process of dispersal," "show a system of interconnected activities," and "undo the hierarchies."[2] As illustrated above, similar ideas have guided the construction of media houses in the past. If indeed, these belong to the past. One of the intriguing aspects of these houses is that they are originally planned and constructed, not only as the result of recent technological and social change, but in an anticipatory, utopian mode, as material predictions of the future of communication. As historical objects, then, these houses may be decoded like Walter Benjamin's arcades: ruins of our vanished dreams of the future, frozen ciphers of the dialectic of old and new, situated "outside" the continuum of history.

The content of this book

The project "Media Houses" originated within a group of scholars from the fields of architecture, media studies, philosophy, and political science. Its overriding aim was to study the esthetic and material manifestations of the mediated center and their relations to societal power. At the outset, three case studies were selected:

- Broadcasting House in London, inaugurated in 1932 as the first purpose-built headquarters of the BBC, now under reconstruction to house the world's largest complex of broadcasting studios.

- The TV centre Ostankino in Moscow, including the tower that in the 1960s was the highest structure in the world, a symbol for the space age and the Soviet state, and a site for power struggles in the post-communist era.

- The new CCTV building in Beijing, designed by Rem Koolhaas, to challenge Western skyscraper aesthetics and position China as world leaders in the use of digital communication.

All of these buildings raised explicit (national) centralistic claims, though their historical origins belonged to different eras of media technology (radio, television, digital media), architectural styles (from modernism to postmodernism), and media systems (British public service, Soviet communism, Chinese post-communism).

During the course of this project, and in preparation for this book, more cases have been added. The study of Bush House and the World Service added the history of a "transnational" network, originally emanating from the British Empire. With Googleplex in Silicon Valley and the InterActiveCorp building in Manhattan, the context was widened, not only to American soil, but to the media landscapes of the Internet.

All individual contributors address the question of how these buildings may be regarded as material and esthetic manifestations of a notion of the mediated center, as well as the countervailing pulls toward decentralization. Their approaches, though, vary considerably, drawing from a wide academic field—ranging over media studies, political science, social theory, cultural studies, and architecture.

In Chapter 2, Staffan Ericson returns to the origins of Broadcasting House, a building conceived in 1932 as a "sound factory" with 22 studios. Its exterior was shaped as a traditional stone castle (a new "Tower of London"), and its interiors were designed by a team of radical modernists, including Wells Coates and Serge Chermayeff. The essay tracks how this "interiorization of the modern" may be linked to contemporary notions of the media (as institution and mechanism of representation), to theories on architecture and media (like Walter Benjamin and Siegfried Giedion), to fantasies about the anxieties of modern life (like the 1934 detective novel *Death at Broadcasting House*), and to architectural practices in the design of modern dwelling (like Coates' 1934 Lawn Road Flats in London). In contrast to the embalming structure of the original building, the ongoing renovation and expansion of Broadcasting House aims at opening up the "heart of the BBC," a space now referring to a "public cyclorama" rather than the inner studio tower. In conclusion, the chapter discusses how architect Richard MacCormac's use of "the interstitial" as a model for social space differs from earlier ideals, and how the historical status of the original Broadcasting House, now presented in old photographs and tours of "heritage spaces" within a digital environment, may be related to the changing eras of media reproducibility (as analyzed by Bernard Stiegler).

14 | STAFFAN ERICSON, KRISTINA RIEGERT, PATRIK ÅKER

In Chapter 3, Kristina Riegert analyzes another 1920s era building, the BBC's World Service headquarters, Bush House, known to millions of listeners throughout the world as the home of the BBC's disembodied voices, as a center from which issued the sounds of Empire: tradition, truth, power, and culture. In many ways, Bush House has expressed the values and ethos of the World Service and its importance for BBC culture can be seen in the motivations for the impending move (and further centralization) to the new Broadcasting House. Based on interviews, and drawing on office design literature, the chapter looks at the way Bush House is perceived by the people actually working there; those working in the international offices and those coming to London from abroad. The chapter traces the ways that technological, political, economic, and cultural changes have influenced the staff and ways of working in Bush House. It describes how the organization of the 33 language services is reflected in the physical layout of the building, and how the ongoing tensions between centralization and decentralization play out in a place that has functioned as a hub for various spokes in the World Service wheel. It is a site for fan pilgrimages from abroad, a place for the induction of foreign personnel into BBC "values," and one providing institutional safety for an increasingly vulnerable occupation.

Chapter 4 moves us into the space age and the 1960s, with its focus on the Ostankino TV tower, opening in Moscow in 1967. This tower served as an important symbol for Soviet society in an age characterized by the space race and satellite communication. As an observation platform, Ostankino differs from its eighteenth-century ancestors found atop churches or cathedrals. Its panorama is offered behind glass in a building shaped like a rocket, belonging to a powerful media institution representing the Communist Party. This chapter discusses the tower in relation to traditions of Russian constructivism, but also to a "mechanism for representation" that bears similarities to McLuhan's description of the "tactual" TV image. The experience provided by a visit to the tower and its surroundings, it is suggested, is one of a specific "organizational complex," producing a subject for the TV age. The post-Soviet era has since then provided this centre with new contexts, from the turbulent years of Yeltsin and the media oligarchs, to Putin's "recentralization" of the Russian media system. Following a fire in 2000—seen by some as a symbol of the failure to commercialize and decentralize media power—the tower was closed for visitors, though the government plans to renovate it. In conclusion, Åker characterizes Ostankino's current status as an historical object (following Susan Buck-Morss' reading of the Moscow metro): projected for the tourism industry rather than for media distribution, linking the country's history with the glorious space age.

As we move from these historical media houses into those constructed for the digital media age, we should point out that all of the former are currently being renovated—not abandoned—which points to historical continuities rather than breaks between old and new media. The fact that costly new media headquarters continue to be built by "starchitects," such as Rem Koolhaas's Beijing project for CCTV, Frank Gehry's Chelsea building for InterActiveCorp, or Renzo Piano's new house for the *New York Times*, demonstrates that old media need to re-brand themselves as much as new. And they tend to do this, in part by including spaces for public access, in part by marketing the interiors of new buildings as "creative" environments for their workers.

Chapter 5 analyzes Googleplex, the headquarters of one of the most powerful media companies in the industry today. Peter Jakobsson and Fredrik Stiernstedt investigate how the architecture of Google's headquarters in Silicon Valley organizes, represents, and performs power in today's "informational culture." The analysis demonstrates that Googleplex is active in establishing Google's claim to power—through techniques related to the principles of information, decentralization, and self-organization, as theorized by Shannon and Weaver, and Norbert Wiener, and through the distinction of "soft" and "hard" architecture—while downplaying the centralization that is achieved through its activities. Google presents itself as being on the receiving end of a communicative relationship and as the connective hub facilitating connectivity instead of the content. Its ideology works to mask its computational capacities and large investments in hardware around the world, while promoting the personal, empowering, and "decentralized" aspects of its "benevolent" software. Typical of the urban sprawl of California, it is not the outside of Googleplex that demonstrates monumentality, but rather the inside. By displaying giant objects from different eras of human history (a dinosaur skeleton and a rocket ship), Google inserts itself "in the new frontier, not by conquering foreign worlds, solar systems or planets but by organizing all knowledge and information."

Another building housing a company at the forefront of the new media industry is Barry Diller's new InterActiveCorp building in New York, designed by Frank Gehry. In Chapter 6, Shannon Mattern asks if this building may represent a fresh approach to the shape of space in a new media landscape—an embodiment of the "scapes" of Arjun Appadurai's global cultural economy. Addressing the InterActiveCorp as a new media workspace, Mattern examines its open-plan landscapes, fanciful color scheme, translucency, and framing of interior and exterior views, all of which purportedly constitute a new type of workspace suited to new media labor. Although the building's form may be more rhizomatic than Euclidean, she argues that its underlying interior architectural and social "protocols" are like the corporate "box's" in their compartmentalization of work functions and reinforcement of hierarchy. In attempting to blend the edges of old and new media and business models—and to represent that blending in architectural form—Mattern argues, the InterActiveCorp building calls attention to the friction between two seemingly incompatible systems, and the extreme difficulty of identifying new symbols for a new political economy.

Sven-Olov Wallenstein's contribution (Chapter 7) analyzes the already well-publicized, long overdue, CCTV center in Beijing (Rem Koolhaas/OMA). In a reading relating to the theories of Fredric Jameson and Slavoj Žižek, Wallenstein suggests that the CCTV building stands as a complex allegory of the role of media in contemporary China, but also more generally, of the culture of current capitalism. On the level of imagery, the building has a clearly iconic status and functions in terms of a "brand" that must unite several contradictory features—the emphasis on openness and communication flows must coexist with an image of centrality and authority. Starting from a discussion on a more easily visible and iconic level, the essay investigates how the idea of a complex transparency is implemented in the structure of the loop, or that of a Moebius strip, one that allows a public trajectory through the edifice to coexist with a closed and sealed-off trajectory for the employees, thus creating a continual sense of public space and communication while at the same time marking the division by impenetrable glass partitions. In this way, production and consumption of media remain separate, and yet they are united in the structure of a building that itself claims to constitute a common space as a kind of "spectacle," or viewing machine, that produces the sense of a political unity while at the same time prohibiting it at every level.

In the final chapter, Helena Mattsson draws together the themes of transparency and "inside"/"outside" of the media from an architectural perspective. She notes that the more the media are questioned as a "public sphere," the more capital media institutions seem willing to invest in building houses that articulate transparency between their physical and internal structures and their audiences. In relation to theories on "brandscapes" and "experience economies," Mattsson discusses how architecture as a technique is used to create experiences of public space and how through varying forms of transparent surfaces, what earlier had been "hidden" media production is now exposed to the public for their amusement. Mattsson describes how this phenomenon plays out in the plans for the new CCTV complex in Beijing and in the new BBC Broadcasting House—buildings that may be seen as examples of "experience architecture," in their almost narcissistic exposure of their own machinery, transgressing the old concept of a democratic, transparent organization and pointing toward a Deleuzian society of control, a regime of exhibitionism where everyday life is on display. The chapter investigates how such public spaces are programmed for the consumption of experiences: how media houses may not only produce programs, but also audiences.

References

Benjamin, W. (1999), *The Arcades Project (Das Passagen-Werk)*, Cambridge, MA: The Belknap Press of Harvard University Press.
Blondheim, M. (2003), "Harold Adams Innis and his Bias of Communication," in Katz, E. & Durham Peters, J., et al (eds.), *Canonic Texts in Media Research*, Cambridge: Polity Press.
Colomina, B. (1994/2000), *Privacy and Publicity. Modern Architecture as Mass Media,* Cambridge, MA: MIT Press.
Couldry, N. (2003). *Media Rituals. A Critical Approach*, London & New York: Routledge.
Couldry, N. & McCarthy, A. (2004), *MediaSpace*, London & New York: Routledge.
Couldry, N. (2004), "Transvaluing Media Studies, or Beyond the Myth of the Mediated Centre," In Couldry, N. & Curran, J. (eds.), *Media and Cultural Theory*, London: Routledge.
Couldry, N. (2006), *Listening Beyond the Echoes: Media, Ethics and Agency in an Uncertain World*, Boulder, CO: Paradigm.
Dayan, D. & Katz, E. (1992), *Media Events. The Live Broadcasting of History*, Cambridge, MA: Harvard University Press.
Fornäs, J. (2006), "Media Passages in Urban Spaces of Consumption," in Jansson, A. & Falkenheimer, J. (eds.), *Geographies of Communication. The Spatial Turn in Media Studies*, Gothenburg: Nordicom
Frampton, K. (1983), "Towards a Critical Regionalism: Six Points for an Architecture of Resistance," in Foster, H. (ed.), *The Anti-Aesthetic*, Seattle, WA: Bay Press.
Giedion, S. (1928/1995), *Building in France, Building in Iron, Building in Ferro-concrete [Bauen in Frankreich]*, Santa Monica, CA: Getty Center for the History of Art and the Humanities.
Giedion, S. (1941), *Space, Time and Architecture: the Growth of a New Tradition*, Cambridge, MA: Harvard University Press.
Habermas, J. (1961/1989), *The Structural Transformation of the Public Sphere. An Inquiry into the Category of Bourgeois Society,* Cambridge, MA: MIT Press.
Hugo, V. (1831), *The Hunchback of Notre Dame*, Book Fifth Chapter II. This Will Kill That. http://www.classicreader.com/book/330/24/ (accessed June 8, 2009).
Innis, H. (1951/2006), *The Bias of Communication*, Toronto: University of Toronto Press.
Jansson, A. & Falkheimer, J. (eds.) (2006), *Geographies of Communication. The Spatial Turn in Media Studies*, Gothenburg: Nordicom.
Jansson, A. & Lagerkvist, A. (eds.) (2009), *Strange Spaces: Explorations Into Mediated Obscurity*, London: Ashgate Publisher.
Jencks, C. (2005), *The Iconic Building,* New York: Rizzoli International Publishers.
Khan-Magomedov, S.O., (1987) *Pioneers of Soviet Architecture*, London: Thames and Hudson Ltd.
Löfgren, O. (2006), "Postscript: Taking Place," in Jansson, A. & Falkheimer J. (eds.) *Geographies of Communication. The Spatial Turn in Media Studies*, Gothenburg: Nordicom.
Martin, R. (2003), *The Organisational Complex. Architecture, Media, and Corporate Space,* Cambridge, MA: MIT Press.
McCarthy, A. (2001), *Ambient Television. Visual Culture and Public Space,* Durham: Duke University Press.
McLuhan, M. (1951/2002), *The Mechanical Bride: Folklore of Industrial Man*, Berkeley, CA: Gingko Press.
McQuire, S. (2008), *The Media City. Media, Architecture and Urban Space,* London: Sage.
Meyrowitz, J. (1985), *No Sense of Place*, New York: Oxford University Press.
Mitchell, W.J. (1995), *City of Bits. Space, Place, and the Infobahn*, Cambridge, MA: MIT Press.

Morley, D. (2000), *Home Territories. Media, Mobility and Identity,* London: Routledge.
Rattenbury, K. (ed.) (2002), *This Is Not Architecture: Media Constructions,* London: Routledge.
Real, M. (1989). *Super Media: A Cultural Studies Approach,* Newbury Park, CA: Sage.
Sassen, S. (1999), "Digital Networks and Power," in Featherstone, M. & Lash, S. (eds.), *Spaces of Culture: City, Nation, World,* London: Sage.
Slaatta, T. (2006), "Urban screens: Towards the convergence of architecture and audiovisual media." *First Monday,* Special Issue #4. Available from: http://firstmonday.org/htbin/cgiwrap/bin/ojs/index.php/fm/issue/view/217
Solomonson, K. (2001), *The Chicago Tribune Tower Competition: Skyscraper Design and Cultural Change in the 1920s,* Chicago: The University of Chicago Press.
Thompson, J.B. (1995), *The Media and Modernity,* Cambridge: Polity Press.
Traub, J. (2004), *The Devil's Playground. A Century of Pleasure and Profit in Times Square,* New York: Random House.
Venturi, R., Scott Brown, D. & Izenour, S. (1972/1998), *Learning from Las Vegas,* revised ed. Cambridge, MA: MIT Press.

Notes

1. Quoted from Colomina (1994, p. 7).
2. According to notes taken at Ole Scheeren's presentation at Tokyo University, hosted by *Theory, Culture & Society*'s 2007 conference: "Ubiquitous Media/Asian Transformations."

CHAPTER TWO

The Interior of the Ubiquitous: Broadcasting House, London

STAFFAN ERICSON

To approach Broadcasting House, you have to reach the northern end of Regent Street, one of the busiest streets in London, and, according to some, the first and longest shopping street in the world. The end of this street is accentuated by a shift from the horizontal to the vertical.

The line of sight is tilted upwards, by three objects pointing toward the sky; dominating the central perspective is the spire of John Nash's nineteenth-century All Souls Church. Slightly to the left is a reproduction of the BBC's radio mast from the 1930s. Slightly to the right is a work of art added in the ongoing extension: the glass ramp of a beam of light, shot into the dark sky at 10 p.m., in commemoration of journalists lost in the line of duty.

What we are looking (up) at, then, is a triad of attempts in supraterrestrial communication. Or, with Mircea Eliade (1957/1987), a triad of attempts in the founding of "sacred space." According to Eliade, "profane space" is formless, fluid, homogenous, chaotic. Sacred space is real, absolute, orienting, organizing. Since the days of primitive habitation, humans have attempted to found their world in the latter by constructing sites (houses, sanctuaries, temples) that are (a) situated at the *Centre of the World* and (b) *opening a link of communication* between different cosmic planes (earth and heaven, life and death). Through history, such links have taken the form of poles, posts, pillars, spires. And this particular triad has some suggestive interferences. The radio mast next to the light ray memorial: a reminder of how the word "medium" in the early days of sound recording and radio was entangled with nineteenth-century spiritualism, i.e., "the art of communicating with the dead." The radio mast next to the church spire is a reminder of how the "natural" interior qualities of sound—listening, hearing, speaking—have been linked to divinity and salvation for thousands of years (Sterne 2003). Symbols of religion will also guide the visitor who enters Broadcasting House. Inside the entrance hall, Eric Gill's sculpture of the biblical sowerman, literally "broadcasting" his seeds (illustrating the parable used by John Durham Peters (1999) in *Speaking into the Air*, to link the communicative ideals of Christianity with those of early mass communication). Over that sculpture, and the doors leading toward the interior, the following Latin inscription is found:

Fig. 1. Broadcasting House, 2006, from Regent Street. Photo by author.

This temple of the arts and muses is dedicated to the ALMIGHTY GOD by the first Governors of Broadcasting in the year 1931, Sir John Reith being Director General. It is their prayer that the good seed sown may bring forth a good harvest, that all things hostile to peace or purity may be banished from this house, and that the people, inclining their ear to whatsoever things are beautiful and honest and of good report, may tread the path of wisdom and uprightness.

Today, this inscription is placed behind a glass wall, fronted by a desk for receptionists and security personnel. Here, sans accreditation, a visitor to Broadcasting House has reached the final destination.

To illustrate how the opposition between sacred and profane space may live on in a de-sacralized world, Eliade offers the example of a church in a modern city:

> The threshold that separates the two spaces also indicates the distance between two modes of being, the profane and the religious. The threshold is the limit, the boundary, the frontier that distinguishes and opposes two worlds—and at the same time the paradoxical place where those worlds communicate, where passage from the profane to the sacred world becomes possible. (Eliade 1957/87, p. 25)

In *The Place of Media Power*, Nick Couldry (2000) suggests a structural analogy between the sacred/profane distinction (here via Durkheim, not Eliade), and a division which Couldry finds crucial in the naturalizing of the media's symbolical power: that between the "media world" (everything "in" the media) and the "ordinary world" (everything "outside" it). His book then explores various ways in which non-media people may interact with media institutions, for instance, when visiting places like the external set of the long-running British television soap *Coronation Street*, which has operated as a tourist site for decades. To Couldry, that location may be described as "a place with 'aura', a 'ritual' place, even a place of 'pilgrimage'" (Couldry 2000, p. 69).

The threshold to Broadcasting House may certainly bring this analogy to mind, for this is not any spatial checkpoint, enforcing any type of social hierarchy. While the physical and electronic obstacles may not appear all that authoritative at first glance, the recognition of the visitor is immediate: there will be no further access without proper preparation. As with the profane and the sacred, we seem to confront an *absolute* distinction, between "two worlds with nothing in common" (Durkheim), or "two modes of being" (Eliade). This distinction is already familiar, active in our minds, actions, and language, as when separating, for instance, media people and ordinary people, stars and fans, production and consumption, the mundane and the magical, the everyday and the holiday. As with the sacred and the profane, there *are* passages to that other side. But these are kept under strict ("ritualistic") control. At Broadcasting House, the reception desk politely informs the visitor: yes, you might cross to the other side, for about one and a half hours, in the company of guides, after applying in advance to the BBC.

To confront the spatial version of this symbolic division is not necessarily to have its "absolute" nature confirmed. Where there is a threshold (like in Eliade's modern church), there is also continuity. Having your physical access denied might be one of these moments when the routine of the inescapable is actually interrupted, "de-naturalised," and even contested. At the very least, a spatial manifestation will bear evidence of historical contingency: this division has to be reconstructed, reproduced, and renovated. Standing at this particular threshold, you can't really miss it, being surrounded by scaffolding, cranes, construction workers, a development site the size of ten football pitches. What is going on here is explained on the BBC's Web site, by current Director General Mark Thompson:

> "We're restoring our original home and expanding it to create the largest live broadcast centre ever."[1]

This decision was made around the turn of the millennium, and the new version of the BBC's first purpose-built headquarters is now expected to be completed in 2012, when London will host the Olympics. The rationale was explained by Greg Dyke, Director General at the time: the new BBC must recognize what its founding fathers had grasped—the symbolic importance of buildings. It was high time for the BBC to put "architecture once again at the heart of [its] strategy" (Jackson 2003, p.14).

Architecture, in general, is said to strive for *permanence*, particularly when housing central social institutions (Brand 1994). To Harold Innis (1951/2006), the Egyptian pyramids were a prime example of *time-binding* media: being heavy, durable, "not suited for transportation." Much like this stone "temple," which also displays manifest connections to what Innis regarded as typical traits for time-binding communication: continuity with religious tradition, an emphasis on sound, listening, orality. On the other hand, it was constructed for an institution with obvious *space-binding* ambitions, in terms of territorial control, and the weightless exercise of such control through radio, that "ethereal medium par excellence" (Milutis 2006, p. x). For the first Christmas at Broadcasting House, Sir John Reith, the director General in the inscription, asked the British king, George V, for a speech. It was scripted by Rudyard Kipling and broadcast live:

> Through one of the marvels of modern science, I am enabled, this Christmas day, to speak to all my people, throughout the Empire. I take it as a good omen that wireless should have reached its present perfection at a time when the Empire has been linked in closer union. For it offers us immense possibilities to make that union closer still.[2]

According to Sir Reith himself, the "wireless" was "manifestly dependent upon the universal ether, a fascinating but illusive, and probably incomprehensible, medium."[3] Defiance of gravity was also signified in the original exterior decorations: in the corporation flag, flattering from the rooftop, portraying "an azure field representing the ether ... broadcasting being represented by a golden ring encircling the globe" (*Broadcasting House* 1932, p. 13), in the bird flocks and wave symbols carved into the stone surrounding the balconies. For the exterior, the BBC asked Eric Gill for a series of four sculptures of Ariel, that "invisible spirit of the air" from

The Tempest, serving as a "personification of broadcasting." The dominant one stands just above the main entrance, portraying the magician Prospero, Ariel's master, about to send him off into the air.

Fig. 2. Prospero and Ariel, over the entrance, Eric Gill, sculptor. Photo by author.

Today, in the midst of renovation, these very sculptures signal "authenticity," "tradition," and, yes, "permanence." The stuff that *auras* are made of, according to Walter Benjamin's (1936/1968) well-known essay on "The Work of Art in the Age of Mechanical Reproduction." So it should come as no surprise: a visitor who raises a camera in the entrance hall of Broadcasting House is approached within seconds with a gentle chide: "sorry, no pictures." Photography, after all, was one of Benjamin's main examples of how media technology would detach the sacred objects from the values of tradition and ritual, how "that which withers in the age of mechanical reproduction is the aura of the work of art" (Benjamin 1936/1968, p. 221). In this case, though, the sacred objects, in the sense of both Durkheim ("things set apart and surrounded by prohibitions") and Eliade (objects that reveal "an absolute fixed point, a center," and thus, "the only *real* and *real-ly* existing space"), are themselves objects of media reproduction.

Back out on Regent Street—access denied, distance confirmed—the ordinary world presents itself again, much like Eliade's profane space: chaotic, fluid, formless. According to Eliade, the founding of sacred space does not emerge out of any human attempt to link to that other side. It is efficacious only when it ritually repeats the creation of a cosmos, when it actually "reproduces the work of the gods" (Eliade

1957/1987, p. 29). In this respect, too, the placing of Prospero, Ariel, and the sowerman seems perfectly appropriate. But how are we to imagine the "ganz Andere" of that other side? What sort of "work" is going on there? A song by Tom Waits pops up, to accompany this visitor's walk down Regent Street:

> "What's he building in there? What the hell is he building in there? We have a right to know."

Before stepping inside to find out, this article will track some of the specific interconnections between (mass) media and (modern) architecture that organized the original interiors of Broadcasting House—spatially, and/or imaginatively—as well as their afterlife in the ongoing renovation. As already indicated above, some of these connections are somewhat paradoxical. And some seem downright scary.

Death at Broadcasting House[4]

Death at Broadcasting House is the title of a detective novel, published in 1934, written by two of the building's first tenants, one of them Val Gielgud, BBC's Head of Production of Drama. The genre is the "whodunit," or classical detective story (Cawelti 1976), often associated with Agatha Christie. In this one, however, there are some interesting departures from the rules. While the crime of a classical detective story is situated within the private sphere, disrupting order by placing dead bodies in the midst of our family circle, this one involves a murder at the heart of a mediated center: the studios of Broadcasting House. During the live broadcast of a radio play, one of the actors, isolated in one of the talk studios, is strangled to death. While the task of a classical detective usually involves tracking past events via material clues and eyewitness accounts from the scene of the crime, this detective faces an intriguing dilemma: Millions have listened in to the live performance of a murder, but no one has seen anything, and not a single clue has been left in the studio. To explain what happened, detective Spears must reconstruct the locality and traces of a crime that have registered only in the ether. But that nevertheless seems to affect our private spheres:

> "You see Spears, this isn´t an ordinary case. You know what broadcasting is. It gets the public in their homes. There are nearly six million people who feel as if anything that happens inside Broadcasting House has happened by their own firesides." (Gielgud & Marvell 1934, p. 121)

An exterior description of the scene of the crime opens this story.

> Broadcasting House has been called a good many names, and described as a good many things. Names and descriptions have varied from the complimentary to the scurrilous, and almost from the sublime to the ridiculous. The building has been compared with a ship, with a fortress, with a towering cliff. . . . Broadcasting House, in short, has been extravagantly laud-

ed and ludicrously damned. But one thing about it remains: if you walk northwards from Oxford Circus for more than fifty yards you cannot miss it. The Round Church ceases to be the dominant architectural figure of the landscape. You stop. Your eyes travel slowly upwards from the bronze entrance doors; pause for a moment questioningly at Prospero and Ariel; continue by way of the flower-bordered balcony of the Director-General's room, past one row of windows after another, to the trellised metal towers upon the roof, and the flagstaff with the Corporation's flag flattering against the sky. You think. Announcers . . . News Bulletins . . . Dance Band Music . . . the Prime Minister speaking from the Guildhall . . . the Derby . . . Wimbledon . . . Gillie Potter . . . Christopher Stone . . . Walford Davies . . . Symphony . . . Concerts . . . Talks . . . Plays . . . Microphones . . . Machinery . . . Actors . . . Engineers . . . 'It's the hell of a big place anyway', you murmur to your companion, with a certain lack of conviction. (Gielgud & Marvell 1934, p. 7f)

Fig. 3. Broadcasting House, early 1940s (the exterior painted dark green, making the building less visible during bomb raids). Postcard from author's collection.

"Response to Tradition," a British modernist manifesto published in 1932 in *The Architectural Review*, opens with an imagined scene from the very same site. The writer is architect Wells Coates, the actual designer of the studio in which this fictitious murder takes place.

> A foreigner, let us say, on a tour of London walks to the top of Regent Street, and finding there four or five architectural critics standing about, points to a building on the corner and says: "What is that?"

> The variety of possible responses to his question might include that it was a building which "expressed its purpose", or its "construction"; or that it displayed very bad manners indeed; or that "expressed" an important aspect of the national life; or that it was an example of unsymmetrical design; or that it "looked like a ship" and was built of Portland stone; or he

might be told what he probably wanted to know, that, indeed, it was "Broadcasting House". Such a collection of verbal responses does not suggest an unfair picture of the state of architectural criticism today. (Coates 1932a, p. 165)

The metaphor of the ship has stuck with the building since. The external referents are actually quite few: the rounded external shape, the antennas/masts, the porthole-like windows at the top. But the ship, according to Michel Foucault (1967/1998), is the "heterotopia par excellence," i.e., the sort of place that, on the one hand, *does* have a real location (unlike the utopia), but that, on the other hand, remains "outside of all places," being strangely linked to, but also neutralizing, or contradicting, *all* other sites. To the editors of *The Architectural Review*, who devoted an entire issue to the opening of Broadcasting House in 1932, this building was not fixed by its geographical location:

> When it is the centre of a great public service, it has a double significance. People will come to London to see it; instead of swooning at Savoy Hill, they will see what to them will be the new Tower of London. On the covers of magazines, on films, in catalogues, in guide books, in all the many means of publicity the new B.B.C. building, its studios, its gadgets, its engineering devices, will appear. Since it is to be the new Tower of London, a focal point and a trade-mark for Broadcasting, it becomes something more than a mere block of offices, enclosing a sound factory. (*The Architectural Review* 1932, p. 43)

In terms of architectural style, the editors saw a mix of old and new.

> The finished building ... represents the outcome of a struggle between moribund traditionalism and inventive modernism. Struggles of this kind are not as a rule conducive to good architecture, and still less to good decoration. But in this case, fortunately, the struggle ended in a victory which largely favoured the modernists; for when it came to organizing the interior of a building of such a necessarily complex plan, the combined brains and help of a corps of architects and engineers were required. (*The Architectural Review* 1932, p. 47)

In other words, *tradition* was here represented by the *exterior*: the solid stone walls and the fenestration with small glass panes suggested the appearance of a medieval, concentric fortress. The *modern* was represented by the *interiors*, the site of the new, exciting technology, occupying the 22 studios, piled in an inner tower, with a huge control room sitting on top. "Whatever the outside looked like," noted the leading architectural critic J. M. Richards, the BBC deserved credit as the first official body to support modern architecture in Britain "by employing a team of the best young designers for the interior equipment and furnishing of studios."[5] According to V. H. Goldsmith (1932), the chair of BBC's "Studio Decorating Committee," their assignment was the outcome of a "battle," in which the principles of modernism—fitness for purpose, form following function—finally had defeated more "anachronistic" ideas: to decorate the studios as "period pieces" (in Venetian style, Jacobean style, etc., for different phases of history) or as varying locations of the Empire (an elephant head for India, a log cabin for Canada, etc.). In the end, only two studios were designed to resemble traditional interiors: one was the religious studio (for believers of any faith, according to the instructions), designed by Edward Maufe, including an artificial window/cyclorama, to mark the presence of infinity. It was rarely used after 1933, since the audience seemed to prefer its sermons delivered "from the atmosphere of an actual church" (Hines 2008, p. 75). In 1940, it was completely burned out, after a bomb attack.

The other was a studio that, according to instructions, should resemble a "small and quiet library, which might be found in an old town or country house." The idea was to accommodate "elderly dons and clergymen" who might be "frightened" by "the naked simplicity of functionalism and metal furniture" (Hines 2008, p. 75). This studio was designed by Dorothy Warren and included props like a fake fireplace. It was scorned as a "concession to the conservatism and weakness of human nature"[6] by Lord Gerald Wellesley, Fellow of the Royal Institute of British Architects, writing for the *BBC Yearbook 1933*.

All other studios were left to that team of young and radical modernists, consisting of Raymond McGrath, Wells Coates, and Serge Chermayeff. In the early 1930s, particularly Coates and Chermayeff stood at the center of a movement (cf. Cohen 2006), committed to breaking the "retrospective stupor"[7] of British design, introducing an architecture that embraced the era of "Steel and Communication" (Coates 1932a). Between 1931 and 1933, these two men visited the German Bauhaus, published articles, participated in exhibitions, formed organizations, designed interiors, and completed houses, still standing as modernist classics. The interior of Broadcasting House was one of their first assignments, and it certainly provided the shock of the new to Lord Wellesley:

> The interior of Broadcasting House is the most important example of untraditional decoration yet completed in this country. The accumulated rubbish or wisdom of the ages has been washed away, and something which is definitely and entirely new has taken its place. Such a phenomenon has never occurred before in the world's history.[8]

Interiorizing the Modern

The "struggle" between old/exterior and new/interior was a topic of interest in Siegfried Giedion's (1928/1995) *Bauen in Frankreich*, and a work it soon came to inspire: Walter Benjamin's (1999) *Passagen-Werk*. Looking back at industrial constructions from the nineteenth century—arcades, railway stations, factories—Giedion saw the traditional and the modern caught in transition:

Fig. 4. Studio 3E, for Religious Services. The central recess is lighted "to produce an effect of infinite distance." From *Broadcasting House* (1932), BBC Photo Library.

Fig. 5. Studio for Religious Services in 1940, burned out after a bomb attack, with surviving statue of St. George (Vernon Hill, sculptor). BBC Photo Library.

> Outwardly, construction still boasts the old pathos, underneath, concealed behind the old facades, the basis of our present existence is taking shape. (Giedion 1928/1995, p. 87)

By the 1930s, however, such masks should be long gone. To Giedion and Benjamin, and to Coates, in his manifesto, stone was the material of old architecture. With steel, glass, concrete, the piled-up wall was no longer an essential element of the structure. From there on, Giedion claimed, modern housing should strive for "the greatest possible overcoming of gravity" and "maximum openness":

> Corbusier's houses are neither spatial nor plastic: air flows through them! ... There is only a single, indivisible space. The shell falls away between interior and exterior. (Giedion 1928/1995, p. 169)

This conception of modern architecture is revisited in Beatriz Colomina's (1994) *Privacy and Publicity: Modern Architecture as Mass Media*. This book declares that "modern architecture only becomes modern with its engagement with the media" (p. 14) and that "the building is a mechanism of representation in its own right" (p. 13). The private homes of Le Corbusier exemplify how the use of windows may transform the home into a camera, directed towards outer forms of life, and transgressing demarcations of inner and outer through light and transparence.

With Broadcasting House, though, something else must surely be going on. For the stony shell of tradition—heavy, closed, monumental—is still there. And while the "falling away" of the shell of *domestic* space may be linked to the breaking up of distinctions between private and public (a main argument in Colomina's book), Broadcasting House is neither private nor domestic. It is planned as the space of a *public service*. And while Colomina tends to link media and architecture in *visual* terms (as when comparing Le Corbusier's interior plans to the mechanisms of a camera), Broadcasting House is planned as a "sound factory."

To Lt. Col. Val Myer, chief architect of the original Broadcasting House, the task of the programme was clear:

> In the case of Broadcasting House, we had first to consider its functions. These are twofold; the actual broadcasting, and the administration of broadcasting. Obviously, the studios, Control Room, and the accommodation of technical equipment come first, with the actual studios as the most important factor of all. Accordingly, it was the planning of the studios which had to be the key to the whole scheme.[9]

And the main concern in that scheme was sound insulation. Every single studio had to be acoustically sealed off from the outside world (and all the other studios). Val Myer's general solution was to erect an inner brick tower for the studios, and to wrap the administrative offices around that tower.

With this plan, the interiorizing of the modern seems less the result of the concealment of tradition, than a series of functions relating to *both* media and architecture.

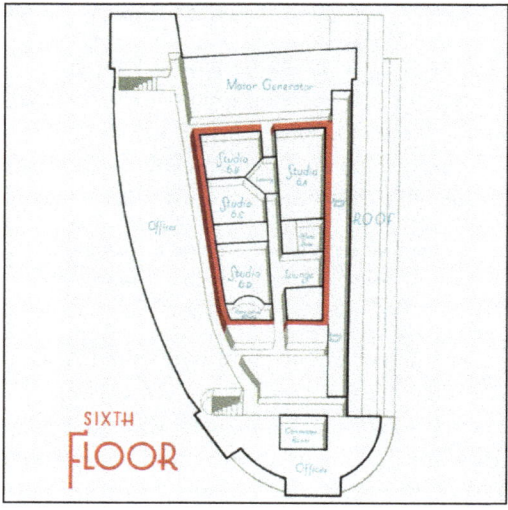

Fig. 6. Plan of Broadcasting House, sixth floor. From *Broadcasting House* (1932), BBC Photo Library.

First, the plan realized a major *technological* step in the development of housing. Since the open air could not "flow" through Broadcasting House, it had to produce its own. With the embalming of the inner tower, each studio had to be supplied with artificial (and quiet) ventilation, humidity, temperature, lighting. According to Kenneth Frampton (1983), historian of architecture, the artificial control of light and climate is technology's most decisive influence on the modern building: from that point on, connection to local context may be cut, and truly universal standardization applied. Broadcasting House was the first building in London to realize this possibility, as a direct result of the demands of media production.

Second, this plan reflected an *ideal model* of the *media institution* at the time. Howard Robertson, Principal of the Architectural Association School, compared the plan of the building with a medieval castle:

> There is the central Donjon, the Keep, which is the inner core, and round it are more public apartments, the service ways, like the outer ring of the defence. In the new building the public might invade the corridors, and even the offices, but the staff of the BBC could take refuge in their inner fastness, lock themselves in, live, cook, eat, circulate, and even produce music, plays, and noises-to-taste, without in any way being disturbed. (*The Architectural Review* 1932, p. 43)

The special need for interior design was derived from this model:

> The new Broadcasting House is unique. It is in essentials a factory for the production and reproduction of sound, but it is not sufficient that it shall behave perfectly as a machine: it is considered vital that the artist shall derive inspiration from his surroundings, and in consequence some form of permanent interior finish or decoration is regarded as an integral part of the scheme. In the coordination of this and a chaos of complicated mechanical equipment lay the architects' task. (*The Architectural Review* 1932, p. liv)

Third, in terms of a "machine," this plan suggests alternative ways of thinking "architecture as mass medium." Returning to the plan (Fig. 6), we may recognize a familiar shape: a human ear, with the studio tower in the position of the inner ear. Though this effect may be unintentional, the plan spatially reproduces what, according to Jonathan Sterne (2003), is the ultimate technological model of sound reproduction since the eighteenth century. Through various mechanisms (the eardrum, the bones of the inner ear, the auditory nerve), the human ear has the capacity to turn incoming sound into something else, and that something else back into sound. The imitation of this "transducing" mechanism was the key to various experiments leading to the telephone (using electricity and phone lines), the gramophone (using tracks and styluses), and the radio (using electromagnetic waves and transmitters/receivers). In this sense, Broadcasting House may actually qualify as a medium, "in its own right" (Colomina): one large-scale, spatially organized, *tympanic machine*.

Making the building perform like one was at any rate a prime task for the team of interior designers, according to V. H. Goldsmith:

> When it is remembered that the position of every piece of ventilating equipment, every lamp, every signal light, microphone lead, bell push, observation window, telephone, and every piece of furniture was fixed dependent on the precise needs of the programme in each individual studio ... that in addition thereto every material used, from quality of paint to nature of fabric, was subject to restriction as to its sound-absorbing or reflecting qualities, its position and area, it will be realized that never have interior designers had to solve a problem more severely conditioned. (Goldsmith 1932, p. 55)

McGrath and Chermayeff designed some of the larger studios, and other spaces with more public functions: like the vaudeville studio (Fig. 7), the "wireless military band" and dance studios (Figs. 8, 9), and the listening rooms (Fig. 10).

Coates was committed to the spaces solely defined by the functions of broadcasting: the control room (Fig. 11), the studios designed for drama, talk, news, gramophones, sound effects (Figs. 12, 13, 14). Including their equipment: Coates designed the air-suspended microphone fitting (Fig. 13) that picked up sonic effects from the walls, floors, and tanks of the effect studio to produce "every conceivable noise" (Fig. 14).

Coates also designed the Dramatic Control Panel (Fig. 15), that mixed incoming sounds from up to eleven studios, into one broadcasted play.

Fig. 7. Vaudeville Studio BA, from the balcony. From *Broadcasting House* (1932), BBC Photo Library.

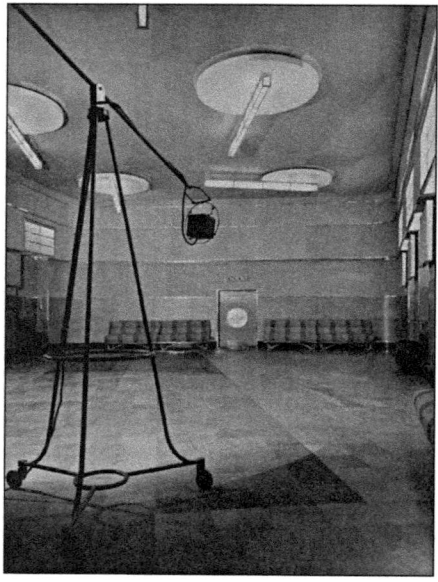

Fig. 8. Studio 8A, for the "Wireless Military Band and other orchestras," From *Broadcasting House* (1932), BBC Photo Library.

THE INTERIOR OF THE UBIQUITOUS: BROADCASTING HOUSE | 33

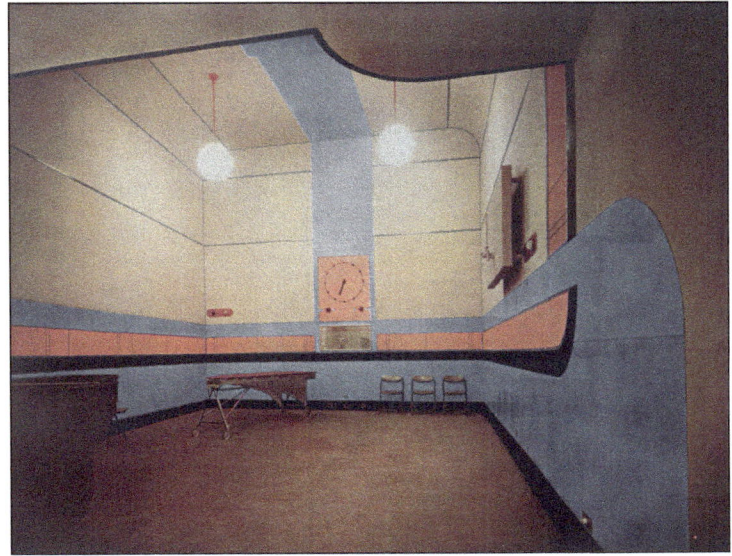

Fig. 9. Dance Band Studio BB. From *The Architectural Review* (August) 1932.

Fig. 10. Listening Hall 2, basement. Gold and silver foil produces the effect of daylight.
From *Broadcasting House* (1932), BBC Photo Library.

Fig. 11. Central Control Room, 8th floor. From *The Architectural Review* (August) 1932.

Fig. 12. News Studio 4b, with separate cubicles for editor and announcer. From *Broadcasting House* (1932), BBC Photo Library.

THE INTERIOR OF THE UBIQUITOUS: BROADCASTING HOUSE | 35

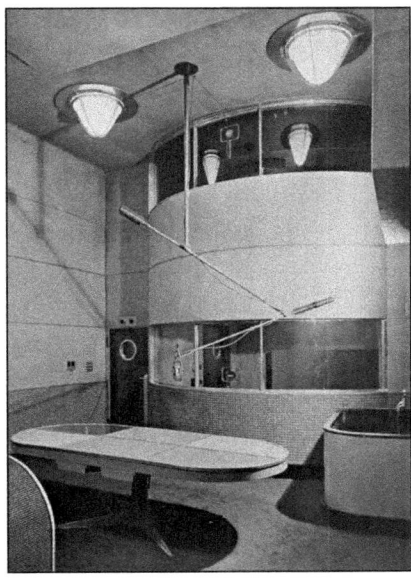

Fig. 13. Studio 6D, for Sound Effects. From *Broadcasting House* (1932), BBC Photo Library.

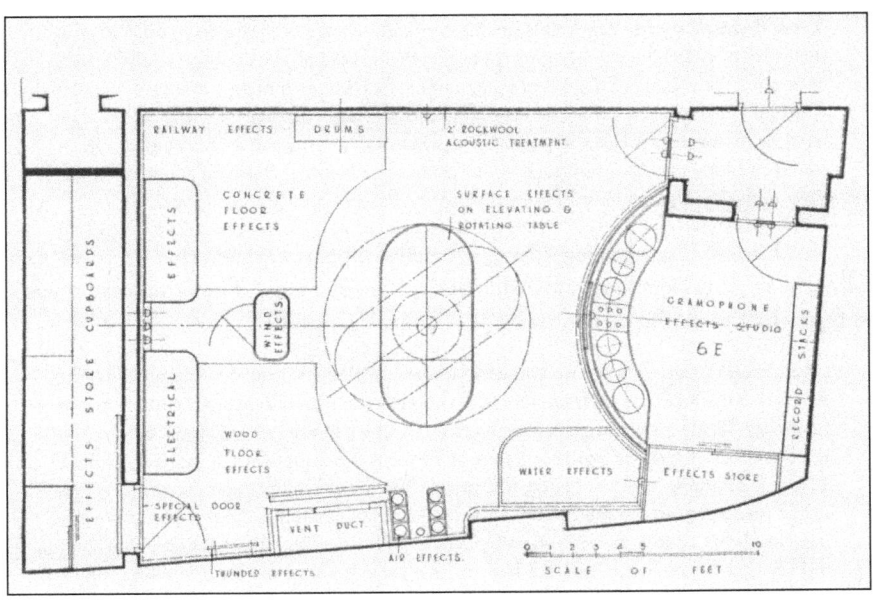

Fig. 14. Plan for Studios 6D and E. From *The Architectural Review* (August) 1932.

Fig. 15. The Dramatic Control Panel, 8th floor. From *The Architectural Review* (August) 1932.

Coates explained the function of this device, in *The Architectural Review*:

> At the dramatic control panel table sits the producer, who gives the actors in other studios their cues by switching on cue lights controlled by the keys on the dramatic control panel, or governs the volume of the sound going out to the ether by turning the control handles which, if necessary, can cut out any studio or actor. Thus, when dramatic effects like rain, wind, or the hoofs of a horse are required, a switch will give the cue to the dramatic effects studio on another floor, and the turning of a control handle will increase the sound or diminish it until the producer cuts it out by turning the handle back. (Coates 1932c)

In *Death at Broadcasting House*, Detective Spears realizes that to solve this crime, he must understand "the inside of that box of tricks." The producer explains to him why the performers must be physically separated:

> "Well," said Caird, "the chief reasons why we use several studios and not one, are two. The first is that by the use of separate studios, the producer can get different acoustic effects for his scenes. That is to say, in a small studio like 7C, which is built as to exclude all echo, you get the effect of a closed room or a dungeon—as in the scene when Parsons was killed. Whereas in a fairly large studio like 6A, you can get the effect of greater spaciousness—as in the scene previous to the murder scene, a ballroom. Secondly, the modern radio play depends for its 'continuity'—if you understand the film analogy—upon the ability to 'fade' one scene at its conclusion into the next. In an elaborate play, therefore, the actors require as many studios as the varying acoustics of the different scenes require, while, in order to avoid their being confused by music or extraneous noises, sound effects have a studio of their own,

gramophone effects one more, and the orchestra providing the orchestral music yet another separate one." (Gielgud & Marvell 1934, p. 78)

The overall attention that the BBC paid to the studios when erecting their first headquarters, and particularly the type of tasks executed by Coates, lends support to a bearing argument in Jonathan Sterne's (2003) book on *The Audible Past*:

> Without studios, and without other social placements of microphones in performative frames that were always real spaces, there was no independent reproducibility of sound. . . . This is contrary to the often-made claim that reproduction decontextualizes performance and deterritorializes sound . . . From the very beginning, recorded sound was a studio art. (Sterne 2003, p. 236)

In such studios, people performed for the machines, not for audiences. The machines were built to reproduce sounds, not eavesdrop on existing, "original" ones. In contrast with discourses that stress "liveness" and "fidelity," Sterne claims that distinctions between copy and original, artificial and real, were irrelevant in the early days of mass-distributed sound reproduction. In contrast with discourses that attribute "no sense of place" (Meyrowitz 1985) to broadcasting, Sterne claims that such events were the product of a reproducibility to which "location was everything."

This argument connects to the plot of *Death at Broadcasting House* and to themes in Walter Benjamin's artwork essay. Here, Benjamin exemplifies the loss of "aura" by a visit to a film studio: a site where an actor performs for the machines and where a visitor never loses sight of the technical equipment. The film spectator, though, will see none of it:

> The mechanical equipment has penetrated so deeply into reality that its pure aspect freed from the foreign substance of equipment is the result of a special procedure, namely the shooting by the specially adjusted camera and the mounting of the shot together with similar ones. The equipment-free aspect of reality here has become the height of artifice; the sight of immediate reality has become an orchid in the land of technology. (Benjamin 1936/1968, p. 233)

According to Benjamin, this "procedure" was unimaginable before film. And according to V. H. Goldsmith, the studios of Broadcasting House could not duplicate the practice of film.

> In the film studio, not only do production and rehearsal precede a 'shot', as they do for some of the work in broadcasting, but 'shots' can be repeated until the desired result is achieved. This repetition of 'shot' is not possible in broadcasting, hence every help must be given to the artist in his one and only actuality. (Goldsmith 1932, p. 53)

In other words, Benjamin's "equipment-free reality" was here to be performed in real time. This was the rationale behind the organization of the studios of

Broadcasting House. And part of the dilemma of detective Spears was that this crime had only left traces in equipment-free reality. But in a chapter titled "The Voices of the Dead," Detective Spears gets a sudden break: he learns that the broadcast has been preserved by a "Blattner-phone", an early steel tape recorder, in order for it to be retransmitted across the British Empire.

Fig. 16. Blattner-phone from 1934. BBC Photo Library.

"Re-transmitted?" repeated Spears. "Do you mean to say that–By Jove!" ... Spears smacked his fist down in the desk in front of him. "You mean you´ve got the play recorded?" he said, and even in his voice there was a thrill of excitement. "You mean you can hear the actual scene over again?" "We can hear that scene", said Caird, "not only over again, but over and over again. As often as you like. I wonder if the murderer thought of that?" (Gielgud & Marvell 1934, p. 38f)

In terms of solid evidence, this playback turns out to be a disappointment. At one point, the listeners think they *might* hear a watch ticking, just seconds before the strangulation—a possible trace of the murderer, since the victim was not wearing one—but, then again, the *natural* appearance of recorded sound is no longer to be trusted, according to the sound effects man:

> You see, in the old days when we started with sound effects, we did our best to make the real noise in front of the microphone. At Savoy Hill, I believe it's true that people fired blank cartridges along the corridors, and even assembled the greater part of an aeroplane and then

dropped it from the ceiling of the studio to get the effect of an aeroplane crash. Now we know better. We wreck ships by crumpling match boxes and create avalanches with a drum and few potatoes. (Gielgud & Marvell 1934, p. 61)

Furthermore, the *locality* of those sounds are already undistinguishable, after being edited at the Dramatic Control Panel, fading and mixing between different studios. The final solution, the detective concludes, is "inseparably connected with the methods and ingredients of broadcast play production" and with "the geography" and "inside working of Broadcasting House" (p. 96). Like the murderer before him (constructing his perfect alibi), this detective must reproduce the full conditions of a "land of technology," as organized by Coates and his colleagues.

Liquidating the Interior

The BBC found its first original, successful radio sitcom formula in 1938, with a show called *Band Waggon*. Its premise is that two comic characters have taken up residence in an imagined flat at the top of Broadcasting House. They actually *live* in that deserted studio, with five hens and one goat. While much of the show sounded like an ordinary variety act—a mix of music and sketches, recorded live, with a studio audience—it provided a mythical space in which the characters could physically intervene in the process of live broadcasting, barracking the announcer, calling for and (mocking) the invisible sound-effect man, and acting as caretakers of the BBC's time signal.

The premise of this show contradicts the preferred scenario for linking media and architecture (cf. Rice 2007), where the "home" (an actual, preexistent site) is being infiltrated, disturbed, or challenged by "the media" (immaterial, siteless). In the career and mind of Coates, however, designing the broadcasting studios of the BBC more or less coincided with a rethinking of domesticity. In an article from 1932, "Furniture Today and Furniture Tomorrow," Coates claims that the modern architect should not be concerned with various styles and fashions, but with "the organisation of a new service."

The natural starting place for this new service must be the scene in which the daily drama of personal life takes place; the interior of the dwelling—the PLAN— and its living-equipment, the furniture. (Coates 1932b, p. 31)

Coates pursued this ideal as chief architect for ISOKON (Isometric Unit Construction), a company set up in 1931 to produce "unit dwellings" with inbuilt furniture and accessories. The most renowned result was Lawn Road Flats, projected and completed between 1930 and 1934.

Fig. 17. Lawn Road Flats, London, 2007. Architect Wells Coates, 1934. Photo by author.

This complex, located in Hampstead, London, consists of thirty "minimal flats" (from 18 to 30 square meters), with adjacent "communal" areas—club, bar, rooftop terrace, garden, garage—including a "very full domestic service"[10] (washing, cleaning, cooking, shoe-shining). Lawn Road Flats attracted some interesting tenants, among them Agatha Christie (!), and the international avant-garde of design: off and on during the 1930s, Lawn Road Flats housed members of the German Bauhaus—Marcel Breuer, Walter Gropius, László Moholy-Nagy—all at some point providing assistance to ISOKON's designs. When Coates died in 1958, the memorial in *The Architectural Review* claimed that Lawn Road Flats was "nearer to the *machine à habiter* than anything Le Corbusier ever designed."[11]

Raymond McGrath noted that the practice of "architecting" rather than "decorating" the studios of Broadcasting House should serve as an "excellent example for interior work other than studios."[12] And there are some tangible correspondences between Coates' organizing of studios (as in Broadcasting House) and his notion of a "machine for living" (as in Lawn Road Flats). In terms of "the plan," Coates organizes his dwellings as *minimal* units, externalizing their points of access (stairs) and social functions (communal spaces), serving them from the outside with all necessities (water, heating, air), and insuring that "conducted sound had been reduced to an absolute minimum."[13] Visually, the open air solutions of Le Corbusier could not be more distant (and complaints of claustrophobia were soon heard from both the tenants of Lawn Road Flats and the artists of BBC). The idea of a "total design" was equally applicable to the studio and the dwelling. In the late 1930s, Coates designed several popular British radio sets for home use.

Fig. 18. Radio, EK Cole Ltd. Model AD-65, designed by Wells Coates, 1932.
Courtesy of V&A images, Victoria and Albert Museum.

To Coates, tables and beds were no more "personal belongings" than heating systems or bathtubs, and the first step of supplying the proper "living-equipment" was obliterating the "old-world dwelling-scene" of our parents:

> How barbaric their habit of overloading was! How seldom did an object stand in the place which correlation points to it! How obtrusive their pictures and ornamental bric-à-brac! (Coates 1932b, p. 32)

Coates presented his most radical proposal of "unit dwelling" in 1947 as a (never realized) plan for production of room units, to be ordered in parts off the shelf, complete to the last light switch, and transportable to the countryside for the weekend. Already in 1932, Coates was arguing for a notion of a modern dwelling that was not fixed by location:

> The love of travel and change, the mobility of the worker himself, grows with every opportunity to indulge in it. The 'home' is no longer a permanent place from one generation to

another. The old phrase about a man's 'appointed place' meant a real territorial limit; now the limits of our experience are expanding with every invention of science. (Coates 1932b, p. 32)

In other words, Coates' idea of modern dwelling was committed to that "structure of feeling" that Raymond Williams (1974/1997) used to explain the development of broadcasting: *mobile privatization*. With his notion of a "furniture of tomorrow," Coates presented the architect with the task of providing "supplies, equipment for the living of a free life":

> There is an important distinction to be realized between what is 'possessed' as an adjunct of personal vanity or wealth (a 'museum-piece' you are told, with a smack of satisfaction) and what is merely included for use in the dwelling-scene for what its efficiency and formal significance is worth in the daily drama and routine of life. In the latter case the article is not valued as a 'personal possession' so much as a means, a medium, for the liberation of individual values and appetencies which alone are the truly 'personal possessions' of a man. (Coates 1932b, p. 33)

Such articles were to be "machine-made" and affordable for "the people." They would reveal "the colossal pretence that has stood for 'art'." In other words, while referring to furniture as a "medium," Coates made similar predictions, and similar distinctions, as Walter Benjamin in his artwork essay, written a few years later.

In his *Passagen-Werk*, Benjamin had already registered the loss of aura through the history of our interior dwellings. He starts out with the bourgeois apartments of the nineteenth century:

> In the style characteristic of the second empire, the apartment becomes a sort of cockpit. The traces of its inhabitant are moulded into the interior. Here is the origin of the detective story, which inquires into these traces and follows these tracks. (Benjamin 1999, p. 20)

With the turn of the century, this sense of the interior was lost. The challenge of the modern was to embrace this loss. In an article from 1933, "Experience and Poverty," Benjamin describes the contemporary as a barbaric, impoverished space, where "naked man …lies screaming like a newborn baby in the dirty diapers of the present" (Benjamin 1996–2003, p. 733). Still, this world would provide housing for its citizens. Benjamin is fascinated by the "stations for living" imagined by poet Paul Scheerbart: "adjustable, movable, glass-covered dwellings of the kind since built by Loos and Corbusier" (p. 733):

> Objects made of glass have no 'aura'. Glass is, in general, the enemy of secrets. It is also the enemy of possession. (Benjamin 1996–2003, p. 734)

This was a "liquidation of the interior" ("1939 exposé," Benjamin 1999, p. 20) that did not lament lost experience, that executed the necessary break with the (always illusory) "dream image" of private life as a space of refuge for the individual.

> If you enter a bourgeois room of the 1880s, for all the coziness it radiates, the strongest impression you receive may well be, "You've got no business here!" And in fact you have no business in that room, for there is no spot on which the owner has not left his mark—the ornaments on the mantelpiece, the antimacassars on the armchairs, the transparencies in the windows. A neat phrase by Brecht helps us out here: "Erase the traces!" is the refrain in the first poem of his *Lesebuch für Städtebewohner*... This has now been achieved by Scheerbart, with his glass, and Bauhaus, with its steel. They have created rooms in which it is hard to leave traces. (Benjamin 1996–2003, p. 734)

And this is the sort of room in which a dead corpse is placed in *Death at Broadcasting House*. The producer and the writer discover it, after the broadcast has ended:

> In the far corner, almost under the microphone standard, lay a man's figure unnaturally crumpled.... Behind the three of them the door shut automatically. 7C was a studio with special acoustic treatment removing all natural echo, and at that moment Rodney Fleming felt acutely the oppressive, almost sinister atmosphere of the room with its single shaded light, its thick carpet and queerly padded walls. The ventilation was perfect, but he felt he wanted to draw unusually deep breaths. (Gielgud & Marvell 1934, p. 17)

Scotland Yard arrives, and the room is properly photographed and searched. But the detective is left without traces to track:

> "This room's as bare as a board.... Here are the contents of the pockets, sir." / ... /There was something indescribably wretched and forlorn about the little pile of coppers: the paper packet of ten Players cigarettes, three quarters empty; the indubitable pawn-ticket; the soiled handkerchief; the three loose keys on a piece of knotted string: the chubbed stump of pencil; and the shabby pigskin pocket book. (Gielgud & Marvell 1934, p. 33)

These are the possessions of modern man, the traces of a crime committed in the interior of the modern. According to this novel, Broadcasting House was not only a marvel of technology, but a scary place to be. Its interiors were soon to produce even stronger images of terror. In George Orwell's *1984* from 1949, Room 101 is the chamber for psychological torture, a room where our imaginary fears will suddenly and inexplicably materialize. The original Room 101 is believed to have been located in Broadcasting House, where Orwell worked during the Second World War. In his novel, this room contains "the worst things in the world," that is, no specific objects at all, since the worst thing imaginable will vary individually: to be buried alive, to drown, or, the fear of the protagonist Winston, to have your face eaten by rats. And perhaps this is the scariest aspect of Room 101: once you enter, your torturers will reveal that they have access to your most private space and your worst inner fears.

Before finally demolishing the interior structure of Broadcasting House, in preparation for the ongoing redevelopment, the BBC asked British artist Rachel Whiteread for a cast of its most infamous space: Room 101.

Fig. 19. Untitled (Room 101). © Rachel Whiteread. Courtesy of Gagosian Gallery. Photo by Mike Bruce.

It is an odd memorial, a countermove to Benjamin's "liquidation of the interior" or the Brechtian motto: "Erase the traces!" In Whiteread's Room 101, the features of interior space are inverted; the metaphor for the worst thing in the world is transformed into an object—"blank" and "ghostly," but material. When asked what would be in her own Room 101 (that is, her worst fear), Whiteread replied: "Outer space."[14]

> "Because there are no walls, no parameters, nothing to relate me to the earth, nothing to stop you going off. I would find that frightening."

About as frightening as Mircea Eliade's "profane space"—borderless, fluid, chaotic. Maybe Whiteread's casting of interiors is a contemporary version of founding sacred space, of establishing a centre of the world. To reconnect with ourselves, rather than the gods, what is needed is not the raising of spires, but the solidification of social space.

Interiorizing the Social

In 2000, the BBC decided to transform Broadcasting House into one "huge, highly efficient global broadcasting machine."[15] After a limited competition, the task was awarded to MacCormac Jamieson Prichard Architects (MJP), led by Richard MacCormac.[16] The demands from the client were clear[17]: in terms of a machine, the building should "go digital," from beginning to end of its production process. In terms of a headquarters, the building should reflect the vision of "One BBC," promoted by Greg Dyke, Director General at the time. And even more important, its expression must break with the model of the closed media institution, where artists occupied an ivory tower. To Dyke, the old Broadcasting House had spoken of a "self confident organisation with a clear vision of its role in the world." But it could not "reflect the values and ethos of the modern BBC":

> "As a building it's patriarchal, even frightening.... today, the BBC needs buildings that connect with our audiences, not buildings that frighten them."[18]

"For the first time," declared the publicity material, "the BBC in central London will have a public face accessible to all—where broadcaster and audience can meet directly."[19] MacCormac compared his ambition with the new British Library:

> This kind of monumentality is not imposed upon us; it is assigned by us . . . You are [now] invited to be a participant, not merely a spectator.[20]

The time had come to let the "shell fall away," to construct a building in one "single, indivisible space," to use Sigfried Giedion's description, from back in the 1920s (Giedion 1928/1995, p. 169). MacCormac's overall strategy, however, did not so much seek the "maximum openness" suggested by Giedion, but the framing of so-called *interstitial* space (Jackson 2003, chapter 4). In natural geography, the interstitial is the shoreline. In MacCormac's architecture, the interstitial is defined as social space, an interface for meetings. From this follows his reinterpretation of the function of the building, not in terms of what the factory produces, but in terms of the social and symbolic organization that it houses (MacCormac 2005).

How, then, is this notion translated into architecture? When describing the interior organization of the new extension, MacCormac tends to refer to public, outside places: the marketplace, the high street, the forum, and the thoroughfare,[21] places where people may interlock, and become physically and visually aware of each other (like they will, it is assumed, inside the new Broadcasting House, on its stairs, circulation routes, and breakout areas). What is being interiorized, then, is not so much modern space, as (old) public space.

To express the interstitial externally, MacCormac enhances the opposites (inside/outside, light/heavy, convex/concave, opacity/transparency) through which this "in-between" may be experienced.

Fig. 20. The new Broadcasting House and Langham Place, when completed in 2012. Computer-generated image, MacCormac Jamieson Prichard Architects, © Hayes Davidson.

The new spire of the artwork, for instance, has the same geometric dimension as that of the church, but it is turned upside down and made transparent. The heavy convexity of the old building is countered and inverted by the air-light concavity of an open-air square or theater, surrounded by a special type of layered glass, prepared to produce a sensation of volume:

> During daylight the patterned areas of the screen will appear relatively opaque and comparable to the Portland stone of Broadcasting House. At twilight the façade behaves like a theatre scrim becoming relatively transparent as interior light levels exceed the level of daylight. The transparency can be reversed or varied by external floodlighting or by images projected on the façade.[22]

What this new building encircles and encapsulates, then, is no longer the keep of the artists, the core of the tympanic machine. The main idea behind the winning solution of MacCormac/MJP was to create an "urban cyclorama" between the old building and the new extension: a "new public space" that would "draw people into the heart of the BBC" (Hines 2008, p. 126).

While waiting for this heart to open up, we may, since 2008, step inside the old one. For one day each month, always on a Sunday (a "day of rest" in live broadcasting), the BBC offers a tour to the interiors of Broadcasting House. It starts out much like this article[23]: In the entrance hall, the guides direct your eyes toward the past (the Gill sculptures, the Latin inscription) while informing you about the oncoming future (how the BBC is "going digital," how the World Service is joining from Bush House, how thousands more are coming from Television Centre, to establish the "largest broadcasting news studio in the world").

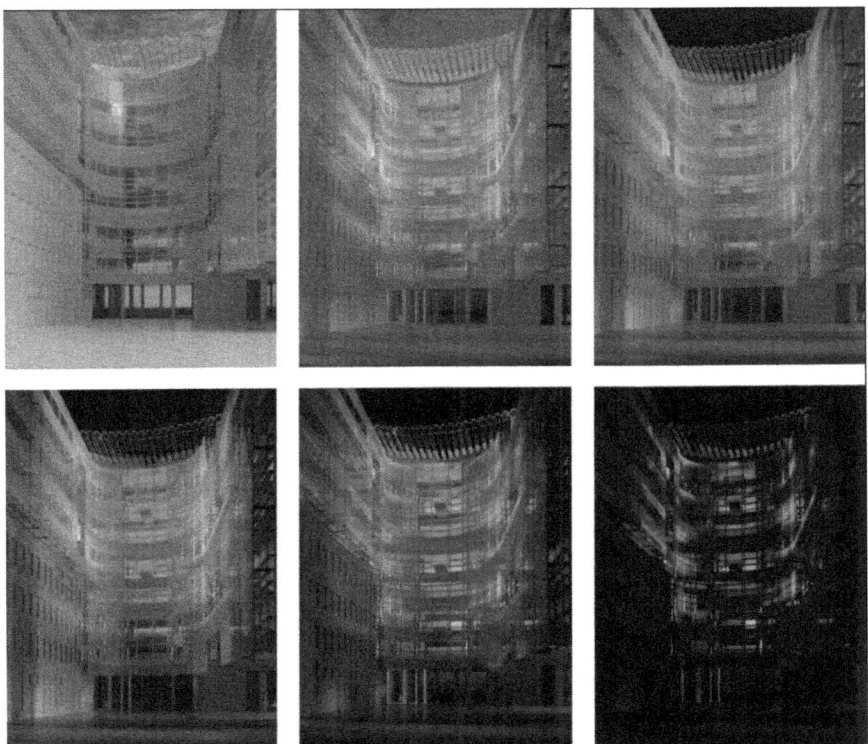

Fig. 21. Study model for exploring the relationship between internal and external lighting in the new cyclorama. © MacCormac Jamieson Prichard Architects.

According to the Web site of BBC Tours,[24] a visitor to Broadcasting House will experience "famous heritage spaces as well as the latest digital workspaces." So what is a "heritage space"? The term refers to the governmental adviser English Heritage and its system for listing buildings with particular architectural and historical interest. Since 1995, Broadcasting House has been listed as a Grade 2*-building, i.e., in the top 8 percent. On their Web page,[25] the English Heritage shows a picture of the front of Broadcasting House and supplies rich information about the exterior design (the sculptures, the Portland Stone, the fenestration, etc.). As for the interiors and the studios, one sentence tells the whole story: the "innovative" and "original" work of Coates, McGrath, Chermayeff, have by now all been "removed."

So what is now being preserved as the proud heritage of the BBC is basically what already in the 1930s signified tradition. While what was considered modern and forward-looking at the time, more or less had vanished within a decade. Its "liquidation" started almost immediately, for a number of reasons. The workforce of the BBC more than doubled within four years after opening Broadcasting House, proving that the scale of their home had been seriously underestimated. Experiments with television started inside Broadcasting House already in 1932, establishing new and different spatial needs. And then the bombs fell from the air, destroying or setting fire to many of the original interiors, calling for a securing of the building's central functions from modern warfare.

The team of MJP architects that entered Broadcasting House in 2002 to start the first phase of renovation thus had an interesting dilemma: by the codes of English Heritage, they were obliged to respect the past. At the same time, they shared the predicament of Detective Spears: traces of that past had already been erased. According to Hines, "accurate measured survey and historic paint analysis" was applied, but remnants of 1932's interiors were difficult to spot: the "intact-looking" turned out to be replacements with "lookalike fixtures and fittings." So "heritage area" came to mean "in the spirit of the original spaces" (Hines 2008, p. 131), mainly referring to spaces like the concert hall, the council chamber, and entrance hall, originally designed in a "classical" style, by Val Myer himself. And the main evidence for reconstructing that "original" spirit existed outside the building: in documents or reproductions (including, one would imagine, the series of photographs displayed in these pages).

In the absence of material traces, the past has to be imagined. The guides of the tour are offering assistance and their references soon display a pattern. There are frequent comments about historical *style*: the "Art Deco" clocks being a preferred object of illustration, though the current ones, as the guides point out, are neither originals nor exact replicas (this would violate the codes of English Heritage). There are plenty of anecdotes about the "funny" lifestyles of the past, many of which, for some reason, illustrate sexual inhibition: Reith's firing of homosexuals, the controversy around the size of Ariel's male organ, the required use of stockings for employed ladies, the separation of sexes when personnel slept over during the bomb raids. The past, it seems, was a place of restraint and *restriction*, and the old studio tower provided a fitting setting: it is referred to as "a box within a box, a rabbit hole," a "maze" with hundreds of doors, every cavity filled with cables and tapes. The *primitive* nature of past technology is another recurrent topic: the material used for sound insulation in those first studios was actually eelgrass. And Val Myer's attempt to isolate the studios from the outer world was a failure from day one: the rumbling of the underground passing below was felt and heard in the studios, in regular intervals.

Most of all, the past is portrayed as a *dark* place. During the visit to the Council Chamber, lighting is dimmed down, to provide some authentic historical atmosphere. The effects of renovation is repeatedly illustrated by the introduction of light: in the concert hall, where the new system of spotlights allow for the production of television, web, and radio, in the new, "open" working spaces, where only windows will separate the producers from that "lovely public plaza" outside, and the view down Regent Street.

Inside the renovated studio tower, the guides refer to the visitors as contemporary radio listeners. We are visiting the site of origin of particular programmes: *Desert Island Disc, Woman's Hour*. The ultimate experience aimed at is clearly stated by one guide when wrapping up her demonstration in one of these rooms:

> There you go. You can now say you have been in the Desert Island Studio.

"Being there"—that original promise of broadcasting. So is a visit to one of those studios really an encounter with its "aura"? In Nick Couldry's study of the tours to the sets of *Coronation Street*, "being there" provides sufficient significance for most of the visitors (Couldry 2000, p. 105). And its essence is getting a sense of that set's "reality *as* a set" (p. 89). In contrast with Benjamin's thesis on the *loss* of aura in the age of mechanical reproduction, what the visitors actually want to obtain is, according to Couldry, "the aura of the place and process of filming itself" (p. 81). An aura, which Couldry, following and quoting Benjamin, grounds in the authenticity of that set's material history: a "testimony to the history which it has experienced." In that respect, the exterior set of *Coronation Street* will deliver more than a "mere studio," where, according to one of the visitors, "you do see [. . .] the unreality" (p. 81), whereas you might actually get your feet wet during a visit to the exterior set, as that visitor has experienced:

> And I stood in a puddle and thought, Oh Crikey! Yes, this is real, it's not covered over, it's always outdoors . . . the actors go out in all weather [. . .] it's real rain and it's real cobbles and it's real dirt (laughs). You don't expect a set to be that real. (Couldry 2000, p. 81)

To Couldry, the rain provides that visitor with a "definitive access" to the aura of the set. It is not entirely clear how such an "access" would correlate to the notion of aura evoked by Benjamin: "the unique phenomenon of *distance* however close it may be" (Benjamin 1936/1968, p. 243, emphasis added). Nevertheless, the studios of Broadcasting House should present a different case: here, we are not visiting the "reality of the fiction" of *Desert Island Disc*. No rain will ever fall inside these studios, and their equipment bears little material testimony to historical experience.

In this studio, "being there" seems to confirm something entirely different than distance to a unique "here and now." Rather the opposite: a denial of absence, of that ever-present, ubiquitous connection, which is not primarily to be applied to the "here and now" of that particular studio, but to the past and the future, and to every other place: *everytime* you listen (or have listened) to *Desert Island Disc*, *wherever* you may be (or have been). What is confirmed, then, by "being there," is not so much the aura of the studio, as the comforting effect suggested by Whiteread's inverted castings: yes, that ubiquitous *does* have an interior.

There is another side to "being there," however, that awaits the visitor to Broadcasting House. The climax of the tour turns out to be a demonstration of a contemporary version of the Dramatic Control Panel, i.e., that "bag of tricks" that baffled detective Spears. The group is led into one of the studios, where they are offered the "opportunity of a lifetime"—stepping inside the process of media production. The setup is the recording of a short segment of radio drama: a horror story, where characters seek refuge in a spooky house. About half of the group members are given assignments, following a script: some are actors, reading lines, some push buttons on computers for prerecorded background noises, some produce sound effects manually (flapping leather gloves in a microphone, for the sound of bat wings). After some quick instructions, the segment is performed in real time, playfully and clumsily, with much laughter. Afterwards, an edited version of the segment is played out, with full-blown sound effects. We now hear how those isolated bits may be integrated into one smooth, apparently authentic, soundscape—so smooth, in fact, that this particular visitor misunderstands the conditions of its production. When exiting, he overhears one of the "actors" noting that the segment had sounded so "real," that he barely recognized his own voice. Could it be that we had listened back to the performances of our particular group, our actual voices, and sound effects? That the dramatic segment actually was remixed, with the visit of every new group? The guides are called back and confronted with this question. They find it odd. Of course it was (our actual performance). If not, what would have been the point of the demonstration?

What, indeed, was the point? Obviously one corresponding with MacCormac's view on monumentality: we were invited as participators, not mere spectators. Maybe also with Eliade's view on sacred space: we were invited to "reproduce the work of the gods," or, at least, to create "equipment-free" reality, in Benjamin's land of technology.

Death at Broadcasting House 2.0

Or were we? Things may of course be complicated, by the fact that Benjamin was writing about the *analogical* reproduction of *images*. And that original Dramatic Control Panel was designed to mix live and prerecorded *sounds*. While this tour has demonstrated sound reproduction within a *digital*, "tapeless" environment, with control panels that are primarily operated visually, editing sounds that *might* be prerecorded, microphoned, or computer-generated (hence, the confusion of this visitor: he did not expect the sounds to be *that* real).

Fig. 22. Studio of *Woman's Hour*, seen from the producer's seat, 2008. Photo © Tim Crocker.

In his article on the "discrete image," Bernard Stiegler (2002) distinguishes three forms of reproducibility: that of the letter (handwritten, then printed), the analog (photographic and cinematographic, as studied by Benjamin), and the digital (the computer-generated image). Each produces its own set of knowledge (of technical conditions of production) and its own intuitive beliefs (relating mental images to material, lasting, image-objects). Their specific epochs have been determined by a play of oppositions, so that the analog is seen as a technology dealing with the continuous, while the digital (and the literate) deals with the discontinuous and discrete. Stiegler's main interest, however, is directed toward the technology that combines two types of reproducibility: the analogical–digital image. With the current and decisive appearance of this object, old conditions of technological knowledge and belief are suspended. We are "plunged" into a moment that is threatening, but also, to Stiegler, potentially liberating (in terms of a "grammaticalization of the visible," which opens new possibilities for reflexivity, analysis, and production).

To identify the "spontaneous belief" invested in analog photography, Stiegler turns to the well-known analysis of Roland Barthes: "The rule is that every analog photo presupposes that what was photographed was (real)" (Stiegler 2002, p. 150). There was always, of course, the possibility of manipulation. But this is accidental, as the rule—with Barthes, the "this was" of the photograph—will not be effaced by such practices.

> I can never simply say: This was not. I *have* to say: *This was*, but there is *something*, however- er, *that is not quite right*. (Stiegler 2002, p. 150)

That belief is grounded in technology. Photosensitive material has been "touched" by luminances, and from there on we may sense a chain, a continuity, so that the photons that once physically emanated from the face of Baudelaire may physically touch us today. With the digital, computer-generated image, the rules change: now manipulation, *not having been*, is the essential attribute. We might still experience an effect of "this was," but if we do, it is accidental. The photons have turned into pixels, reducible to zeros and ones, to be treated as calculations. As a result, "touch is blurred, the chain becomes complicated" (Stiegler 2002, p. 153). Digitization has introduced manipulation into the image-object itself.

This line of reasoning may also be applied to sound. According to Eric Rothenbuhler and John Durham Peters (1997), there is a fundamental difference between sound that is analogically reproduced (with phonographs, tape recorders, and Blattner-phones) and sound that is digitally reproduced:

> Analog playback ... has a continuous physical relation to the original music recorded, while the digital has not. There is an unbroken chain from the sound in the living room to the original sound as recorded. (Rothenbuhler & Peters 1997, p. 252)

While the vinyl record and the magnetic tape display physical traces of the vibrations of sound waves, the CD is a device for storing data, according to conventions agreed upon by the commercial industry. The implications of this difference are then further elaborated, in what the authors call a "thought experiment": analog sound is fundamentally natural, while digital is fundamentally arbitrary ("copies without original"). Analog is an indexical trace, while digital measures whatever information the convention designs. Analog is designed for the pursuit of transcendence, while digital is designed for the pursuit of profit. Analog retains "the otherness of past times," while digital fixes it in a code. Analog registers the passing of time (records grow old, have "a body with a voice"), while digital obscures it (CDs either work or they don't). Analog speaks from that other side, "out of the grave," while digital does not recognize a mortal mechanism. As such, the digital is a poor witness to historicity, while the analog may support a "hermeneutics of testimony" (Ricoeur), based on singularity, uniqueness, embodiment, and mortality.

And the Blattner-phone tape, to return to *Death at Broadcasting House*, finally delivered the trace that the detective needed (the victim deviates from the script in one single word, thus revealing his hidden connection to the murderer, when he entered the studio). Listening back to the voice of a man whose corpse was lying on a mortuary slab was a horrifying experience to the producer of the play.

> To Caird there had always seemed something repellent and almost indecent about the attempts of spiritualists to pierce the veil of the hypothetical after-life, and to drag back the

voices of the dead to make suburban holidays over ouija boards and equivalent tomfooleries. Neither had he been able to reconcile himself entirely to the continued use, for purposes of entertainment, of the gramophone records of the voices of celebrated artists after their death. And though he had suggested the replay of this blatterphone record of Parsons's murder, now that he actually heard it, he experienced both fear and disgust, combined with an overwhelming conviction that the use of such a method must be unlucky and might well be something worse . . . (Gielgud & Marvell 1934, p. 57)

To Stiegler, the analog image produces a fear of phantoms. The analogical-digital image does not so much replace our knowledge of *this was*, as it destabilizes it. According to its own, intuitive knowledge: "*perhaps* this was not." For there still *is* a photograph, which means that the "chain of memorial light" is not *absolutely* broken, that some part of the image *has* been touched—though we cannot really say which one, and how. Like those pictures of the future Broadcasting House (Fig. 20, p. 45), the old building and the church spire look real enough, but "something is not quite right" (yes, the church spire has actually been pushed to the right, for a better view of the new, public place). And those people moving about in that open place, the light that is falling on them, and on Prospero—it seems to come from another world. With the analogico-digital image, even phantoms become indistinct. Still, Stiegler finds things to be afraid of:

> What *else* are we afraid of in the analogico-digital? We are afraid of a *night light*. Barthes too, already, spoke of a night: the night of the past that I didn't live. The light of photography comes to us from the night of a past that I didn't live, but once (*un jour*) this night was day (*cette nuit fut le jour*). It has irreversibly become night, this is what the past is (and the phantom). But the day has to have touched the silver halides first. With analog light, the silver luminances still have to do with touch and with life—with a past life. With the digital photo, this light, from out of the night, *no longer comes entirely from the day*, it doesn't come from a past day that would simply have become night (like the photons emanating from Baudelaire's face). It comes from Hades, from the realm of the dead, from the underground: it is an electric light, set free by materials from deep within the belly of the earth. (Stiegler 2002, p. 152 f)

In 1932, the BBC published a book with over 100 photographs of the brand new interiors of Broadcasting House (some are illustrating this chapter). According to Richard MacCormac, seventy years later, these pictures appear "spooky—like a German expressionist film-set."[26] A deserted film-set, one might add. For what is lacking in them is people: not a trace of a living soul—not even a corpse!—in any one of these studios. In Benjamin's artwork essay, the withdrawal of man from the photographic image was an early sign of the withering of aura and ritual value. To Benjamin, the Parisian street exteriors of nineteenth-century photographer Atget looked "empty," "voiceless; the city in these pictures is swept clean like a house which has not yet found its new tenant" (Benjamin 1931/1980, p. 210). The city resembled "the scene of a crime" and the photos existed for "the purpose of establishing evidence" (Benjamin 1936/1968, p. 226).

So what are we looking at, in those pictures of the old interiors of Broadcasting House? Not equipment-free reality, but the material and technological conditions of its production. Not phantoms, but the spaces and machines for reproducing the "voices of the dead." Spaces and machines that are precisely "voiceless," uninhabited. And we are seeing them through a strange light, a "nightlight," that *actually never was day* (daylight being absent in the interiors of Broadcasting House). It is like we are looking at an *analog* image of that *digital* light, an all-electric "this was," coming straight from the underground:

> a night still deeper even than that of a past, a night of past that was never present: the weft of our dreams, of these dreams of which Prospero says we are made. (Stiegler 2002, p. 154 f)

This light may now present us with the future "heart of the BBC," Prospero still standing as its guard. Through images that are essentially analog-digital, representing spaces that are intuitively interstitial (in between past and present, sacred and profane, mediated and ordinary, interior and exterior, public and private). Its surface may look like solid stone during the day, transparent screen during the night, and its tenants, missing from those old pictures, may appear from out of a computer-generated future. This is a tympanic machine that may no longer reproduce the vibrations of our inner ears, and these are "voices from the other side" that may be the outcome of calculations.

If so, what we are looking at, in those old pictures, is what Siegfried Giedion once saw in the interiors of nineteenth-century industry buildings: how "the basis of our present existence is taking shape" (1928/1995, p. 87). And that is spooky.

References

The Architectural Review (1932): August.
Benjamin, W. (1931/1980): "A Short History of Photography", in Trachtenberg, A. (ed.), *Classic Essays on Photography*, New Haven, CT: Leete's Island Books.
Benjamin, W. (1933): "Experience and Powerty" ("Erfahrung und Armut"), in *Selected Writings (1996–2003)*, Cambridge, MA: The Belknap Press of Harvard University Press.
Benjamin, W. (1936/1968): "The Work of Art in the Age of Mechanical Reproduction" in *Illuminations*, New York: Schocken Books.
Benjamin, W. (1999): *The Arcades Project (Das Passagen-Werk)*, Cambridge, MA: The Belknap Press of Harvard University Press.
Broadcasting House (1932), London: British Broadcasting Corporation.
Blondheim, M. (2003): "Harold Adams Innis and his Bias of Communication", in Katz, E., Durham Peters, J., et al. (eds.), *Canonic Texts in Media Research*, Cambridge: Polity Press.
Brand, S. (1994): *How Buildings Learn. What Happens After They're Built.* London: Penguin.

Cawelti, J. (1976): *Adventure, Mystery, Romance. Formula Stories as Art and Popular Culture.* Chicago, IL: University of Chicago Press.
Coates, W. (1932a): "Response to Tradition" in *Architectural Review,* November.
Coates, W. (1932b): "Furniture Today and Furniture Tomorrow," in *Architectural Review*, July.
Coates, W. (1932c): "The Dramatic Control Panel No 1", Plate IV, *Architectural Review*, August.
Cohen, D. (2006): *Household Gods. The British and Their Possessions.* New Haven, CT: Yale University Press.
Cohn, L. (1999): *The Door to a Secret Room. A Portrait of Wells Coates,* Aldershot: Scolar Press.
Colomina, B. (1994/2000): *Privacy and Publicity. Modern Architecture as Mass Media.* Cambridge, MA: MIT Press.
Couldry, N. (2000): *The Place of Media Power: Pilgrims and Witnesses of the Media Age.* London & New York: Routledge.
Dayan, D. & E. Katz (1992): *Media Events. The Live Broadcasting of History.* Cambridge, MA: Harvard University Press.
Eliade, M. (1957/1987): *The Sacred and the Profane. The Nature of Religion.* Orlando & London: Harcourt Inc.
Foucault, M. (1967/1998): "Of Other Spaces" in Mirzoeff, N. (ed.), *The Visual Culture Reader,* London & New York: Routledge.
Frampton, K. (1983): "Towards a Critical Regionalism: Six Points for an Architecture of Resistance," in *The Anti-Aesthetic*, Foster, H. (ed.), Seattle, WA: Bay Press.
Giedion, S. (1928/1995): *Building in France, Building in Iron, Building in Ferro-concrete (Bauen in Frankreich),* Santa Monica, CA: Getty Center for the History of Art and the Humanities.
Gielgud, V. & H. Marvell (1934): *Death at Broadcasting House*, London and Manchester: A Cherry Tree Book, Withy Grove Press Limited.
Goldsmith, V. H. (1932): "The Studio Interiors," in *Architectural Review*, August.
Hines, M. (2008): *The Story of Broadcasting House: Home of the BBC.* London and New York: Merrell.
Innis, H. (1951/2006): *The Bias of Communication,* Toronto: University of Toronto Press.
Jackson, N. (2003): *Building the BBC: A Return to Form*, London: BBC.
Jansson, A. & Lagerkuist, A. (eds.)(2009) *Strange Spaces: Explorations into Mediated Obscurity,* London: Ashgate Publisher
MacCormac, R. (2005): "Private View II: When Art Meets Architecture", *TATEetc*, Issue 5, Autumn 2005.
Meyrowitz, J. (1985): *No Sense of Place*, New York: Oxford University Press.
Milutis, J. (2006): *Ether. The Nothing That Connects Everything*, Minneapolis and London: University of Minnesota Press.
Peters J.D., (1999): *Speaking Into the Air*. Chicago, IL: University of Chicago Press.
Rice, C. (2007): *The Emergence of the Interior. Architecture, Modernity, Domesticity,* London and New York: Routledge.
Rothenbuhler, E. & J. D. Peters (1997): "Defining Phonography: An Experiment in Theory," *The Musical Quarterly* 1997, 81 (2).
Sterne, J. (2003): *The Audible Past: Cultural Origins of Sound Reproduction*, Durham and London: Duke University Press.
Stiegler, B. (2002): "The Discrete Image," in Derrida, J. and Stiegler, B. (eds.), *Echographies of Television*, Cambridge: Polity Press.
Williams, R. (1974/1997): *Television: Technology and Cultural Form*. London: Routledge.

Notes

1. http://www.bbc.co.uk/pressoffice/keyfacts/stories/bh_development.shtml. [June 23, 2009].
2. CD-disc (1997): Radio Collection BBC: 75 years of the BBC, BBC Worldwide Ltd.
3. J C W Reith: ""Broadcasting," *Quarterly Review* 242 (1924), quoted from Peters, J.D.(1999), p. 103.
4. A shorter version of this article has been previously published, as "Death at a Broadcasting House" in Jansson & Lagerkvist (2009).
5. Quoted from Hines (2008), p. 53.
6. Quoted from Hines (2008), p. 75.
7. Chermayeff's phrase, from a 1931 speech on "A New Spirit and Idealism," delivered at Heal's, a store for modern furnishing in London.
8. Quoted from http://www.miketodd.net/other/bhhistory/bh_1932b.htm. [June 23, 2009].
9. *BBC Handbook 1932*, quoted from http://www.miketodd.net/other/bhhistory/bh_1932b.htm. [June 23, 2009].
10. Publicity material for Lawn Road Flats, quoted from Cohn 1999, p. 159.
11. J. M. Richards: "Wells Coates 1895-1958", *The Architectural Review* (1958) December.
12. Quoted from Hines (2008), p. 52.
13. Presentation of Lawn Road Flats in *The Architectural Review* (1934), August, quoted from Cohn 1999, p. 167.
14. *Independent* on Sunday, November 16, 2003.
15. The words of John Smith in 2000, at the time serving as BCCs Director of Finance. http://news.bbc.co.uk/2/hi/entertainment/998847.stm. [June 23, 2009].
16. In late 2005, when the renovation of the old building was nearly finished, the BBC issued a statement that the second phase of the project would be handled by another firm (Sheppard Robson), due to "creative differences" between the construction team/BBC and MJParchitects/MacCormac. In 2008, correspondence between MacCormac and the BBCs Director General was made public, under the information act: http://www.bdonline.co.uk/story.asp?storyCode=3116414. [June 23, 2009].The open disagreement concerns the use of supporting columns, in the new, large news room. But MacCormac also claims that his aspirations to create a "work of architecture" of iconic status have been compromised in too many ways—"in the name of fitness for purpose, whatever that is!"—and that the extension might end up "no better than a spec office building," which would be a "disaster" for the BBC. The BBC chooses not to overturn the judgement of the construction team, and the press describes MacCormac's following departure as a "sacking."
17. Personal interview with architect Mark Hines, October 2008, London. Hines, at the time a member of MJP architects, led the renovation of Broadcasting House. His book *The Story of Broadcasting House: Home of the BBC* (Hines 2008) appeared after this article had been conceived. It provides a full account, in words and pictures, of events that this article only sketches.
18. Speech given at the British Property Federation Conference in 2003, http://www.bbc.co.uk/pressoffice/pressreleases/stories/2003/01_january/27/property_speech.shtml. [June 23, 2009].
19. http://www.bbc.co.uk/pressoffice/keyfacts/stories/bh_development.shtml. [June 23, 2009].
20. Quoted from Hines, 2008, p. 142.
21. Notes from a talk given by MacCormac on Broadcasting House, February 2004. http://www.cityofsound.com/blog/2005/12/index.html. [June 23, 2009].
22. "Surface," Richard MacCormac, http://www.mjparchitects.co.uk/essay/Surface.pdf. [June 23, 2009].
23. The writer attended this tour on November 5, 2008.

24. http://www.bbc.co.uk/tours/details/details_bh.shtml. [June 23, 2009].
25. http://www.imagesofengland.org.uk/Details/Default.aspx?id=424540&mode=quick. [June 23, 2009].
26. Notes from a talk given by MacCormac on Broadcasting House, February 2004. http://www.city-ofsound.com/blog/2005/12/index.html. [June 23, 2009].

CHAPTER THREE

The End of the Iconic Home of Empire:
Pondering the Move of the BBC World Service from Bush House

KRISTINA RIEGERT

> Yet Bush House remains embedded in our perceptions as a BBC building as much as Broadcasting House or the Television Centre, and to millions of listeners it is still the only building the BBC has.—Mary Welch (1992, p. 180)

> "Buildings fulfil needs; architecture fulfils desires. In contemporary Western society, the paradigm of need has been surpassed by the paradigm of desires, as the acquisition of basic goods has been replaced by a search for emotional satisfaction, a quest for identity, the ability to distinguish oneself, and the aspiration to belong. Just as products are judged by their representational value, architecture must provide environments that people can relate to emotionally . . . —Anna Klingmann (2007, p. 312)

The BBC World Service is now finally slated to move out of its iconic home, Bush House, to the newly renovated Broadcasting House, marketed to become the "largest live broadcast centre in the world." Until recently, Bush House was known to audiences throughout the world as the location of the BBC's disembodied voices, as a center from which issued the sounds of tradition, truth, power, and culture. In this mobile digital media era, the BBC is centralizing further to Broadcasting House and strengthening some of its international offices outside the United Kingdom. Thus, there is reason to reflect on what Bush House has meant to the World Service, the ways the organization will change with its move to Broadcasting House, and what the twin trends of centralization and decentralization tell us about the BBC as media organization.

This chapter focuses on Bush House as a physical representation of the World Service ethos and tradition, not only in the sense of how buildings are used to influence behavior, but just as importantly how social behavior influences buildings (Hall & Hall 1975; Baldry 1999). Bush House is here considered as a center for value production and organizational cohesion in an organization with offices around the world. A specific focus is on the ways that the cultural and social organization of the 33 language services are reflected in the physical layout of the building. From the World Service staff's point of view, what are the advantages and problems of Bush House and how do they view the move from Bush House? How have technological, political, and cultural changes influenced ways of working in the building and the relationship between the center and its international offices? Finally, there is a discussion of what Bush House as a building represents to its audiences, wholly found outside of the UK. Media buildings are of a paradoxical nature: they are material manifestations of that which is ephemeral, and they represent a concentration of that which is dispersed. For the millions of listeners around the world, Bush House and London represent the very center of the historic imperial power Britain. Naturally, one wonders who gains access to Bush House and under what conditions? Does Bush House facilitate contact with its worldwide audiences?

This research is based around interviews with several types of World Service staff: I have called them technical managers (TM), coordinating managers (CM), and managing editors (ME) based on their job description and in order to preserve their anonymity.* Those interviewed were based in different language services, as well as more centrally placed departments.[1] Other materials include secondary sources, mainly from previous World Service staff about the organization, but also architectural and sociological theories about space, place, and office planning. Architectural psychologist David Canter said that a "sense of place" is gained from the interaction between the physical locale, the activities linked to this locale, and the way the subject constructs meaning about the place and its activities (Groat & Wang 2002, p. 77). Likewise this analysis attempts to uncover what kind of place Bush House is through the subjective experiences of the World Service staff, how their activities influence, and are influenced by, the building and what this says about the organization as a whole.

Bush House as the Unlikely Representative of BBC Tradition

Bush House is in many ways similar to the World Service, which Walker describes as "particularly British in the haphazard way in which it developed, [and] its character derives ultimately from decisions made as long ago as the 1920s when the wireless was in its infancy . . ." (Walker 1992, p. 13). Yet, one of the first things World

Service staff will tell you about Bush House is that it was not conceived as a broadcasting headquarters and that the BBC has never owned the building. Some say it was once a hotel, an office, or a "world" trade center. In fact, it was the brainchild of American businessman Irving T. Bush, who contracted the well-known New York architect Harvey Corbett of Helemle and Corbett A.I.A. to build a high class "office and showroom building" for traders from all over the world. Today, the building is comprised of Centre Block, the northwest and northeast wings, and the southeast and southwest wings, built from 1923 to 1935. The southwest wing has never been let to the BBC. The BBC European Service moved to the southeast wing in 1941, and other parts of what was then called the Overseas Service successively took over more floors and wings as it expanded broadcasting hours and language services during the Second World War.

Centre Block is the most grand, with its arresting neoclassical columns, and high portico, although the Travertine marble interior and mahogany details can be found in the other wings as well. Lord Balfour officially opened it in 1925, when the statues still standing above the entrance columns—situated at the end of the tree-lined thoroughfare Kingsway—were finished. The American sculptor Malvina Hoffman said she was asked to "interpret the concept of England and America holding a torch over a Celtic altar" with the inscription "Dedicated to the Friendship of English-Speaking Peoples" (Welch 1992, p. 173).

Fig. 1. Bush House Centre Block Entrance. Photo by author.

Several of those interviewed commented that this statue is not very representative of the World Service; in actuality Bush House is more like a mini-United Nations, or a "Tower of Babel" because of the over thirty languages spoken in the building and broadcast from its premises. A less well-intentioned interpretation by critics of the BBC might even see the statue as representing the partnership of cultural imperialism over the *non-English*-speaking peoples. Another interpretation of the building from the architecture correspondent for the *Guardian,* John Glancey, defines it as typically "American." He describes Bush House as a twentieth-century Roman temple, as "a Masonic temple from somewhere in the United States," that it is "Hollywood Art Deco" and "very very American"—implying that it is somewhat ostentatious (BBC Radio World Service 2008).

Former Managing Director John Tusa had another view; he wrote that the two male figures of the statue facing in different directions symbolized the "physical and psychological location of the BBC External Services" in between academe, in the guise of the London School of Economics on one side of Bush House, and the Foreign and Commonwealth Office, on the other. "The twin polarities of academe and government exercise their respective attractions very explicitly over Bush House" (Tusa 1990, p. 100). Here, he was alluding not only to the World Service in terms of benefiting from scholarly expertise and that of foreign dignitaries willing to grace the airwaves with their presence, but also of government influence. Like many other managing directors of the BBC, Tusa argued forcefully for the will and the ability of the BBC to successfully fend off attempts at editorial interference by the British and other governments.[2] Being in the "psychological" middle, he argued, means that the BBC can utilize outside expertise, while retaining enough authority to be autonomous. Clearly, placing Bush House in this illustrious company lends the World Service authority, something augmented by the building's imposing edifice and its magnificent façade.

If the façade of buildings sends messages or symbolizes one thing to the outside world, what does it mean to those who work inside? One of the staff interviewed said that when he first saw Bush House he felt a sense of awe and humility—it was more like a cathedral and a church than a media house, he maintained. "But at that time, I guess the physical appearance of the building also sent a message, today that is relatively unimportant, I mean you could be sitting in a garage" (ME1).[3] This is an interesting point, since this statement assumes that buildings are no longer used to brand media organizations. It also assumes that a building's features do not affect those working there. For many others interviewed, however, the grandeur of Bush House instilled in them a sense of pride. A member of the technical staff described thus,

It is very majestic, it's very imposing, you feel like you are working in an important place. When you walk through the door you feel like you are doing something important. You are working in a landmark. People all over the world know what you are talking about when you talk about Bush House. (TM1)

Fig. 2. Front Entrance, detail. Photo by author.

Authority also tends to come from longevity—another staff member commented that the building's age ran parallel to the history of the BBC. The age of the building instills in those working there a sense of the legacy of their predecessors, a sense of stability, and of the BBC brand name that has withstood the test of time. Several interviewees contrasted the World Service ethos with the rest of the BBC, saying that the World Service was more old-fashioned, just as Bush House was less renovated than other BBC buildings. Indeed, the move from tape to digital was made as late as 2005, so that, for example, the terror attacks of 9/11 were reported using tape. From the point of view of one technical manager,

TM2: So I'd say working in here, even from a non-technical point of view, the décor, you get a sense of history, a sense of kind of tradition . . . . And I think it affects how you see yourself and how you see the World Service.

KR: How? How do you mean affect?

TM2: You see yourself as part of a longer tradition . . . [of] the BBC and the World Service, a very good tradition of being the best, and also being something that maybe generations of people would have listened to. So maybe when people come here, they come here already with an idea of what it will be like in their heads. . . . I think people don't really think of it as a new, challenging broadcaster, the World Service. They would think of something that had been around for eighty years or something along those lines, something that was always there . . . . When people do come here, they're less surprised to see it [Bush House] being archaic in many ways. (Author's parenthesis).

So, to paraphrase architect Sir Richard MacCormac, if architecture is to buildings like clothing is to identity, what kind of identity does Bush House communicate about World Service? According to those who are or have worked in the World Service, Bush House communicates history, grandeur, authority, and integrity outwardly, placing the brand name of the BBC in the thick of those with the knowledge and ability to shape views of the world. It inspires pride and awe in its employees, and gives a sense of a legacy, so employees feel they are part of a tradition handed down from generation to generation. In that tradition, values such as trustworthiness take precedence over values such as challenging or new.

From the Inside Out: Silos, Tunnels, Cubby-Holes, and Cables

Whereas the age of Bush House is seen positively in one sense, it was also considered a drawback in the practical sense. A common anecdote told to newcomers is that it takes two years to be able to find one's way around the building. Finding one's way is said to be like going through a maze, there are long walks between the wings (outside across the car park or underground), and the building was planned "irrationally" (the front and the back of the building are said to be on different levels). Also mentioned as drawbacks were the "rat's nest" of cables within the walls and the constant renovation of different floors and sections in order to fit the needs of the changing organization. The phrase "There's only so much you can do to a building" sums up the time and expense that have gone into renovating different parts of the building over the years.

One person likened it to a hotel: a series of smaller rooms and corridors with larger landing areas. With a lot of smaller offices that feel like private spaces, people don't move about freely. There are few open office spaces, which was said to hinder communication between language services and sometimes within a language service if it is large and various parts are not colocated (which is not always the case). The physical layout of the building can therefore *not* be said to encourage relationships and connections between different language services.[4] Instead, the physical space, the fixed structure of the building, can more be likened to "cozy" office environments, where language services have little physical contact with people from other language services.

In 2005, the outgoing head of the World Service Nigel Chapman launched the "biggest transformation" of the World Service since the end of the Second World War. In his speech to staff, he outlined the closure of nine European language services (and the Thai service), the launch of new television services for Arabic and Persian audiences, the expansion of new media (or the "tri-media" platform), more FM presence around the world, the strengthening of international offices, as well as increased marketing.[5] The move from Bush House to the new renovated Broadcasting House complex is part of this change. The Arabic (television, radio, and online) and Persian (television) services were already operating there in 2008; but the entire World Service will not have moved until 2012.

The location of the 33 different language services of the World Service in the building reflects the maze-like properties of Bush House itself, but even more it seems to reflect the pragmatic (or haphazard, as some describe it) way that organizational change has taken place throughout the decades. This means, for example, that the "central" news desk is located in the Northeast Wing, that the Head of the Persian/Pashto service has some of his tri-media staff in the new Broadcasting House complex called Egton House.[6] The African languages—previously spread out in different wings according to language—are now for the very first time trying to adjust to each other in one large open office space. It also means that, in the latest reorganization of regions, Brazilian Portuguese is now in the same region as Macedonian, although being in the same region does not necessarily mean being in the same building. This, despite the recent attempts to colocate people from the same language service and to group related languages together, such as in the new South Asia Hub (for more on this, see later discussion).

The irony of these physical moves are, of course, that digitalization and email now make it easier for communication to take place without people leaving their desks, as one interviewee put it (ME1). On the other hand, signs of hierarchy and prestige in an organization tend to be expressed spatially even in a digitalized world. Baldry (1999) observed that the amount of territory/space a worker has, and the amount of control the worker has over her immediate working environment, is directly related to the amount of prestige or place in the hierarchy that person has in the organization. Interesting then that none of the interviewees thought that language services' location in the building had anything to do with prestige or hierarchy. Location seemed rather to reflect the growth of certain language services at the cost of others. Those services with an historical legacy and that are relatively large are more likely to be colocated than those that have recently expanded.

When architect Sir Richard MacCormac was planning the renovation of Broadcasting House, he visited Bush House and was, according to accounts, struck by someone who said that their important meetings took place in the hallways and landings. MacCormac therefore reportedly planned large thoroughfares, with sitting areas for informal meetings at Broadcasting House (see Ericson, in this volume).[7] As will be discussed more below, open spaces for casual encounters constitute a major theme in contemporary architectural literature on new offices (Duffy 1997; Arnold, Hascher, Jeska & Klauck 2002). According to those interviewed for this chapter, however, Bush House was not considered a terribly easy place for spontaneous mingling, and it was seldom that people interact with those from other language services in hallways.

Fig. 3. One possible meeting place in a landing in Bush House. Photo by author.

Where did people meet up in Bush House then? Several spoke nostalgically of the club, a mainly male affair in the basement of Centre Block as a meeting place for people after their shift. After a smoking ban was instituted, people began to congregate in the car park between the wings, but smoking was banned there too. While the club is still there, the pub culture seems to have given way to the gym culture—which takes up half the basement. Outside of special events and parties to mark anniversaries of the organization or holidays, the role of BBC Training was mentioned by several as a natural meeting place for interaction between language services. In addition, editorial meetings or the monthly meetings of the Service Heads

Network promote the sharing of needs, concerns, and innovations between language services.

The coordinating managers interviewed said that a World Service objective is to get people out of their offices and interact more across language services (whether these be in hallways or not). This would, according to them, create efficiencies between different departments, encourage the exchange of knowledge and ideas, resulting in mutual learning and the avoidance of a replication of efforts. In this context, several people brought up the common BBC metaphor of a silo mentality. The silo can be thought of as people working in their own worlds, in "parallel isolation," within their own language group, unaware perhaps of similar work being done in other language services or parts of the BBC. There has been a conscious effort on behalf of the BBC management to tackle this problem on many levels; in this context the focus is on the architectural level. Within the BBC as a whole, organizational changes have been introduced to decrease the number of people doing the same things in different parts of the organization.[8] Correspondingly there has been an increase in the number of platforms that journalists work in (filing for radio, online, and television), which increases the need for editorial coordination. World Service staff are, for example, now more often utilized by domestic BBC as experts and reporters on different parts of the world. This is part of the ongoing centralization of the BBC, which is the subject of the next section.

Bush or Broadcasting House: London as the Center for the World of BBC

The move of the World Service to Broadcasting House is part of an overall BBC strategy, described by Jackson (2003) in *Building the BBC: A Return to Form*, to create efficiencies within the organization by centralizing and to brand the BBC with buildings that the organization deems appropriate to its status as a heritage cultural institution. Due to the increased competition in a digital world, the strategy of utilizing the BBC brand name seems an integral part of the organization's renewal.[9] The BBC's international activities and reputation appear to be considered great assets by the government since the BBC forms a key in one of Britain's most successful export industries—television (BBC 1992, p. 23).

Thus, the newly renovated Broadcasting House will bring the domestic parts of the BBC and World Service together for the first time under one (in fact several) roofs. Despite the different sources of funding for the World Service and the rest of the BBC, Newsgathering and correspondents already share content, and this should be further increased, according to one coordinating manager. Yet, at the same time, the language of the World Service public statements also emphasizes getting closer to international audiences, and local markets, and being sensitive to local conditions. Several recent managing directors of the World Service have been trying to effect a paradigm shift from being a "London-based organization" that happens to have international centers to an "international organization" (CM3). How are these notions of centralization and decentralization played out in practice?

There is no question, according to those interviewed, that London and Bush House are thought of as the social center of the World Service. Bush House is the center in a number of ways. First, in terms of efficiencies, the point was made that a single central infrastructure keeps from duplicating facilities in different locations. Technologically, the international offices are connected through London, the systems they use are London-based, and this can lead to frustrations as the Internet connections can at times be slower than if local offices used local connections (TM1). Locally hired technical staff in offices outside the UK cannot advance freely in terms of moving "up" from their own part of the world to London.[10] In terms of content, although there are large offices in places like Nairobi, Delhi, and Kabul, which produce an increasing amount of material on a day-to-day basis, it is still "centered, and based, and edited, and put together here," in London, as one coordinating manager said. While the notion of getting closer to audiences, closer to the news on the ground, and to the markets around the world is an important goal for the World Service, it is still an international news service that does not compete with local broadcasters, except in cases of failed states, and crisis-ridden areas where there is little information to be had (CM4).

Indeed in terms of news content, mentioning on air that the broadcast is coming from Bush House or from London (with the use of Big Ben's gongs) can still be found in the opening sequence or as a signature for some language services. While there is an ongoing discussion about the value of "London calling," those that still use this signature perceive London as part of the BBC brand—one that conveys certain values to audiences. As one editor put it,

> BBC Arabic is known across the Arab world as the London station sometimes. It's a local way of referring to it .... Broadcasters started their bulletins with 'This is London' which is 'Hunah London'. I was just thinking about it because still whenever I go to the Arab world ... people still refer to us as London. And its not in a political sense, its just like ... Nokia is a little town in Finland but when people say Nokia they don't mean the town or Finland or very few of them actually know that Nokia exists in Finland and 'Hunah London' is a brand associated with BBC Arabic as an operation, as an organization, as a medium and a broadcaster, with all the values associated with it. So people come to, you know, the mother operation, to the hub where everything is taking place and yeah, it is the center. (ME2)

Since the BBC brand conveys values such as quality, impartiality, and truth (see next section), being geographically distant, especially from areas of conflict, tends to reinforce the image of credibility. In this case, distance from audiences adds to the authority of the World Service. One of the editorial managers was not favorable to the current climate of decentralization to international offices, because in his experience of war in his home country, it was very difficult for the World Service staff to remain unaffected by "the ocean of emotion" in these conflict areas.

> If you ... are broadcasting to very troubled or unstable countries or regions, I think its safer to keep away from those areas. They [language services] have to have very good sources of information, they have to have, um, as the French would say Intel, you know someone to send you information and reports, etc. But the gist of the thing has to be in London for their own good and for the good of the program. (ME1)(Author's brackets)

This focus on London as a place to keep journalists safe feeds into another point made by an editorial manager about the purpose of having a central headquarters for the staff:

> The iconic nature of the building reinforces their sense of belonging and purpose and journalists often engage in work that does not make them popular and indeed sometimes it makes them vulnerable. Working in a strong environment where they have the ready support of colleagues helps them maintain their confidence and professionalism ... providing a safe environment where they can exercise the profession independently is important. (ME4)

Thus, whether in Bush or in Broadcasting House there is a perceived need for the World Service to have a central hub in London despite the efforts to improve the capacities of the international offices. This is not only due to technological and practical reasons (although these seem less and less valid in the age of mobile digital media), but also because distance from the thick of conflicts emphasizes the credibility of the organization and provides a sense of security for journalists in an increasingly vulnerable occupation. Noteworthy in the above are references to professionalism and to BBC values. This is perhaps one of the most important reasons for the retention of London as the heart of the organization—to steep the staff recruited from around the world in BBC values and to continue the training at various points in their careers.

Inculcating BBC Values

The much-vaunted "BBC values" are a mantra for the organization and for its funder, the UK Foreign and Commonwealth office. These editorial values, perhaps stated differently in various documents and changing in emphasis over the years, all have to do with objectivity, impartiality, accuracy, fairness, independence, and quality, nowadays expressed as creativity and innovation. These were recently reiterated by the outgoing Director of the World Service Nigel Chapman as "integrity, honesty, a passion to broadcast the truth, without fear or favour," and an "unflagging insistence on 'getting it right'" (Chapman 2005, pp. 11–12).

Jean Seaton (2008) suggests that the BBC's "journey to the truth" is made by way of tools that are means to an end—these means are practices such as impartiality, fairness, freedom of speech, independence, objectivity, and pluralism, among other things. That said, it would do well to remember, as former World Service staff member Graham Mytton does, that the World Service inherently reflects the Western political and cultural values of its home nation. The paradox is that it depends on a formerly imperial, Cold War British state, while at the same time retaining a world-renowned reputation for objectivity and independence (Mytton 2008; cf. Baumann & Gillespie 2007). He credits the latter with the fact that the BBC does best in places where the media are not free—thus implying that this independence is relative. Yet, he worries about the creeping emphasis on Britain in current World Service documents where the main goal reads: "To be the world's best known, most creative, and most respected voice in international news, thereby bringing benefit to the UK, and to the whole BBC" (Chapman 2005, p. 3). Previous World Service goal statements, he says, laid emphasis on freedom of information as a basic human right, and the basis for the BBC's contribution to the world.[11] He concludes that the tensions between the BBC's *de facto* relationship to the state and the fierce defense by its staff of their editorial independence make it difficult to determine just how independent the World Service is.[12]

So, how do editorial independence and BBC values play out in practice? According to Seaton (2008), it has to do with day-to-day editorial work, a process of constant vigilance, of always double-checking facts, continuous editorial discussion of judgment calls, internal reviews, defense from governments' interference, in short, by trial and error. Important in this respect, and mentioned by several people, was the central role of recruitment and training in the process of inculcating BBC values:

> You know everybody we recruit here is trained to be a BBC journalist, and trained to understand and to work in BBC values of impartiality and accuracy and so forth. And sometimes, it can personally be quite difficult for them, but that is the culture that overrides all others here—the BBC Culture. And that is a reason or one of the reasons why we in the World Service, a) do have a center, and are not just a succession of bureaus that are scattered around in different countries, that are sort of autonomous, there must be an organizing center, and b) why we in the World Service are very much at the heart of the BBC as a corporation, as a journalistic organization and that can only, we can only benefit from being in with the rest of the BBC, and because the rest of the BBC will benefit from having such a wealth of different cultures and outlooks, to help in reporting the world so that we don't just impose some kind of Anglo-centric outlook on the world on our reporting. (CM1)

Two things should be noted from this coordinating manager: that a center is needed to cultivate BBC values and that the World Service representing people from all over the world will enrich the new center of the BBC in Broadcasting House.[13] It also points to the role of training. As mentioned before, the role of BBC Training is known as a central place where people from different language services work with each other. This happens not only during their "induction training" [sic], but at different stages during their careers, for editorial as well as technical staff. Its central location at the bottom of Center Block in Bush House, near the canteen, also promotes casual drop-ins for technological advice on the go.[14]

The socialization into the BBC culture and values refers both to those working in Bush House and those working in the international offices, although the latter do not receive the same amount of training as the former for various reasons (CM3). Recruitment to the language services focuses on those living outside the UK because of their knowledge, experience, and contacts on the ground in the countries they are covering—in this way they are seen to enrich the World Service (the center). It was put forward by several people that the type of person that wants to work for the BBC already holds similar values and standards, and may be highly trained in their own regions—still, they must be socialized into the "ethos and style" of the BBC, because although

> ... you have to be very, very careful here because I appreciate fair is different to different people, but whatever fairness is, if you could do it purely, is trying to help journalists here have an editorial understanding of what is balanced journalism, how to get two sides of the story, which might be different from how they have been brought up .... (CM3)

Training includes legal issues, libel, data protection, protection of sources, as well as exercises in judgment. Trainees assessed the day's news agenda; they were asked what sources, guests, and experts should be used, and how they would put together typical BBC programs. There is a rigorous disciplinarity inherent in this socialization into BBC values; however, it was pointed out that training was also meant bring together different perspectives and to debate these values "so that people really own them" (CM3).

The South Asia Hub: Technology and Perceptions of Personal Space

Previously, the point was made that the move from Bush to Broadcasting House is seen by the managerial staff as an opportunity for architecture to direct change in entrenched organizational and thought patterns—using terms such as increasing "creativity" and "synergy" across divisional boundaries. On the other hand, quite a few of the interviewees said that the main motivator for the move itself was probably to save money and increase efficiencies of space—to put more people into less space.

In 2007, an experimental section called the South Asia Hub was opened in Bush House. Originally introduced as the "Production House of the Future," it had a radically different floor plan and was conceived in order to solve some of the technical problems envisioned with the move to Broadcasting House (TM1, CM2). The hub houses the South Asia language services (i.e., Hindi, Urdu, Bengali, Sinhalese, and Nepalese), which have their desks in an open-plan landscape—there are no private offices on the floor, the editors sit among the staff. In the middle are the studios and control rooms, which consist of two glassed-in booths, with desks surrounding them. These booths can alternate as control rooms or recording studios according to need (see Fig. 4). According to interviewees, the hub is similar to the floor plans in Egton House (in the new Broadcasting House complex), and as such they represent a significant departure from the series of offices along small corridors that characterize Bush House.

Fig. 4. Detail of South Asia Hub from inside one of the glass booths. Photo by author.

The plans for Broadcasting House call for open-plan landscapes, lounges for BBC personnel who work outside the building and furnished thoroughfares for spontaneous meetings. These elements are also ubiquitous in the architectural literature on office building design, where the new information society worker is said to need "creative environments" to prosper. According to Duffy (1997, pp. 17–18), whereas the old Taylorist office was hierarchical, standardized, and closely supervised, the new ways of working are "more interactive than old office routines, and give people far more control over the timing, the content, the tools, and the place of work" (Ibid. p. 46). In this mobile digital world, the office is now "where you are," or where the "screen" is, and the effort has been in "humanizing" offices by breaking down barriers between formal and informal working (Ibid., pp. 56–59). The incorporation of new communication technologies into office design has in practice meant open-plan office landscapes with the elimination of private offices for management (i.e., to flatten hierarchies) and de-personalizing workspaces, such as the use of "hot-desks," which are computers strategically placed in various locations for anyone to use. There are often open lounge spaces where people can come into contact in an informal setting.[15]

While the concepts of "flexibility" and "creativity" in new office designs are clearly technology-driven, they must be traced to broader changes in the working conditions and organizational culture of the network society (Castells 1996; Baldry et al. 2007). The flat hierarchies and open-planned landscapes of new office design can be seen in light of Gilles Deleuze's notion of "societies of control," whereby control has become "free-floating" and is exerted through access to information, flexibly, fluidly, interactively in order to administrate populations. As Fiona Allon puts it, "Control is precisely about flexible management, self-organization and an incessant mobility between different networks of control and between different times, spaces and registers of experience" (Allon 2004, p. 271). She relates this development to the "networked" house (home) as being a site of control, whereby the division between work and leisure disappears since work can be performed anytime. Others have noted the reverse, how especially the dot.com industries adopt a logic incorporating the notion of play into the office to encourage workers to stay after hours (Ross 2004, see Jakobsson and Stiernstedt in this volume).

In the introduction to a book on "creative office design," Matthew Stewart wrote, "Nearly every architect interviewed for this book mentioned the impact of new technologies as the primary driver of change in office design, particularly with respect to the profound effect on communication behaviours (2004, p. 5). That said, Chris Baldry (1999, pp. 549–551) worries that technology-dominated office design and the mantra of flexibility ignores the cost in human resources. For example, the de-personalization of the work spaces (hot desks, touchdown desks, nonterritorial offices) strip workers of a sense of their own space and control, therefore undermining commitment and emotional well-being.

The experiences of those working in the South Asian Hub after the first six months appear to confirm Baldry's concerns. The new hub has had its share of technical and human problems, and according to the technical staff, it is the latter that have been most potent (TM1, TM2). The move of these language services into one large open-planned office has meant the flattening of previous hierarchies, which provoked controversies around the placement of desks and proximity to toilets, but above all, the lack of privacy. This means, "when you come to work, you are kind of, on show. You adopt a certain persona at work and here you have to be that person all the time, there is no getting away from it" (TM1).

It could be asked how much this working space has been technology-driven and in what sense the cultural and social sensibilities of the different languages services were taken into account in the design. The ways the new office blurs the boundaries between work time and private time is also perceived to be a problem for World Service journalists who work on night shifts, in an operation that is on call 24 hours a day. These people cannot "simply step outside into the city at all hours of the night for a breath of fresh air," so the need for private space is perhaps greater, according to one technical manager (TM2). Arnold (2002) points out that office work organized around spatial flexibility requires a stronger social bond among employees, due to the breakdown of spatial separation between the work sphere and private sphere. In the case of Bush House, this bond has not been formed because these teams had not previously worked in the same space.

Furthermore, studies from the 1970s and 1980s demonstrate that moves to open-planned offices fail to support the claims of greater efficiency and improved communication by open landscape advocates (Becker 1981, p. 106). In fact, those office workers experienced a decline in autonomy, as supervisors and coworkers could interfere with the worker's discretion, there was a decrease in manager feedback due to the elimination of private spaces, not to mention the difficulties workers had in concentration. Becker (1981, p. 108) cites a study by Clearwater that found that workers felt that the new open-planned office made them feel more insecure and vulnerable rather than eliminating internal barriers and increasing information flow. While these offices were not media organizations, and these studies were carried out in the precomputer period, it is worth questioning why the "new office" literature does not take into account studies of how open, more anonymous physical spaces of today may affect workers or whether it is simply technology and economic considerations that are driving modern building design.

In the above, it can be concluded that technology is one very important driver in the organization of physical and social space. This is further emphasized by speculation among coordinating and editorial managers (CM3, ME3) about how the present organization can be reorganized to allow closer proximity between different media platforms, or according to the type of content (news or feature programs) produced, rather than the current physical location of workers by languages and single (radio or online) platforms. Clearly, the multicultural, multiethnic nature of the World Service makes it even more important to take the human aspect into account in the shift to technologically driven working environments.

Tourism as Public Access?

There is a paradox in that architectural design in the twenty-first century foregrounds transparent buildings that display inside production to the outside, while media organizations are engaged in work that makes them potential targets of security threats.[16] How has Bush House been involved in the relationship of the World Service to its audiences? Here it should be recalled that unlike many other media houses, the audiences for the World Service are not in London, and not even in Britain.[17] Bush House has very limited accessibility to the public because of space and security restrictions; however, it is a site of interest on the open-top red tourist bus routes (with loudspeakers trumpeting the building) and for individual tourists who stand outside and take pictures of the building.

Among those who are invited inside are foreign dignitaries, intellectuals, artists, decision-makers, or famous personalities from outside the UK. There is much anecdotal evidence of Bush House being a port of call for foreign dignitaries who are interested in visiting the language service of their country: "prime ministers and ministers from overseas who make themselves available to our broadcasters when they visit London are too numerous to mention" (Tusa 1990, p. 101; Mansell 1982). Those interviewed for this study also spoke of being asked from time to time to show people around Bush House when "big shots" came from overseas. This is a testimony not only to the BBC's reputation among foreign elites, but of their desire to experience media power from the inside. Couldry says that the boundary that separates media production processes from the public helps to maintain and legitimate "the enormous concentration of symbolic power in media institutions" despite it being at odds with the notion that the media should be a space that members of the public are able to access (Couldry 2003, p. 83).

Aside from the "big shots" who asked to see Bush House there is a category of regular, longtime listeners from all parts of the world who are interested in seeing Bush House, according to several interviewed. In the documentary *London Calling: Winners and Losers* (2007), fans of the famous Russian veteran emigré Seva Novgorodtsev organized a week-long charter trip to London and Bush House to become studio guests of the Russian Service (they even brought him a birthday gift). Some of these very same fans returned to protest outside of Bush House when the World Service decided to cancel Novgorodtsev's Saturday evening feature program that had aired since 1992.

According to Sandvoss (2005, p. 61), fans seek out "physically manifest places" in the search for unmediated experience; in going beyond "mere consumption and fantasy" they are creating a "new relationship between the object of fandom and the self." These fans are seeking "a sense of place" in the world and, in this case, could be interpreted as trying to connect their own lives to the disembodied radio voices they have grown up with. Whatever their motivation, for the Russian fans or just curious tourists who make a special trip to take pictures of Bush House from the outside, such "media pilgrimages" serve to reinforce the position of London and, of Bush House, as particularly significant, as "having a privileged status in networks of symbolic production" (Couldry 2003, p. 80) (see also Ericson's chapter in this volume).

Conclusion

In pondering the move from Bush to Broadcasting House, this chapter has focused on how Bush House as a physical place communicates the ethos of the BBC World Service. It was noted that while the exterior reinforced notions of historical legacy, grandeur, of integrity and of authority, the interior was a warren of corridors and offices, which has developed haphazardly as the organization has grown and changed. The physical layout has not encouraged crossovers and connections between the language services, and thus tended to reinforce the famous BBC metaphor of a silo mentality. The senior management of the World Service wants to use the move to Broadcasting House to remove entrenched organizational patterns and promote change. However, it was shown by previous research on open-planned offices, if cultural and social sensitivities are not addressed in this transition, this type of solution may pose problems in an organization with over 33 languages and many more nationalities.

A second aspect looked at above consists of the tensions between decentralization and centralization in a number of senses. One sense is how the World Service is merging with other parts of the BBC in London, at the same time that it is trying to further strengthen its "international offices overseas." Clearly, there is an effort to direct attention away from the organization's imperial past, to reject suggestions that the Foreign Office has any editorial influence or that the BBC exists to serve Britain. At the same time, the induction into "BBC values" and the centrality of the technical systems limit an equal exchange between the center and its offices outside the UK. The organization remains centered in London—even if "London Calling" is passé—and Bush House is the center of the World Service. There are clearly good reasons for this in terms of journalism: it is an increasingly dangerous occupation and the organization wants to be seen to be speaking with one voice, while retaining journalistic credibility through distance from conflicts. Yet, taken together these developments at the BBC World Service do tend to reinforce Couldry's charge of the "myth of the mediated centre," writ large, in global terms. London is a center for the "right" social values shared by the world, and the BBC as a media organization is a "natural" place for the symbolic production representing those values.

References

Allon, F. (2004), 'An Ontology of Everyday Control: Media Flows and 'Smart' Living in the Absolute Present' in *Mediaspace: Place, Scale and Culture in a Media Age*, eds. N. Couldry & A. McCarthy, London: Routledge.
Arnold, T., Hascher, R., Jeska, S., & Klauck, B. (2002), *Office Buildings: A Design Manual*, Basel: Birkhäuser.
Arnold, T. (2002), 'The New Work Environments: Appearance and Reality' in Arnold, T, Hascher, R., Jeska, S., & Klauck, B., eds. *Office Buildings: A Design Manual*, Basel: Birkhäuser.
Baldry, C., Bain, P., Taylor, P., Hyman, J., Scholarios, D., Marks, A., Watson, A., Gilbert, K., Gall, G., & Bunzell, D. (2007), *The Meaning of Work in the New Economy*, Basingstoke: Palgrave.
Baldry, C. (1999), 'Space—The Final Frontier,' *Sociology*, Vol. 33, no. 3, August, pp. 535–553.
Baumann, G. & Gillespie, M. (2007), 'Diasporic Citizenships, Cosmopolitanisms, and the Paradox of Mediated Objectivity: An Interdisciplinary Study of the BBC World Service, Diasporas@The World Service Project, Available from: http://www.open.ac.uk/socialsciences/diasporas/publications.htm [June 18, 2009].
BBC (1992), *Extending Choice: The BBC's role in the New Broadcasting Age,* London: British Broadcasting Corporation.
BBC Radio World Service (2008), 'Take a Tour of Bush House'. September 20. 10 minute sound recording. Available from: <http://www.bbc.co.uk/worldservice/news/2008/09/080919_bush_house_wwt_sl.shtml> [March 13, 2009].
Becker, F. (1981), *Work Space: Creating Environments in Organizations*, Westport, CT: Praeger.
Born, G. (2004), *Uncertain Vision: Birt, Dyke and the Reinvention of the BBC,* London: Secker & Warburg.
Castells, M. (1996) *The Rise of the Network Society: Economy, Society and Culture.* Malden: Blackwell, MA.
Chapman, N. (2005), 'Transforming BBC World Service for a Digital Age: A Strategy for 2010 and Beyond', October 25, 2005, pp. 1–13. <www.bbc.co.uk/worldservice/2010/docs/051025_fullspeech.pdf> [March 12, 2009].
Couldry, N. (2003), *Media Rituals: A Critical Approach*, London: Routledge.
Deleuze, G. (2006), 'Postscript on the Societies of Control' libcom.org. September 4. Originally published by OCTOBER 59, Winder 1992. Cambridge, MA: MIT Press, pp. 3–7. Available from: <http://libcom.org/library/postscript-on-the-societies-of-control-gilles-deleuze> [February 24, 2009].
Duffy, F. (1997), *The New Office*. London: Conran.
Groat, L. & Wang, D. (2002), *Architectural Research Methods*, New York: John Wiley and Sons.
Hall, M. & Hall, E. (1975), *The Fourth Dimension in Architecture: The Impact of Building on Behavior,* Santa Fe, NM: Sunstone Press.
Holmwood, L. (2008), 'World Service Dropped Report on Piracy after Foreign Office Request.' *The Guardian*. 4 December. Available from: <http://www.guardian.co.uk/media/2008/dec/04/bbc-world-service-piracy> [June 11, 2009].
Jackson, N. (2003), *Building the BBC: A Return to Form*. London: BBC.
Klingmann, A. (2007), *Brandscapes*. Cambridge, MA: MIT Press.
Küng-Shankleman, L. (2000), *Inside the BBC and CNN: Managing Media Organisations*, London: Routledge.
London Calling: Part 3. Winners and Losers (2007), BBC Documentary, First aired on BBC World, December 2007.

Mansell, G. (1982), *Let Truth Be Told: 50 Years of BBC External Broadcasting*, London: Weidenfeld & Nicolson.

Mytton, G. (2008), 'The BBC and Its Cultural, Social and Political Framework', *Historical Journal of Film, Radio and Television*, Vol. 28, No. 4, pp. 569–581.

Ross, A. (2004), 'Dot.com Urbanism,' in *Mediaspace: Place, Scale and Culture in a Media Age*, eds. N. Couldry & A. McCarthy, London: Routledge.

Sandvoss, C. (2005), *Fans: The Mirror of Consumption*, Cambridge: Polity.

Shaw, D. (2003), 'On the Bombers Trail' *BBC News*, British Broadcasting Corporation, April 8, 2003 <http://news.bbc.co.uk/2/hi/uk_news/2906263.stm> [June 13, 2009].

Seaton, J. (2008), 'Journeys to Truth: The BBC as a Pragmatic Ethical Engineer at Home and Abroad,' *Historical Journal of Film, Radio and Television*, October, Vol. 28, no. 4, pp. 441–451.

Stewart, M. (2004), *The Other Office: Creative Workplace Design*, Amsterdam: Frame Publishers.

Tusa, J. (1990), *Conversations with the World*, London: BBC Books.

Walker, A. (1992), *A Skyful of Freedom: 60 Years of the BBC World Service*, London: Broadside Books Ltd.

Welch, M. (1992), "The Story of Bush House" in Walker, A., *A Skyful of Freedom: 60 Years of the BBC World Service*, London: Broadside Books Ltd.

Notes

*This chapter is based on a research partnership with the Arts and Humanities Research Council funded project entitled "Tuning In: Diasporic Contact Zones at the BBC World Service" project (Grant Award Reference: AH/ES58693/1). The project is based at The Open University, Milton Keynes and led by Professor Marie Gillespie. I am grateful to Marie for assisting me in the research design, and especially with the execution of this project.

1. There were ten in-depth interviews with people of different ages, and different positions and nationalities. Nine followed the same questionnaire. One interview was spontaneous and not all questions could be asked. Certain questions were asked only of those in the departments where the answers were relevant. One interview was done by email. To preserve anonymity, their quotes will be attributed with characters denoting job position, Editorial Managers include one regional head, heads of language services and those dealing with editorial work (ME), Coordinating Managers are those who are mainly tasked with coordination, such as between the World Service and parts of the Global News Division, Training or Business Continuity (CM) and Technical Managers (TM) are those working mainly with technology. Although all were from the managerial staff, efforts were made to include editorial, coordinating, or technical staff in equal measure. One limitation here is lack of interviews from those working in the international offices.
2. This is not surprising since the BBC World Service is wholly funded by a Foreign and Commonwealth Office Grant-in-Aid programme. This fact has also led to the criticism of it being "the mouthpiece of imperialism" (see Walker 1992).
3. ME denotes Managing Editor. There are four managing editors, which are denoted by ME1 through ME4, four Coordinating Managers (CM 1 through CM4) and two Technical Managers interviewed here (TM1 and TM2).
4. The extent to which the BBC provides sites for transnational intradiasporic contact is an important issue for the Tuning in: Diasporic Contact Zones at the World Service. See http://www.open.ac.uk/socialsciences/diasporas/

5. See "Transforming BBC World Service for a digital age: a strategy for 2010 and beyond" www.bbc.co.uk/worldservice/2010/docs/051025_fullspeech.pdf. [October 25, 2005].
6. Tri-media is a term used at the BBC to signify that a service exists in radio, television and online.
7. For an account of MacCormac's vision, see http://www.cityofsound.com/blog/2005/12/notes_richard_m.html.
8. During the unpopular Birt Era (1992-2000), this was handled through increased centralization and "bi-medialization," see Georgina Born's book, *Uncertain Vision: Birt, Dyke and the Reinvention of the BBC*.
9. Lucy Küng-Shankleman (2000, pp. 167-177) did her research mainly in the 1990s and found that while the BBC brand was exceedingly important internally for broadcasting creativity and excellence, marketing was found wanting. This is something that obviously has moved up the priority list, at least at the World Service.
10. This according to TM1, although one of the major reasons for this has to do with visas rather than BBC policy.
11. The promotion of Britain is provocative in the eyes of one senior coordinating manager who said, "Our purpose is to bring credit and value back to Britain, to the British taxpayers who fund us, but not through being a sort of British values or a British culture in the way that some of other international broadcasters try to do, I mean the primary way we bring credit back to Britain is because we are a trustworthy source of news . . . but it is very much internationally focused as well and what is important to our audiences . . ." (CM1).
12. As this chapter was being written, a controversy broke out about this very issue. See Holmwood (2008). For historical accounts of these problems, see Mansell (1982).
13. Several others interviewed were worried about losing what is "better" about the World Service when merged with the rest of the BBC. Reasons given were that the World Service continued to rigorously adhere to the more old-fashioned aspects of editorial values, the quality was better, it was a friendlier workplace, and that the WS contributes more to the BBC than they get back from it (TM2, CM2, ME1).
14. CM3 strongly expressed the belief that Training would be as centrally located in the Broadcasting House complex as it was in Bush House.
15. For the personalization of workspaces as a sign of control and hierarchy, see Baldry (1999).
16. Indeed, the BBC's Television Centre in West London was targeted by IRA bombers in 2003. See Shaw (2003).
17. The World Service had, in 2007, 33 languages, 183 million listeners and 12 million international online news users around the world.

CHAPTER FOUR

Ostankino TV Tower, Moscow: An Obsession with Space

PATRIK ÅKER

Ostankino TV Tower was built between 1963 and 1967 as part of the Ostankino TV center, at that time, the largest television center in the world. The center included studios and offices for radio and TV production and was planned and built together with the tower for GOSTELERADIO, an organization controlled by the Communist party. The whole idea behind this complex was to integrate and centralize media production and distribution. With the introduction of color TV, on the eve of the 50th anniversary of the October Revolution, the Ostankino Tower started transmissions of radio and TV programs. At 537 meters, it was the highest building in the world, a position it held until 1977, and it is still today the tallest free-standing building in Europe.[1]

One year after the opening of the Ostankino TV Tower in 1967, the first visitors took the elevators 337 meters up, entered the observation deck, enjoyed the panorama over Moscow, and perhaps had something to eat in the rotating restaurant ("The Seventh Heaven").

The public experience of viewing panoramas seems to have a relatively long history. It is traceable at least back to the Enlightenment of the eighteenth century and the invention of panorama painting. This art form introduced a new way of seeing, combining the realism of the central perspective with endless viewing positions, a democratic way of seeing for a mass audience. It has been claimed that "television of today is a direct descendant of the panorama" (Oettermann 1997, p. 44).

Fig. 1. A postcard of the Ostankino Tower. Photo by Nikolai Rahmanov.

Fig. 2. One of the architects behind Ostankino Tower and production center (to the right)–Leonid Batalov–in front of his creation. Printed with kind permission from Andrei Batalov.

OSTANKINO TV TOWER, MOSCOW | 83

Fig. 3. The architect Leonid Batalov inside the production center. Printed with kind permission from Andrei Batalov.

Fig. 4. The observation deck at Ostankino. Printed with kind permission from Andrei Batalov.

Fig. 5. The restaurant "Seventh Heaven" at the top of the Ostankino TV Tower. Printed with kind permission from Andrei Batalov.

Incidentally, one of the oldest current affairs programs on television, running since 1953, is the BBC's *Panorama*.

Stephen Oettermann describes the time of the invention of the panorama painting as one characterized by a "see-fever," observation platforms were put up all over Europe, many of them on top of churches and cathedrals. More than 150 years later, the world witnessed a new explosion of observation platforms, now built as transmission towers for national media organizations in different parts of the world (Crowley & Pavitt 2008). Ostankino is a prominent part of that development. In what way is Ostankino's TV Tower a descendant of the panorama tradition, a continuation of the "see-fever" of the Enlightenment? What are the differences between the panoramas offered from the observation deck of a TV tower and that of a church? And how can we understand the tower today, forty years after its completion?

This chapter places the Ostankino Tower in a specific Russian history of media towers characterized by "de-materialization" and discusses the ways in which the tower can be understood as a "mechanism for representation" in relation to television at the end of the 1960s. Further on, it discusses the Ostankino TV center as an "organizational complex" in relation to centralization/decentralization, demarcations between inside and outside, and how this has changed in the postcommunist era. The chapter also attempts to analyze how Ostankino, both as a symbol and a material structure, has been used in power struggles at certain critical points since the breakdown of the Soviet Union.

Russian Media Towers

The Russian history of twentieth-century architecture includes a tradition from the 1920s of what could be called *media towers*, their function being to integrate different forms of media distribution, their structure expressing de-materialization, the opposite of solidness and weight (Buck-Morss 2002, pp. 134–140).

Fig. 6. The engineer Vladimir Shukhov's radio tower in Moscow from 1922.
Photo by Staffan Ericson.

The radio tower designed by the engineer Vladimir Shukhov was completed in Moscow in 1922. It is famous because of its so-called hyperbolic structure: a network of iron bars creates a pattern like a woven basket, making the construction very light (at the time, its weight was compared with that of the much heavier Eiffel Tower, another steel construction). In 1924, the Vesnin brothers, leaders in the Constructivist movement, proposed a tower of glass and steel as the new headquarters for the newspaper *Pravda* in Moscow (see "Introduction" to this volume). Another famous but never realized building was designed by Vladimir Tatlin:

Monument to the Third International (1919). This is also a tower, with an information center at the top, including telegraph, radio masts, and a spotlight projecting revolutionary slogans against the sky. Tatlin's tower was not only planned as a rational building for the party administration; it was a metaphor for a whole new society, "a telescope pointing at the polestar," and "the control-room of the spaceship Earth" (Ekbom 1986, p. 142ff.).

The Ostankino Tower can be seen in the light of this tradition. When Khrushchev came to power after Stalin's death in 1953, there was a revived interest in the constructivism of the 1920s, which under the Stalin era had been regarded as a part of international modernism, and thus a despised Western architecture (Ockman 1993, p. 184). Khrushchev turned his back on Stalin's monuments, with their ornaments and "pastry-cook facades," to highlight architecture that celebrated function.

Fig. 7. A sketch from the end of the 1950s with the planned Ostankino Tower in front and Shukhov's radio tower in the background. Printed with kind permission from Andrei Batalov.

In an early sketch of the planned Ostankino Tower from the end of the 1950s, it is placed in front of the Shukhov tower (Fig. 7). The first, and most obvious, interpretation is that a new tower is going to replace the old radio tower with its limited capacity for television transmissions. From an architectural perspective, the picture also indicates the connection between the new tower and the Constructivist movement—of which the Shukhov tower is a prominent part. Marginalized, to the left in the drawing, is one of Stalin's skyscrapers, used as a landmark but not as a symbol to be connected to the new modern tower. Together with the two towers in the center of the picture, there is a power plant and what looks like American cars (on one of them it says Ford, a company that was used as a prototype for the rationalization and centralization of the Soviet industry in the 1920s). For Lewis H. Siegelbaum, who has written about cars during the Soviet era, the design of the cars in the 1950s, often inspired by American models, were "less ponderous, sleeker, and

Fig. 8. The base at Ostankino Tower. Photo by Staffan Ericson.

Fig. 9. The entrance hall at Ostankino Tower. Printed with kind permission from Andrei Batalov.

more modern in the way that much of the Soviet Union would be in the post-Stalin era" (Siegelbaum 2008, p. 30). In that way the cars are used as signs for a new modern society of which the Ostankino Tower is a part.²

The cars, together with the people moving around the tower and the dramatic sky behind, signal motion and speed. When building Ostankino, the illusion of motion could be accomplished by the use of formable reinforced concrete. In post-Stalinist architecture, it became the material of the time. The motives were both economic and esthetic—reducing costs by using standardized preproduced sections, reintroducing the flexibility of expression of early modernism.³

Writing in the late 1920s, Giedion sees reinforced concrete as a development of the dematerialization found in iron constructions such as the Eiffel Tower. The use of concrete as a "skeleton" would produce buildings with "the feeling of walking in clouds" (Giedion 1928/1995, 168ff). At Ostankino, the skeleton is reduced to just one hollow bone. The idea behind the construction to Ostankino came from thin and high floor lamps, standing with a shallow but heavy and broad base. At Ostankino, parts of this base are not visible. thus, considering its height, it creates the impression of a slim and light building.

A unique construction with 149 steel wires—hidden under the concrete surface—holds the parts together and anchors them to the ground. Early on, there were doubts about the stability of the tower; for some months, the project was stopped because of such apprehensions.

As in early constructivism, Ostankino is celebrated because of its advanced technical solutions. The tower was made into a symbol for Soviet science and engineering in a period characterized by the Cold War and space race. Therefore, it was the engineer not the architect who was given the greatest recognition. In the case of Ostankino, the engineer Nikolai Nikitin was awarded the prestigious Lenin Prize, and he is the one celebrated on the wall in the entrance hall of the tower, while the architects Leonid Batalov and Dmitry Burdin play a more marginal role in the Russian history of the tower.

The Tactual Panorama

Compared to the Eiffel Tower, the inside is clearly separated from the outside at Ostankino, by the closed concrete tube and by the glass screens of the observation deck. With parts of the floor also being of glass, the visitor may really get the experience of "walking in the clouds."

But the visitor will not, as in the Eiffel Tower, sense the air streaming through the building: this panorama must be enjoyed through a glass screen. Marshall McLuhan, probably the most influential media theorist of the 1960s, has compared the TV image with a nightly panorama of a city landscape:

Fig. 10. The glass floor at Ostankino's observation deck. Photo by the author.

From the air at night, the seeming chaos of the urban area manifests itself as a delicate embroidery on a dark velvet ground. Gyorgy Kepes has developed these aerial effects of the city at night as a new art form of "landscape by light through" rather than "light on." His new electric landscapes have complete congruity with the TV image, which also exists by light *through* rather than by light *on*. (McLuhan 1964/2007, p. 140)

If the glass at Ostankino's observation deck has similarities to the TV screen—linking a specific technology of representation to a specific architectural expression—it may also present a different "bird's-eye view" than the one offered the visitor at the top of the cathedral, e.g., in Hugo's *The Hunchback of Notre Dame* (1831). Hugo's book was written during the widespread "see-fever" and during the heyday of print culture. Symptomatically, Hugo reads the panorama over Paris as "a chronicle in stone." According to McLuhan, television must break with literate culture:

The literate man, accustomed to an environment in which the visual sense is extended everywhere as a principle of organization … The visual stress on continuity, uniformity, and connectedness, as it derives from literacy, confronts us with the great technological means of implementing continuity and lineality by fragmented repetition. The ancient world found this means in the brick, whether for wall or road. The repetitive, uniform brick, indispensable agent of road and wall, of cities and empires, is an extension, via letters, of the visual sense. *The brick wall is not a mosaic form,* and neither is the mosaic form a visual structure.

> The mosaic can be seen as dancing can, but is not structured visually; nor is it an extension of the visual power. For the mosaic is not uniform, continuous, or repetitive. It is discontinuous, skew, and nonlinear, like the tactual TV image. (McLuhan 1964/2007, p. 364f)

This would mean that a visitor to Ostankino in the television age is *not* primarily there to *read* Moscow, objectively and detached, as a linear history. But is it possible to understand an *observation* deck at the world's highest tower as something else than an extension of the eye? According to McLuhan TV is " . . . an extension of the sense of touch, which involves maximal interplay of all the senses . . . " (p. 370)—this is why the TV image is called "tactual." The TV viewer will experience the outside as inside (p. 357), and the outside is coming *through* the screen, toward an involved and participating viewer, much like in McLuhan's descriptions of the oral culture—an unmediated interaction with all senses in balance. This experience of "being there," of "touching the real," could be what puzzles Joe Milutis when reflecting on one of the legendary moments of television—the moon landing in 1969: " . . . there was really nothing to see, yet here was a television event of the highest order" (Milutis 2006, p. 120). What is anticipated is that the viewer will "fill in the picture," participate and engage with all senses. Likewise, a visit to the top of the Ostankino Tower will involve a *whole* bodily experience. In line with Jonathan Crary (1999), this can be understood as shaping an attraction for the medium, i.e., television, which cannot be separated from power relations.

Space Age and Television

So what was the experience of visiting Ostankino like, at the time of its opening? How was the visitor prepared for the tactual panorama provided by the tower, as a "mechanism for representation"?

The tower is situated in the former Ostankino Park, which has remained from the time of the tsars with the Ostankino castle opposite, an area used for recreation by Muscovites. Another part of Ostankino Park contains the All-Union Exhibition of the Achievements of the National Economy (today it has reclaimed its old name All-Russia Exhibition Center), best described as "Moscow's Disneyland" (Siegelbaum 2008, p. 30). This exhibition occupied a huge area and included pavilions representing the different regions in the Soviet Union and prominent fields in society. One of these fields was outer space and a Space Pavilion was opened in 1966. In front of this pavilion, a full size copy of Yuri Gagarin's rocket was erected. At the closest metro station, the monument of "The Conquerors of Space," a rocket rising into the sky on a 100 meter stream of titanium, was inaugurated in 1964. (In 1981, to celebrate the 20th anniversary of Gagarin's space flight, a space museum was located in the base of the monument.)

Fig. 11. A woman with a baby carriage in the surrounding park from the time of the tsars. Printed with kind permission from Andrei Batalov.

Fig. 12. A copy of Gagarin's rocket in the All-Russia Exhibition Center with Ostankino Tower in the background. Photo by the author.

Fig. 13. The monument "The Conquerors of Space" with Ostankino as a relief. Photo by the author.

Fig. 14. Ostankino Tower. Photo by Staffan Ericson.

Given this context, it is possible to say that the visitor entered the Ostankino Tower with the experience of living in the space age.

This is also reinforced by the architecture. From the outside, the tower may look like a huge antenna or transmitter, but it also resembles a *rocket*. The column is ornamented with horizontal sections, or rings, in different sizes (serving an important function, as equipment can be attached to them). According to the architects, Batalov and Burdin, these rings signified the upwards acceleration of a space rocket.

Taking the elevators equaled preparing for the launch of a space flight, and entering the observation deck was taking the cosmonaut's position. The dream of conquering outer space in the early Soviet State, expressed in, for instance, Tatlin's tower, finally got its monument with Ostankino, where visitors were able to enter the "control-room of spaceship *Earth*." Or, finally, the realization of Joe Milutis' characterization of the new kind of monumentalism found in the model of Tatlin's tower: "Steel and glass and concrete could be used to signify that we actually existed in the clouds" (Milutis 2006, p. 96).

From the beginning of the eighteenth century, panoramic vision has been connected to mobility. Giuliana Bruno (2002) sees the cinema as an inheritor, a kind of "panoramic wallpaper" with "its spatial roots in the new 'fashions' of spatiality that marked the rise of modernity ... the new vision was a travelling one ..." (p. 171). However, as mentioned earlier, enjoying panoramas is not only related to media representations but also to physical travelling. The eighteenth century introduced "the Grand Tour" and people started to travel around in Europe to "broaden one's horizons." Oettermann's thesis is that the panorama painting was the "pictorial expression or 'symbolic form' of a specifically modern, bourgeois view of nature and the world..." (Oettermann 1997, p. 7). This also resulted in observation platforms all over Europe, expressing a new way of seeing the rural and urban landscapes, in tune with the progression of natural sciences in the Enlightenment. Instead of looking up at God, the bourgeoisie viewer looked down to discover and experience natural and social landscapes.

Oettermann's characteristic of the eighteenth century traveller is that of a person schooled in, what McLuhan would call, the literate culture. It is likely that the visitor to Ostankino replaces this viewer. When looking down from Ostankino the height makes it hard to "read" the landscape below and therefore the visitor was not primarily there to get an overview. The main attraction could be the feeling "that we existed in the clouds." Instead of looking up at God, the sky became the place for communication and global connectedness. A connectedness that could be experienced, not read.

The tower is also a reminder that television, as a technology, is space-biased in a very concrete way. Satellites placed in space are needed for distribution of signals over huge areas. The tower had state-of-the-art solutions for the technological distribution of TV: its height permitted the transmission of signals over the Moscow area, its relay equipment made it possible to synchronize broadcasts all over the Union. In the Soviet Union, the world's first national network of satellite communication was a prerequisite for conquering difficult terrain and 11 time zones (Downing 1985). The launching of this satellite system coincided with the construction of the Ostankino Tower.

The Tower as Part of an Organizational Complex

At the time of the inauguration of the tower in 1967, the BBC planned a live intercontinental satellite broadcast: *Our World*. The theme for this broadcast was the "population explosion" and the threat of world starvation. The humanitarian theme was supposed to engage people all around the world. To create the impression of a "global village," the viewers were offered a *panorama* over the planet Earth, and live shots of four childbirths from different places. The studio was "constructed as a portal to the world 'out there'," using multiple screens, space-age sounds, floor-light, minimalist design, and a 3-D model of Earth (Parks 2005, chapter 1).

In the Soviet Union, this utopian panorama was never broadcast: their decision to withdraw from participation referred to the West's support of Israeli attacks during the "Six-Day War" in the Middle East. Two years later, the first moon landing was not distributed by the Soviet satellites. For years to come, the internationalization of satellite communication developed according to a Cold War logic, with on the one hand, the U.S.-dominated Intelsat system, on the other, the Russian Intersputnik system (Downing 1985).

Media scholar Lisa Parks has noted that media studies have tended to disregard the "military-industrial-information complexes" of which satellite communication, and thereby television, is a part (Parks 2005, p. 7). Parks argues that satellite TV must be understood as a "site of convergence" between such different spheres as entertainment, science, education, and the military—all of which have shaped what she calls the "televisual" (Parks 2005, p. 12). Perhaps this is a truism when applied to a state-controlled and propaganda-oriented media system such as the one in the Soviet Union. All of these activities are present and distributed at Ostankino. Besides the convergence of "visual" material, including a center for national meteorological observations, the tower was equipped with "a system for radio-frequency voice communication for the basic Ministries and offices" and "special radio communication for the head of the State, government and operating bodies."

Kristin Roth-Ey (2007) has described the building of the Ostankino TV center as "finding a home" for Soviet television. Until then there had been no clear ideas about how to use this new medium. For Roth-Ey, this has a specific reason: television threatened the Soviet tradition of public meetings face-to-face. It was assumed that the control over the audience was lost. Because of this, the development of Soviet television was at first shaped by a decentralized process through local initiatives with limited central regulations. Local investments were foremost due to television as a symbol for modernity, and having equipment for production and distribution of television gave status to the region. When the Soviet state began to realize the importance of television,[4] it determined that the viewer should be schooled to become active and engaged, much in tune with McLuhan's vision about television. One way to stimulate this was to include television sets in public spaces and make arrangements for collective viewing.

In the light of this history, the opening of the Ostankino center in 1967 may be understood as both a centralization of television by the Soviet authorities and an emphasis on the collective part of the new medium (inviting the public to the site). The latter is underlined in the rhetoric around the building process, which says that the center was built "with materials and labor from the entire country" (Roth-Ey 2007, p. 305). When Ostankino was celebrated as "a home" for Soviet television, the site offered a "convergence" between leisure and entertainment (the park, visiting the tower) and education, science, politics, and the military (producing the "right" programs, equipment for observations, communication among those in power). How is it possible to understand this "organizational complex" in relation to distinctions between inside and outside?

Reinhold Martin (2003) uses the term "organizational complex" to describe the American corporate architecture of the 1950s and 1960s. Martin understands these buildings as both "mythical" and "real," as strategies for organizing social space:

> The system's phantasmagorias—with built architecture also counted prominently among these—likewise constitute an indelibly real system of images, with indelibly real consequences. Far from simply staging a spectacle that screens out the structural logic of corporate power by coaxing the spectator-user into a state of passive distraction, architecture works here actively to integrate spaces and subjects into naturalized organizations, specifically to the degree that it is "reduced" to corporate image. (Martin 2003, p. 4)

According to Martin, this is articulated in the corporate buildings as they seem to promote "de-hierarchized interactivity." A form of decentralized power may also be at work at Ostankino, but in contrast to the buildings analyzed by Martin, the "mythical" can be separated from the "real" decentralization.

The inside of the television center's tower is organized to reduce all obstructions and to secure a pure and joyful experience of the tactual panorama. Hidden from sight are the technical devices for transmission of signals and the administration of the tower. Even though there are spaces for meetings, there is no evidence that they were open to the public. It is as Roland Barthes says about the Eiffel Tower: " . . . there is nothing to see *inside* the Tower" (Barthes 1979/1997, p. 86). What is more, the openness of the *distribution* tower will not include the processes of *production* going on in the nearby TV center. This partial blindness could be related to an innovation contemporary to the panorama—the *panopticon*. It is common to think about the panopticon—designed to confine—in relation to surveillance and control (Crary 1999, Foucault 1979) and the panorama in relation to mobility and transport (Bruno 2002, Friedberg 1998). According to Oettermann, the two inventions are different sides of the same coin:

> As "school of vision," the panorama and panopticon are at the same time identical and antithetical: in the panorama the observer is schooled in a way of seeing that is taught to prisoners in the panopticon. (Oettermann 1997, p. 41)

Fig. 15. Inside the base at Ostankino Tower. A hall for "lectures and meetings." Printed with kind permission from Andrei Batalov.

Just like the warden in the observation tower remains out of sight for the prisoner, the system of power being served by Ostankino will remain out of sight for the visitor. And if the panorama of the Ostankino Tower is tactual, it is not primarily about seeing; its mechanism of representation will not really serve panoptical observations. If it is neither panopticon nor panorama, how can we best understand this mechanism?

When Martin examines the "organizational complex" as self-controlling organisms, he departs from Gyorgy Kepes and his electric landscapes, the same reference McLuhan uses to describe the TV screen. There is also a striking resemblance between the office buildings Martin studies, built in curtain wall architecture,[5] and the TV center at Ostankino, which the visitor to the tower sees "as a mosaic below." In one drawing by the architects (including only Batalov and almost a whole collective of architects[6]), the production center looks like an illustration of one of Kepes' electronic landscapes that "exist by light through" (Fig. 16).

For Martin, Kepes' landscape is congruent with Norbert Wiener's cybernetics:

> This new landscape also belongs to what Kepes calls a shift from "thing-seeing" to "pattern-seeing," where the body into which this sensorium is embedded is decisively flattened. What was once a "thing" in space, an organism made up of carefully arranged functional organs, has become, for Wiener as well as for many biologists, a communications network linked to other networks in all directions, a "pattern." (Martin 2003, p. 40)

The cybernetic patterns are universal and there are continuities between "organic" biological patterns and scientific/technological ones. To accomplish this congruity, Martin gives the following description of Kepes' mission: "the alienation of the scientific specialist was to be overcome by the retrained eye of the artist" (Martin 2003, p. 67). And what is more: "In order to sustain this effect, the media through which images were transmitted had to be naturalized." In McLuhan's world, it is TV and not the artist that will shape the "congruity"—the global village—and facilitate for the TV viewer the experience of the outside as inside, thus naturalizing the medium. In a passage about the congruity between Kepes' work and the TV screen, McLuhan writes about a near future when electronic simulations can bypass languages and create a global "consciousness-without-walls" (McLuhan 1964/2007, p. 141).

The 1960s was the heyday of cybernetics in the Soviet Union, and it became, during the Khrushchev period, the "science in the service of communism" until the beginning of the 1970s (Gerovitch 2002, p. 4).[7] And if, as Martin argues, the curtain wall is the congenial architectural expression of cybernetics, that theory's importance is evident in the production center. But the cybernetic thought of bridging the gap between nature and technology and torn down walls in a "de-hierarchisized interactivity" is not easily applied to Ostankino as an "organizational complex."

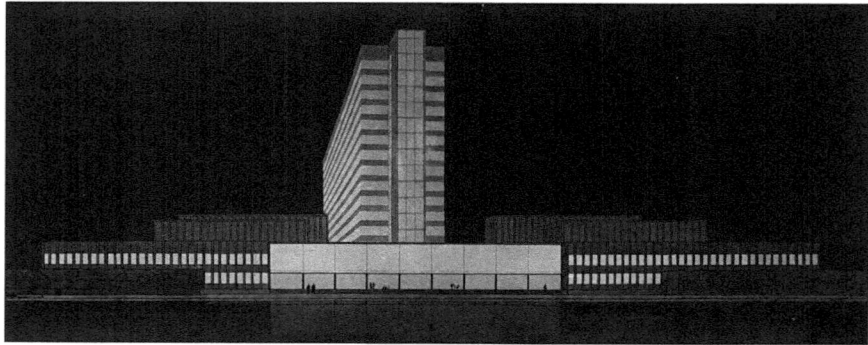

Fig. 16. An early sketch of the production center. Printed with kind permission from Andrei Batalov.

Fig. 17. The production center in one architectural drawing from Leonid Batalov's archive. Printed with kind permission from Andrei Batalov.

Instead the complex seems to be caught between two organizational principles, what Gilles Deleuze and Félix Guattari (1975/1986) call the "old, imperial, despotic bureaucracy" and the "new capitalist or socialist bureaucracy" (p. 75). Deleuze and Guattari exemplify these two bureaucracies with two different states of architecture: the old is found in the central tower, and the new in buildings with contiguous hallways and corridors interrelated in complex ways. An early example of how these bureaucracies are intertwined is according to Deleuze and Guattari found in the Russian constructivist projects of the 1920s, for instance, Tatlin's Tower: "It seems that the most modern functionalism more or less voluntarily reactivated the most archaic or mythical forms" (Deleuze & Guattari 1975/1986, p. 75). When Soviet television "found a home" at Ostankino the integration of production, distribution and the audience "reactivated" this mix of two organizational principles, articulated in the production center (new) and the tower (old). The idea of decentralization found in McLuhan's thoughts about television could then be used in this organizational complex to conceal the "system of power that it serves."

The ability for the visitor to "come inside" strengthens the illusion of a mediated center of society during the space age (offering the position of the cosmonaut at the top, Moscow as a mosaic below, the tower being "a portal to the world 'out there'," a "global village" with everyone empathically engaged over geographical borders). But this being inside does not involve actual participation, the visitor does not contribute to the distribution of entertainment and information and remains an outsider to all the real functions of the tower. As a mechanism for representation, Ostankino may perhaps be best understood as a part of a larger "organizational complex," its architecture and surroundings producing the subject for the TV age.

Fig. 18. The completed center with children playing in the swimming pool in the foreground. Printed with kind permission from Andrei Batalov.

The Tower as a Ruin

In one of the early drawings of Ostankino Tower, from the end of the 1950s, there are wall paintings on the inside of the base (Fig. 19). These paintings show different fields in Soviet society such as sports, agriculture, and the military. Mother Russia rises above the ordinary people, and further up, above her, activities in space take place. Even if the content in the wall paintings is interesting—announcing a global social order about outer space, a cosmology—the most interesting aspect is that there are paintings on the concrete surface at all. If the building of Ostankino in certain ways marked a return to the 1920s constructivism, it is no surprise that this ornamentation was taken away from the final building.

Constructivism, seen as part of the international modernism movement, broke with history and that is what, for instance, Walter Benjamin celebrated in his *Arcades Project* (1999). For Benjamin, modernism in architecture was a revolutionary break up, an awakening from the dream world of capitalism. The architecture in the capitalist society was covered with ornamentation, creating a false consciousness by concealing the structure of the building and thereby keeping the collective asleep.

Fig. 19. An early drawing of Ostankino's base with wall painting. Printed with kind permission from Andrei Batalov.

But Benjamin's thoughts about modern architecture can lead us in another direction applied to the time for the planning of Ostankino. Was the return to Russian constructivism at the end of the 1950s a way to create a dreamworld of socialism by keeping the collective asleep? Could it be that the unmasked skeleton architecture created by steel, concrete, and glass in constructivism, as part of the modernism movement in Europe, had a particular history that Khrushchev used or that the "awakened architecture" of the 1920s as a historical style was turned into a dreamworld for the masses?[8] In another way, the return to the Constructivist movement was only half-hearted, at least considering Ostankino. The tower *was* ornamented to create an illusion of speed, and the whole building was thought of as an icon of a rocket.

Accepting the architecture of Ostankino as part of that specific celebrated history *and* as ornamented makes it possible to understand the tower in a similar way to Susan Buck-Morss' (2002) reading of the Moscow metro. The metro stations were covered with ornamentation used by Stalin to create luxurious underground castles accessible to all. For Buck-Morss, in her Benjamin-inspired reading, the dreamworld found in the Moscow metro became crucial for a collective awakening: "The gap between the utopian promise believed in by children and the dystopian actuality that they experience as adults can indeed generate a force for collective awakening" (Buck-Morss 2002, p. 209).

Buck-Morss' reading of the Moscow metro has a prehistory in her earlier book, *The Dialectics of Seeing* (1989), about Benjamin's *Arcades Project,* where she gives the following description of Benjamin's analysis:

> ...the theory is unique in its approach to modern society, because it takes mass culture seriously not merely as the source of the phantasmagoria of false consciousness, but as the source of collective energy to overcome it. (Buck-Morss 1989, p. 253)

Buck-Morss explains Benjamin's theory by adopting a model where one axis is "waking-dream" and the other is "petrified nature-transitory nature", (1989, p. 210f). This gives her four fields that can be used to describe objects: (1) fossil, (2) fetish, (3) wish image, and (4) ruin. The following part of this chapter will analyze the Ostankino Tower's postcommunist history with the help of this model. First, some thoughts about how Buck-Morss' four perspectives can be applied to the tower:

1. The fossil places the object in its ur-history—in the case of Ostankino, it can be the tower as an observation platform and the widespread see-fever that took place at the end of the eighteenth century. Another ur-history is the myth of the Tower of Babel in the Bible (Genesis 11: 1–9). According to the myth, the Babylonians built a city with a mighty tower, reaching the heavens "to make a name for themselves." God disrupted the work, because it was an expression of human overweening pride, by confusing the language so people could not understand each other and scattered them all over the earth. The "global village" of the 1960s can be understood in line with the efforts made by the Babylonians.

2. The *fetish* works as a dream world keeping the collective asleep, the Moscow metro was a fetish or phantasmagoria, and it is possible that visits to the tower/rocket during the space age had a similar attraction.

3. The *wish image* is the "dream form" of the potential of "a collective political action." It is, for example, likely that childhood visits to the tower lives on as bright memories of a promising future among people in postcommunist Russia, much like Buck-Morss' understanding of the function of memories of the Moscow metro.

4. The *ruin* is "the wish image of the past ... as rubble, in the present." This means that the childhood memories and stories about the tower can awaken the adult and turn it into a ruin. There are a couple of incidents at Ostankino during the postcommunist era that indicate these kinds of clashes between the "utopian promise" of the tower and the realities of the Russian society.

The purpose for the remainder of this chapter is to analyze how these four perspectives overlap in different ways during the recent history of the Ostankino Tower, from the postcommunist era until today, and what this tells us about the tower's function as an (historical) object.

Ostankino as a Real and Symbolic Center during the Postcommunist Era

In 1993, the Russian president Boris Yeltsin was subject to a coup d'état. Former vice president Aleksandr Rutskoy encouraged his followers to assault two targets: the Parliament and the Ostankino TV center. The military supported Yeltsin and stopped the attack. According to official information, 147 people were killed in the battles involving Ostankino. John Downing describes this event as an extreme example of the power struggles among the Russian elite at the time: "Battle was never joined in order for the public to have access to media, merely for the parliamentary forces to have 'their' media to balance the Yeltsin administration's media dominance." (Downing 1996, p. 142). The main reasons the communists and ultranationalists wanted to dethrone Yeltsin was that he had become autocratic and that his reforms toward a capitalistic market economy had led the country to ruin. Yeltsin's victory at the battles around Ostankino strengthened his power and made it possible to continue his privatization of state property. This had major importance for the rise of the "Russian oligarchs," a small business elite who became private owners in, not least, the media industry.

Brian McNair describes this development as the world's first "media-ocracy," a social condition in which politics is " . . . indistinguishable from—economic power vested in the media and culture industries, and in which the traditional barriers separating political and cultural power dissolve" (McNair 2000, 88f). The support from the "media-ocracy" is a common explanation to why Yeltsin managed to win the presidential election in 1996 despite growing unpopularity among the Russian people.

Yeltsin's privatization of the media industry totally changed the Ostankino TV center. From the 1960s to the beginning of the 1990s TV production for the first four then five offered channels was headed by GOSTELERADIO.[9] From the 1990s their monopoly of media production was broken, and the commercialization of the Russian media began. Today, Ostankino hosts 22 TV channels and about as many radio channels, all financed by advertisements, representing everything from the state to private enterprises. In its relatively concentrated area, this center represents a development that makes Russia particularly interesting for today's media researchers, according to Brian McNair: " . . . it allows us to witness what happens when the attempt is made to build a politically and economically independent media system from the ruins of a state-controlled, propaganda-oriented one . . ." (McNair 2000, p. 79).

Commercialization of the Russian media leads us to another important incident at Ostankino, a story that made world news at the end of August 2000: a fire on top of the tower involving three casualties. It shut down TV and radio broadcasting for those 15 million living in the area. The official explanation referred to a short circuit and that the work of the fire brigade was complicated by an overcrowded interior. This accident coincided with the wreck of the atomic submarine *Kursk*: both incidents came to symbolize neglected maintenance and a state economy close to ruin. The silence from the TV center also became evidence that the state had lost political and social control. At the time, the commercialization and decentralization of Russian media was blamed: according to the World Socialist Web Site, the fire was caused by an overload in the equipment of the tower, not adapted for "contemporary capitalism."[10]

There are several news articles after the fire describing how addicted especially elderly people were getting to (especially commercial) television. When the screen turned blank, they felt an emptiness as if a companion were lost. However, there are examples of the opposite:

> The Internet news sites traffic surged, print media sales went up, videotapes sold better. People enjoyed the amazingly pleasant weather that reigned in and around the capital for a whole week; they spent more time outdoors and socialising.[11]

From this perspective, the silence from the Ostankino Tower was more threatening for the media and the medio-cracy than for the people living in the area. The importance of a mediated center for the political sphere can explain Vladimir Putin's actions when he took over as president in 2000.

Fig. 20. The fire at top of Ostankino in 2000. Photo by Sergey Chirikov/Epa/SCANPIX.

After the fire, voices from both the political and the media sphere suggested that Ostankino should be substituted with a more flexible, decentralized structure, in tune with the development of digital media. But for Putin, the fire at Ostankino could be used as a symbol for the turbulent and unstable Yeltsin years. Putin and his government decided to launch a restoration of the tower, with grants from European Bank for Reconstruction and Development, adapting it for the future.

The material structure of Ostankino has thus been reintroduced into new historical contexts: political, cultural, and technological. In this new situation, it is tempting to say that opening the tower for the public is not the primary goal. The fire has kept the tower closed to visitors since 2000. The Putin era has been described as the completion of the "oligarchs' era" and re-centralization of Russian media, with increased state activities and reinvestments.[12] In this context, the permanence of the tower itself—a symbol for stability—may be more important than the experience its interiors might offer. The renovation and digitalization concern the equipment in the tower, not the way it expresses dominant thoughts about today's media. One side of the renovation is the Russian government's investments in the new digital media infrastructure—and thereby gaining control over media distribution. According to Gennady Sklyar, general director of Russian Television and Radio Broadcasting Network (RTRN), founded in 2001, new media towers adopted for digital distribution are planned all over Russia (including observation decks).[13] Ostankino is of course an important part of that development. The tower is still a state property, it is part of the RTRN, and has been separated from the TV center, which is managed as a commercial business, lending production space to all media companies that are willing to pay.

How can we then understand the tower as a ruin—the wish image of the past as rubble in the present—in the battles of 1993 and in relation to the fire in year 2000? The incidents clearly start political discussions and actions but they do not lead to a new order. The battle in 1993 seems to be a power struggle at the top of society and not so much about democratic access to the media. After these struggles, it was "business as usual" between political power and media power. The fire in 2000 was immediately used by those in power as an expression of the former government's mistakes, but at the same time the quick decision to renovate the tower manifested that the new government had the answer to the problems. The Finnish TV journalist Ann-Britt Kaca noticed that Putin's use of the fire was miles away from "TV towers as symbols and catalysts of revolution" as in Poland and the Baltic States in the years around the fall of the Soviet Union.[14] For example, at the Vilnius TV tower in Lithuania there are memorials of victims of the Soviet military attack in 1991. Seen in this light the incidents at Ostankino have been used instead for consolidation of political power and have not contributed to an awakened transition.

But this battle is not completely won. Still demonstrations are held around the tower that can be described as a kind of awakening, where the role of the tower in today's media landscape is questioned.[15] And maybe the tower was a ruin already when it was completed in 1967. The period called "Khrushchev's thaw" after years of Stalin's hard rule ended when Khrushchev was forced from power in 1964 and Brezhnev took over. During Brezhnev's rule, the media again became more regulated (Downing 1996, p. 44). That is why Ostankino immediately got nicknames such as "the syringe" or "the needle" among critical circles (Roth-Ey 2007), signaling that it has more to do with control of the mind than offering a tactual panorama.

Ostankino as an Historical Object

One way to draw attention from the tower as a ruin is to place it in a continuous mythic history. There is some evidence of ongoing activities in that direction. The renovation and adoption to today's media are part of an invisible *inside*. But the director of the tower has great plans for the future. It is said that the observation deck will be reopened in the near future, and there are ideas about a "cultural center" close to the tower, attracting people of all ages.[16] Even the area surrounding the tower is going through refurbishments. The space museum close to the nearest metro station has been totally renovated and reopened in 2009. The monument "Conquerors of Space" is surrounded by a recently restored space park with statues of prominent people and events in the Soviet Russian space program. It is again possible to walk in this park with the Ostankino Tower in relief as the background. But this return to what was once the future creates a different experience from that of the 1960s. Today the tower is part of a proud Russian history, not a manifestation of future achievements. If the tower ever should be reopened, it is likely that nostalgia for the space age of the 1960s will be the main attraction, rather than the utopian ideas of decentralization that were once connected to satellite television.

Fig. 21. The man "holding his hand" on the tower is Sergey Korolev, the mastermind behind the Soviet space program. Photo by the author.

The tower is now a member of an organization called World Federation of Great Towers (WFGT)—including the CN Tower in Toronto (which took Ostankino's place as the highest tower in the world in 1977) and the Eiffel Tower (once saved by its importance for radio transmissions)—with the explicit goal of strengthening the member towers' role as tourist attractions. In autumn 2008,

Ostankino hosted the organization's annual conference, and at the opening party, the tower was turned into a screen when a light and sound show was projected at it (September 15). The tower was ornamented with media projections and written into a specific history.[17]

The show is worth a description because McLuhan's "tactual panorama" of the 1960s can be said to be turned inside out—the tower is transformed into a projection screen characterized by "light on." The light show also raises questions about media globalization in relation to media production and distribution.

It begins with a story of the building process where laser beams mark different parts of the buildings, giving them significant dates of different years during the 1960s. The engineer Nikitin is celebrated as the man behind the building, and a new interpretation is given the design of the tower in the comparison of it to an upturned lily. This comparison is the beginning of a part of the show that projects exotic flowers, animals, and birds—peacocks, with their "eyes" on the feathers, connote the tower as an eye. This first part of the light show celebrates the tower as a link to a magical world.

The next part is a celebration of (American) popular culture. Visualizations of communication signals are followed by popular international characters from movies for children such as Disney's *Alice in Wonderland* and *Pinocchio*, and *Tom & Jerry* are chasing each other around the tower. After this Elvis, and music stars like Michael Jackson and Madonna, cover the tower, followed by clips of stars from Hollywood movies. In the last part of the show, the focus shifts from the tower as a sender and receiver of popular content to, what can be called, its original context. A floodlight is searching in the grass around the tower and finally finds a cosmonaut walking towards the tower, waving at the audience. The projection turns the tower into a rocket and a countdown starts. At zero, the rocket/tower is virtually launched into space and the silence that follows is interrupted by the characteristic beeps associated with the *Sputnik* satellite. Stars and planets indicate that we are now in outer space. John Lennon starts singing his "Imagine" and the word "peace" is projected on different spots all over the tower. To reconnect to the organization WFGT and to reach a climax, flags from the member countries replace outer space and icons of the member towers circulate at Ostankino's base, at the same time a (real) firework display takes place beside the tower.

As an expression of the globalization of media content, the light show is a sign of U.S. victory when it comes to "soft power." It is also easy to relate the show to the commercialization of the media that started in the 1990s and an excitement over previously unavailable content (Jakubowicz 2007, p. 220). The exposé over (mainly) American popular culture that ends with the rocket provides a history that works through "back to the future." And moving back to the future is made possible by moving beyond a Cold War logic and into the utopia of a "global village," by showing media content that is internationally known. It is not the tower as part of media production at Ostankino that is celebrated, but instead its importance for distribution of global entertainment. The light show also connects Ostankino to the space age and the 1960s satellite communication technology in a very direct way, when the cosmonaut approaches the tower and it is turned into a rocket and launched to space. If the space age was a symbolic battle between two opposite world systems, then the Americans are definitely crowned as the winners in the battle of presenting the most attractive lifestyle.

When the tower is used as a screen, transporting the audience to outer space, it also turns the tower into an *object* connected to that era. Turning the tower into a space-age object gives it a new status as fetish. We now watch the *history* of the promises of satellite television communication and the tower is used as a film screen. There are good reasons to believe that the possibility to come inside and take part of a tactual panorama is an outdated illusion about television. That the tower as a "mechanism of representation," once employed in its initial (mythological) decentralization, i.e., the tactual panorama of television shaping an involved and participating viewer, has been lost to history. TV is still important with regard to people's media consumption, but in the commercialized media system with strong state control, TV's role seems to be reduced to broadcasting entertainment. According to Elena Degtereva, there has been an increase of entertainment on TV along with Putin's re-centralization of the media system, since it is "both profitable and politically safe for mass media" (Degtereva 2007, p. 218).

Today, the tower's association with television makes it a rather weak symbol in a media landscape where the Internet has become the most important arena for participation and involvement (Jakubowicz, p. 295). Even if studies have shown that the Russian state has developed "soft" ways to control Web sites (Fossato, Lloyd & Verkhovsky 2008), new communication technology is associated with interaction and participation that today is hard to connect to a huge communication tower designed to offer a guided path to the observation deck. The development of Russian television during the postcommunist era undermines its importance as "a mediated center."

Ostankino's Separation from Television

But how can we then understand the tower's function today? Ostankino as part of the organization WFGT can give a clue. Most member-towers in the organization were built for distribution of communication, and they are still used for that purpose, but today these technological aspects are highly separated from the marketing of the towers. In other words, the towers are separated from the media organizations for whom they receive and transmit signals. This separation is also important in considering the kind of experience the towers offer their visitors. Plans for the future at Ostankino involve new media technology, making it possible to see the panorama over Moscow even when the weather is bad, and there are other "media solutions" being discussed, such as experiencing what the view would look like during different parts of the day by providing interactive screens at the observation deck.[18]

This "digitalization" of the observation deck has not so much to do with expressing the symbolic power of the media or producing the TV subject. Instead media technology is intended to be used and integrated to intensify the panorama experience when visiting the tower. It can also be understood as an integration of the symbolic form (at the eighteenth century, it was the panorama painting) and the observation platform. Thereby the distinction between real and virtual dissolves, with the goal of making the panorama more "readable."

As such, the future plans for Ostankino leave traces, the tower as a *fossil*, of the eighteenth century and the observation platforms as part of the emerging travelling in Europe. In today's well-developed travel industry, Ostankino can become an important landmark as well as a trademark for the city tourism of Moscow. In the experience industry, the Soviet Russian space program is an attractive history to attach to the tower, as is done in the light show described earlier and by the nearby renovated space park. Besides being important for the tourism industry, it can also work in another direction—it turns the tower into a dream image of the country's glorious history and thereby distracts attention from the tower as a ruin. Renovating the tower is also a concrete way of keeping it from decaying, from becoming a material ruin.

In this way, ongoing work (e.g., in relation to the organization WFGT) attempts to highlight the tower as a cultural resource to be used in branding to attract tourists. From this perspective, the tower is turned into a *fetish* but not necessarily in relation to television. One evidence for this is the strict separation between the production center and the distribution tower. At the end of the 1960s, the tactual panorama and its utopian idea of decentralization could be established by the huge Ostankino complex integrating both production and distribution—even if highly separated, the visitors were invited to this common site; it was thought of as a whole. Today this idea of an organizational complex is gone.

In relation to literature about media globalization, the Russian government's decision to invest in media infrastructure, with the Ostankino Tower as an important node, is an example of the continuing importance of national frames when it comes to control of the media (Curran & Park 2000). In this process, the fire at Ostankino in 2000 served as a reminder of the recent failure of an attempt to commercialize media and thereby, in a way, decentralize media power (i.e., by Yeltsin, the oligarchs). Putin and his government could then use the tower as a *ruin* to propagate for the need to start a recentralization of the media. This can be understood as a strategy to meet changes in the commercial media industry with companies working over national borders (Flew 2007).

What seems to be of importance in this process is control over distribution, not production. And in this new digital infrastructure, distribution is not connected to a specific medium, and in that way the Ostankino Tower, if opened again, will not serve its initial role as "a mechanism for representation." There is no longer an organizational complex related to utopian ideas about TV's role in society and therefore a necessary social space for a *wish image* in relation to television is closed in future plans for the Ostankino Tower. What thus remains is its importance for media distribution in general. The irony being that the tower unintentionally, if turned into a part of the experience industry, will be a congenial expression for today's Russian media system with entertainment intertwined with strong state control.

References

Barthes, R. (1979/1997), *The Eiffel Tower and Other Mythologies*, Berkeley: University of California Press.
Benjamin, W. (1999): *The Arcades Project (Das Passagen-Werk)*, Cambridge, MA: The Belknap Press of Harvard University Press.
Bruno, G. (2002), *Atlas of Emotion. Journeys in Art, Architecture, and Film*, New York: Verso.
Buck-Morss, S. (2002), *Dreamworld and Catastrophe. The Passing of Mass Utopia in East and West*, Cambridge, MA and London: MIT Press.
Buck-Morss, S. (1989), *The Dialectics of Seeing. Walter Benjamin and the Arcades Project*, Cambridge, MA and London: MIT Press.
Crary, J. (1999), *Suspensions of Perception. Attention, Spectacle, and Modern Culture*, Cambridge, MA and London: MIT Press.
Crowley, D. & J. Pavitt (2008), *Cold War Modern. Design 1945–1970*, London: V & A Publishing.
Curran, J. & M.-J. Park (ed.) (2000), *De-westernizing Media Studies*, London: Routledge.
Degtereva, E. (2007), "Changing Programming Strategies of State, Public and Commercial TV Channels. The Cases of Russia and Sweden", in Vartanova, E. (ed.) *Media and Change*, Moscow: Faculty of Journalism, Moscow State University.
Deleuze, G. & F. Guattari (1975/1986), *Kafka. Toward a Minor Literature*, Minneapolis & London: University of Minnesota Press.
Downing, J. (1985), "The Intersputnik System and Soviet Television," *Soviet Studies*, vol. 37, No. 4. pp. 465-483.
Downing, J. (1996), *Internationalizing Media Theory. Transition, Power, Culture*, London: Sage Publications.
Ekbom, T. (1986), *Tatlins Torn och Andra Texter*, Stockholm: Bonniers.
Flew, T. (2007), *Understanding Global Media*, Hampshire & New York: Palgrave Macmillan.
Fossato, F., Lloyd, J. & A. Verkhovsky (2008), *Web That Failed: How Opposition Politics and Independent Initiatives Are Failing on the Internet in Russia*, Oxford: Reuters Institute for the Study of Journalism.
Foucault, M. (1979), *Discipline and Punish: the Birth of the Prison*, New York: Vintage Books.

Friedberg, A. (1998), "The Mobilized and Virtual Gaze in Modernity: Flâneur/Flâneuse," in Mirzoeff, N. (ed.), *The Visual Culture Reader*, London & New York: Routledge.
Gerovitch, S. (2002), *From Newspeak to Cyberspeak*, Cambridge, MA: MIT Press.
Giedion, S. (1928/1995): *Building in France, Building in Iron, Building in Ferro-concrete (Bauen in Frankreich)*, Santa Monica, CA: Getty Center for the History of Art and the Humanities.
Hugo, V. (1831), *The Hunchback of Notre Dame*. www.classicreader.com/book/330/16/
Ikonnikov, A. (1988), *Russian Architecture of the Soviet Period*, Moscow: Raduga Publishers.
Jakubowicz, K. (2007), Rude Awakening. Social and Media Change in Central and Eastern Europe, Cresskill, NJ: Hampton Press.
Margolin, V. (1997), *The Struggle for Utopia: Rodchenko, Lissitzky, Moholy-Nagy 1917–1946*, Chicago, IL: University of Chicago Press.
Martin, R. (2003), *The Organizational Complex. Architecture, Media, and Corporate Space*, Cambridge, MA: MIT Press.
McLuhan, M. (1964/2007), *Understanding Media. The Extensions of Man*, London & New York: Routledge.
McNair, B. (2000), "Power, Profit, Corruption, and Lies: The Russian Media in the 1990s," in Curran, J. & M-J. Park (ed.) *De-westernizing Media Studies*, London: Routledge.
Milutis, J. (2006), *Ether. The Nothing That Connects Everything*, Minneapolis & London: University of Minnesota Press.
Ockman, J., ed. (1993), *Architecture Culture 1943–1968: A Documentary Anthology*, New York: Columbia University Graduate School of Architecture, Planning, and Preservation.
Oettermann, S. (1997), *The Panorama. History of a Mass Medium*, New York: Zone Books.
Parks, L. (2005), *Cultures in Orbit. Satellites and the Televisual*, Durham & London: Duke University Press.
Roth-Ey, K. (2007), "Finding a Home for Television in the USSR, 1950–1970," in *Slavic Review* 66, no. 2 (Summer 2007).
Siegelbaum, L. H. (2008), *Cars for Comrades. The Life of the Soviet Automobile*, Ithaca, NY: Cornell University Press.

Notes

1. When it comes to Soviet architecture of the 1960s in general, and notably the Ostankino Tower, the sources are few, it is just mentioned in architectural overviews. The Russian TV channel NTV has an electronic archive about the TV center and their story is available on the Web site http://special.newsru.com/ostankino/62.html. However, during a visit to Moscow in 2007, the Media House project came in contact with Andrei Batalov, the son of Leonid Batalov, one of the architects of the tower and the production center. It turned out that Andrei Batalov had inherited his father's archive, which he was kind enough to make accessible for the project. The old photographs and sketches in this chapter come from that archive.
2. What also comes to mind is Susan Buck-Morss' argument throughout her book *Dreamworld and Catastrophe* (2002), that the Soviet Union was always a mirror of Western capitalism.
3. For the connection between European modernism and Russian constructivism, see Margolin (1997).
4. One story says that this happened during Khrushchev's travel to the United States in 1959 (Roth-Ey 2007, p. 287). Maybe he then also identified the main problem with television that came to characterize the discussions around the medium during the 1960s—that it seemed to stimulate individualization.

5. Nonbearing wall of glass or metal attached to the buildings structure.
6. The production center was constructed by the architects Leonid Batalov, Victor Zharov, Yakov Zakaryan, Leonid Solovyov, Karo Shekhoyan, and the engineer A. Levenshtein (Ikonnikov 1988, p. 292).
7. During the 1960s, it was common in U.S. political and military discourses to speak about the "Soviet cybernetic threat" due to the conviction of the theory's ability to create a sustainable society and a way for the Soviet Union to achieve world domination (see, for instance, www.airpower.maxwell.af.mil/airchronicles/aureview/1967/mar-apr/sleeper.html)
8. This question has a prehistory. Victor Margolin (1997) writes about how the Russian avant-garde of the 1920s, Rodchenko and Lissitzky, invented "revolutionary forms"—"awakened architecture"—that at the end of the decade "were called to serve the state" and ended up representing the regime.
9. At the time of the Olympic Games in Moscow in 1980 the center was expanded with another building for studios and offices and new technological equipment was installed. The architect behind this building was, once again, Leonid Batalov. In the beginning of the 1980s a new administrative building, including an art gallery and a concert hall, was constructed near the tower.
10. http://www.wsws.org/articles/2000/aug2000/mosc-a30
11. http://weekly.ahram.org.eg/2000/502/in4.htm
12. Interview with Professor Yassen Zassoursky, Faculty of Journalism, Moscow State University, February 28, 2007.
13. Gennady Sklyar at World Federation of Great Towers (WFGT) conference in Moscow, September 15, 2008.
14. www.mediachannel.org/views/oped/kaca.shtml
15. For example, demonstrations for media freedom and freedom of speech May 20, 2007 (see http://www.rferl.org/content/Article/1347563.html).
16. Sergey Trubitsin, Deputy General Director of RTRN and Director of MRC (Moscow Regional Centre) at the WFGT conference in Moscow (September 15, 2008).
17. This show did not attract a large audience, but was aimed at those attending the conference and those working at Ostankino Tower, around 150 people. There did not seem to be any public announcements. But still the show must be of importance; it had a prominent audience (this is how the administration behind Ostankino like to "sell" the tower) and was very well accomplished. Afterwards, the show was celebrated with a prize because it was said to be the highest light projection ever.
18. Solutions delegates talked about this at the WFGT conference in September 2008.

CHAPTER FIVE

Googleplex and Informational Culture

PETER JAKOBSSON AND FREDRIK STIERNSTEDT

Introduction

Google is the world's most used search engine and the second most visited web page on the Internet (Halavais 2009, p. 6). The company is arguably a center of power in the contemporary global media culture (van Couvering 2008; Vaidhyanathan 2007) and the search engine is part of our "technological unconscious" (Thrift 2004) by providing an infrastructure of knowledge that is becoming increasingly integrated into the everyday life of a great part of the world's population. This chapter sets out to explore the headquarters of Google, Googleplex, which is situated in Silicon Valley and aims to answer the question of what kind of centrality is represented and performed in the building and what it can tell us about the presumably decentralized world of digital information?

Googleplex was adapted for the company in 2004 by the San Francisco-based architect Clive Wilkinson. The house had previously been the home of Silicon Graphics, but was rebuilt for Google. This chapter will place Googleplex in an historical and architectural context, throwing light on the tradition from which it springs: a mode of building and city planning that incorporated information theory and cybernetics in the American postwar era. Furthermore, we will approach Googleplex through its surroundings, the functional and monumental aspects of the building, and as immaterial and mediated architecture. Googleplex will be explored as a metaphor for the role of the search engine in informational culture, as a mechanism of representation, expressing the ways Google itself seeks to be perceived, and as a materialization of how dominance and power are performed and executed in the digital era.

The theoretical starting point of this chapter is the supposition that centrality in the digital era is achieved through the ability to connect, to be an effective transportation hub, transporting information and suppressing noise. Central to this achievement is the ability to transform things into information. In each part of the chapter, the analyses show how Googleplex, through all aspects of its architecture—the "main street," the transparency, the hidden server halls—manages its operation not only by transporting information, but also by turning people and objects *into* information or putting them in a position where they can be handled and organized *as* information. The way this is accomplished is indeed decentralized, but only with the effect of increasing Google's gravitational pull. Googleplex illustrates how power in an informational culture is constituted by the ability to dissolve matter into information—to animate that culture by providing the raw material it feeds on and provide the material substrate that allows it to live on and reproduce.

Fig. 1. Googleplex as seen from the air. Photo courtesy of Google Inc.

Informational Culture

Looking at the ambitions of Google, one finds that those are to: "organize the world's information and make it universally accessible and useful" (Google.com

2008a). Setting the self-aggrandizement aside, this points to the company's place in a cultural order that is centered on the concept of information. Borrowing Tiziana Terranova's concept of "informational culture" (Terranova 2004), we see this as an order in which cultural processes are "increasingly taking on the attributes of information—they are increasingly grasped and conceived in terms of their informational dynamics" (ibid., p. 7). The concept of an informational culture is, however, double-sided in that it has become both an active force in contemporary culture and an ideological construction that obscures the dynamics of power in society. A society built on technologies that are the direct result of theoretical innovations like those of Shannon & Weaver and Norbert Wiener, and at the same time a society that has incorporated the justifications and the rationality of these scientific theories into the political and economic systems. The feedback processes between the different spheres—culture, economy, and politics—have expanded the number of domains guided by—and arguably best theorized in—informational terms. Against this background, we will outline four principles guiding this informational culture and point to how they can be used to understand Google as a global center of the information age: signal-to-noise ratio, decentralization, self-organization, and informatization (cf. Terranova 2004).

Shannon & Weaver's mathematical theory of communication (1949) proposes that communication can be understood as the relation between signal and noise. Their theory allows for an understanding of communication that disregards the content of messages and describes communication in purely mathematical terms. Whereas the original theory was developed to allow for analogue signals to travel vast distances, the kind of noise that threatens us on the Web today is instead the amount of information. The problem of *signal-to-noise ratio* in the age of digital communication is not related to distances but to selection, a problem that can be solved not by measuring but by counting. The patent that set Google off (Page & Brin 2001) was a solution to precisely this problem, how to find the relevant information in a sea of noise.[1]

Google solved the problem of relevance by applying two of the other principles of informational cultures: *decentralization* and *self-organization*. Wiener (1948) set out to describe how humans as well as societies could be understood as consisting of a number of smaller entities that through intercommunication and feedback processes contributed to the integrity of the organism. Decentralization and self-organization have since been central concepts within everything from artificial intelligence (AI) research to architecture (as will be explored further in this chapter). In order to understand the kind of decentralized and self-organizing systems under consideration here, however, we have to move beyond the work of Wiener and engage the concept of emergence (Johnson 2001) and "soft control" (Terranova 2004). Wiener was primarily interested in the role that feedback processes had in the survival of the organism. In capitalist markets in an informational culture, decentralization and self-organization are also means of creating value. Emergence is when systems governed by relatively simple rules show signs of complex behavior. What Google's founders realized was that the Internet, when looked at from a bird's- eye view, showed certain patterns resulting from such behavior. All the links between different Web pages, when taken as a whole, constituted a pattern in which some pages attracted much more links than others. From the individual activities of Internet users emerged a pattern that, when treated mathematically, gave Google a way to calculate the relevance of a specific Web page. The Google algorithm is thus not only an algorithm for valorization of Web content but consequently also an instrument for control of and extracting value from the Internet. In total, this amounts to what Terranova (2004) theorizes as soft control and the way it is linked to value production in decentralized networks. This kind of control operates only at the start and end points in a given system, exploiting the creative freedom and movements within its given limits. On the Internet, this means the format of the content entered into the system (binary code, HTML code, etc.) and a mechanism for selecting relevant material (the Google algorithm). In an organization like a company, it means internalization of company values by the staff with instruments for surveying and selecting what kind of work is valuable to the company.

Signal-to-noise ratio, decentralization, and self-organization, as described here, are thus important themes in the following analysis. These three are, however, reliant on yet another principle: *informatization*, the fourth and perhaps most important principle for our understanding of informational cultures. From Google's point of view, the successful application of the above-mentioned principles is based on the premise that things—people and objects—are available *as* information. The organizing principles of informational governance are only effective if the world can be grasped and understood as information, rather than as continuous flows and statistical variations. It is from this principle that we may view the many ways Google gathers and transfers once noncomputable existences *into* information.

From these principles—signal-to-noise ratio, decentralization, self-organization, and informatization—we can consider the centrality of Google as well as the company's attempts to downplay this centrality. The company's centrality can be assessed through its power to organize content rather than produce it, to suppress noise through decentralized modes of value production. Through storing, reading, analyzing, and organizing the sum total of communicative production on the Internet, Google has managed to create pseudoindividual connections with a majority of all Internet users and supply them with ranked information on all things searchable. On the other hand, organization is also an act of production; selection and presentation are primary also in traditional media companies' production of "content." Through Google's dependence on the content created by others and the apparent neutrality of their *technological* and *mathematical* modes of selection, the company claims to be guided by other beliefs and principles than mass media companies. But the informational milieu created by the company is not that different. Neither are the organizational powers of the company dependent on a single software algorithm, nor are they weightless, immaterial, and imbued with a mathematical rationality. In the following parts of this chapter, we will see how this power is achieved and performed on several levels—metaphorical, representational, and material—within Google as an organization and especially through the company's headquarters, Googleplex. We will, however, start by placing the company and its architecture in its proper historical and geographical place.

Californian Architecture and Ideology

Silicon Valley has in many ways been the birthplace of the U.S. computer industry (Lécuyer 2006; Saxenian 1994). Closely intertwined with Stanford University, the industrial park has grown rapidly over the years and has attracted a high density of immigrants from India and China who work in the software industry. With this in mind, it is no wonder that it was here that Google took off as the result of the work of two Stanford postgraduates, Sergey Brin and Larry Page: Brin, the descendant of two generations of professors in mathematics at Moscow University, and Page, the son of a pioneer within the nascent field of computer science in the 1960s (Vise 2005). It is here, in the Valley, that the 47,000-square-meter campus/office/laboratory/playground that is Googleplex was built in 2004. As with other success stories before and since, its founders both went to Stanford, started off in a rented garage, got financial backing from the venture capitalists on Sand Hill Road, and were eventually introduced into the stock market, making its founders very wealthy. In contrast to other information and communication technology (ICT)-related businesses, however, Google has decided to stay in the Valley instead of moving to downtown San Francisco. This sent the message that Google is more about technology than content (Graham & Guy 2002).

Google shares not only its myth of origin with other companies in the Valley, but also a corporate culture imbued with a mix of technological savvy and liberal ideals, typical of this region. It is the progressive, multicultural, post-hippie America described by Jean Baudrillard in his 1986 travelogue as a place with a slower "pace of work, decentralization, air conditioning, soft technologies. Paradise. But a very slight modification, a change of just a few degrees, would suffice to make it seem like hell" (Baudrillard 1986/1993, p. 46). For Baudrillard, Silicon Valley is a place that is "post-orgy," wrapped in "a foetal tranquillity [sic]," a world without passions where all is organized, in a "total decentring, total community." For Baudrillard, this decentralized community is a mental as well as a physical state that seeks to make all ruptures impossible. The "community" Baudrillard sees in the Valley is not organized to "converge [everything] on a single point" (ibid., p. 46), which is obvious in the city planning and architecture as well as in the ideology of "dogmatic pluralism" of Silicon Valley. For Baudrillard, this is the opposite of the organization of European cities, which often gravitate towards a single, defined, and visible centre (or even downtown San Francisco, which is shaped by the centralization of production characteristic of the nineteenth-century industrial capitalist city [Soja 1989, p. 193]). And for Baudrillard, "by that very token, it also becomes impossible to hold a demonstration: where could you assemble" in a place absent of squares or other distinct and open centers? (Baudrillard 1986/1993, p. 44). The architecture of the Valley, then, is one lacking spaces for conflict; decentralization in this way creates concurrence, making it impossible for ruptures or disagreements to be played out in the cityscape. In other words, the seemingly centrifugal forces of Silicon Valley converge with its opposite: the centripetal force of the total community, effectively negating the need for an *agora*.

A well-known description of the ideals of this community is found in Richard Barbrook and Andy Cameron's 1995 account of "The Californian Ideology":

> the bizarre fusion of the cultural bohemianism of San Francisco with the hi-tech industries of the Silicon Valley. [. . .] the Californian Ideology promiscuously combines the freewheeling spirit of the hippies and the entrepreneurial zeal of the yuppies. This amalgamation of opposites has been achieved through a profound faith in the emancipatory potential of the new information technologies. In the digital utopia, everybody will be both hip and rich. (Barbrook & Cameron 1995, without paging)

Google, with its motto "Don't be evil," is one of the companies embodying the technologically deterministic liberalism of this ideology. In interviews and written statements, the company's founders, Larry Page and Sergey Brin, often speak of their ambition to "change the world" (Battelle 2005, p. 66). What they actually mean by this assertion is quite diffuse, but what it indicates is that for them Google is a project and a company with a utopian stance. The perpetual drive to "organize all information" could also be seen as placing Google, if not geographically, then at least ideologically in the middle of Silicon Valley. As stated by Larry Page in a 2004 interview, "everything that Google does shall have positive social consequences" (Sheff 2004). This idea of pragmatic mathematics serving a liberal cause is widespread, not only in the history of Silicon Valley but in the American history of ideas in general. Google could hence be seen as perpetuating a line of work that goes through Norbert Wiener's cybernetics and the notion of engineering, and applied mathematics as not only a scientific but a social endeavour (Wiener 1950). The architecture of Silicon Valley and Googleplex materializes this ideology in several ways.

From an historical perspective, the style of office buildings and city planning in Silicon Valley constitutes part of what Reinhold Martin (2005) calls the "organizational complex," the "aesthetic and technological extension of what has been known since the early 1960s as the 'military-industrial complex'" (ibid., pp. 3–4). The American modernism in the architecture of the 1940s, 1950s, and 1960s was a mix of the previous avant-garde and experimental esthetics of the early twentieth century, and the military and techno-scientific developments of the war years, altering the very fabric of modernity. New materials like aluminum and plastics made possible several rationalizations in construction work—a connection between the war industry and peacetime housing, made explicit in a 1943 advertisement for the George E. Ream Company, announcing: "Plywood for war, later for peace" (in Buisson & Billard 2004). This era saw the "dispersal of urban infrastructures into an increasingly horizontal network of communication and transportation lines [. . .] a development of a systems-based notion of organization in architecture" (Martin 2005, pp. 7–8). This was a direct result of the developments in cybernetics and information theory during the war that "hurled towards a peacetime industry dedicated to the individual" (Buisson & Billard 2004, p. 24). The decentralization of postwar America, in which suburbs and business parks spread across the landscape, was in a similar fashion a logical consequence of the Cold War and the fear of atomic warfare in which "dissemination [in space] is seen as a deterrent from bombardment" (ibid.). A decentralization that was planned and calculated by cyberneticians like Norbert Wiener, who together with Karl Deutsch and Giorgio de Santillana, published an article in *Life* in December 1950 titled "How U.S. Cities Can Prepare for Atomic War." According to Reinhold Martin, Wiener was the primary author of the plan and the text proposed that the city is to be understood as a giant "communicative organism." In a draft version of the article, Wiener and the other authors wrote that "the danger of blocked communications in a city subject to emergency conditions is analogous to the danger of blocked communications in the human body" (in Martin 2005, p. 28). The solution to such a problem would, according to the three authors, be to create dispersed and decentralized cities, "reaching outward to maintain equilibrium and to overcome the entropic effects of traffic jams and communications breakdowns in the wake of nuclear bombardment" (ibid).

Accordingly, Googleplex is not to be found in the center of either Silicon Valley or Mountain View, the name of the suburb where it is located, since there is actually no center in which to be located. Driving through this sprawling landscape and its meandering suburban streets, you unwittingly arrive at the entrance of the main building before you even know it is there. However, Google's domain is not limited to the four buildings that make up the core of Googleplex; instead, it is spread out over several blocks of low buildings:

> Google's sprawling, cheerfully dystopian campus at Mountain View may intimidate the first-time visitor. But there's no need to fear. The easy rule of thumb dictates that the most con-

centrated power centres gravitate toward the middle (where the engineers and their excellent cafeterias reside). (valleywag.com 2007, without paging)

Yes, the seemingly unorganized architecture does indeed have centers. Although the free bus service and various cafés are important to Google, it is the four buildings that make up the actual Googleplex that grab the attention of most visitors. This is where the company has spent its resources and is intent on making a statement. Otherwise, Googleplex lives seemingly in symbiosis with its environment, fitting snugly among the other hi-tech companies in the vicinity, with only the logos distinguishing one office building from the other.

Fig. 2. Googeplex main entrance. Photo courtesy of Tim Trueman.

The American modernism in the architecture of the 1950s and 1960s, influenced to a high degree by information theory, cybernetics and techno-scientific engineering, is in many ways a distinctively Californian modernism (Buisson & Billard 2004). The prime example of this is the Case Study Houses of the 1950s and 1960s, which can be seen as the leisure equivalent to the office buildings in Silicon Valley. The Case Study Houses were a result of the California-based *Arts & Architecture* magazine, which, in the 1940s, commissioned major architects of the day, including Richard Neutra, Raphael Soriano, Craig Ellwood, Charles and Ray Eames, Pierre Koenig, and Eero Saarinen, to design and build inexpensive and efficient model homes for the U.S. residential housing boom. The boom was in part caused by the end of the Second World War and the return of millions of soldiers. For them, home ownership was made possible by the institution of the GI Bill of Rights, which allowed former soldiers to benefit from loans that covered the entire cost of a house without the need for an initial contribution (ibid., p. 31). The solution to the housing problem was hence a radically individualistic one, and owning one's home was seen—by John Entenza, editor of *Arts & Architecture*—as a "tool of man's fulfilment" (Buisson & Billard 2004, p. 24) and an important part of the American ideology in general—so important that the government favored the acquisition of single-family homes through exemption from certain taxes (ibid.).

The Case Study Houses were a product of, as well as a performer in, not only the American individualist and consumerist ideology, but also the ideologies of techno-scientific engineering. The announcement for the Case Study House program, published in the *Arts & Architecture* magazine in January 1945, reads that "it is important [that we] arrive at a 'good' solution to each problem, which in the overall program will be general enough to be of practical assistance to the average American in search of a home in which he can afford to live" (Entenza 1945). The goal was to, repeating the famous motto of Le Corbusier, create "machine[s] for living" (Buisson & Billard 2004, p. 37). Rational and functional houses, possible to operate without the help of servants, saturated with the latest technologies, housing not only people but the new media of the day. Television sets were embedded in the architecture and television screens entrenched in the walls of several of the houses. The houses themselves were also thought to function as media for facilitating communication. In the very first Case Study House (by Julius Ralph Davidson), the architecture included perforated wall openings between several of the rooms so that the inhabitants could see and be seen, as well as easily talk to each other: the building was meant to make communication easier between family members and, in cybernetic terms, foster intercommunication and feedback processes contributing to the integrity and maintenance of the family organism.

The esthetics of the Case Study Houses have continued creating one of several styles of architecture specific to California, one exuding functionality, transparency, low-story houses in simple materials, saturated with communication media and transgressing the binaries of outside/inside (Buisson & Billard 2004). The announcement of the Case Study House Program in *Arts & Architecture* magazine also echoes in California-based Googleplex architect Clive Wilkinson's statement that the engineers of Google "needed to see clear-cut reasoning" (Chang 2006) behind design decisions, and it was when he realized this and began to present his plans as a series of solutions that Google became receptive:

> The workplace is ideally a mirror of the organization in the same way that the human body represents how its organs collaborate as a multifaceted machine [. . .] The first task is to clarify the workings of the machine, but the second, equally important point is that individ-

uals should feel some sense of ownership and belonging—of possessing and being possessed by the company. (Quoted in Chen 2006, without paging)

In this quote, Wilkinson furthers the notion of Googleplex as a "machine for working," extending Le Corbusier's motto with the language of cybernetics to support his ideas. But he also envisages the workplace as a machine for living, promoting a workplace "architecture of togetherness [in which] the sociability factor is integral" (ibid.). This brings to mind the Baudrillardian notion of "total community" in which electronic tribalism achieves a perfected illustration by the company itself possessing the worker, through the architecture. Other features of Californian modernism embodied in the Case Study Houses and—as we will see below—furthered in Googleplex are, for example, the way that the Google headquarters are constructed to enhance communication: the incorporation of new media in the building; the thematics of inside vs. outside; the functionality and simplicity of the architecture; and the way in which Googleplex, just like the Case Study Houses, has become intensively mediated, to the extent that one can see the building as a "prop for the media" (Colomina 1996).

The Functions of Googleplex

Passing by the piano, lava lamps, and the live projection of current search queries from around the world that meet the visitor walking through the main entrance of Googleplex, one soon finds oneself in a space where transparent, glass offices line virtually the entire building perimeter. But what kind of work is done here? How is it organized? And in what way does the building partake in the organization of work at Google?

Within the software industry in general and at Google in particular, the dream of "working as a hobby" has been taken to its utmost extreme (e.g., Ross 2004). In an article published in the journal *Metropolis Magazine* in July 2006, journalist Jade Chang describes the working day of Google employee Corin Anderson:

> Each day he sits in the midst of figurines, Legos, and stuffed animals, eyes fixed on his computer screen and earphones strapped on, for hours at a stretch. When he wants a snack, he walks to the fully stocked micro-kitchen, maybe breaking open a bag of organic potato chips or grabbing a handful of trail mix. Twenty percent of the time—with his employer's full approval—he works on projects of his own devising that are only tangentially related to his job. And strangest of all, come nightfall he often has no desire to go home, preferring to get dinner, gratis, in one of the employee cafés, followed by a few hours playing a strategic card game with some colleagues in a small meeting room. (Chang 2006, without paging).

The image seems to be working. Every 25 seconds Google receives a job application from yet another hopeful young engineer eager to live the dream of becoming a Google programmer. Clive Wilkinson has explained that the main idea of Googleplex is to make it feel like "an average American city." And most certainly, many of the activities and services of a city are to be found in Googleplex (leisure activities as well as hairdressers, medical doctors, daycare centers, etc.). Google has also published several pictures from Googleplex on its Web site, showing employees taking part in the simple pleasures of consumption, as well as seemingly combining work and leisure. This image serves the purpose of expressing the "nicety" and everydayness of Google's operations and implicitly the nicety of Google as a technology.

Work at Googleplex is organized in a flat and decentralized manner, with a couple of devices for managing the relationship between everyday work and the overall goals of the company. One of those devices is Googletts, small groups of Googlers working independently on their own projects. With a system resembling the freedom found in academia to pursue one's own goals, each employee has 20 percent of the working week to dedicate entirely to projects of his or her own choosing. With the trust that good and interesting work will attract attention, it is up to the employees to seek out the teams and projects they find interesting. This way, groups will increase and decrease in mass in a self-regulative manner without too much intervention. Google's mail service is one of the products developed within this system. This manner of organization of work is not far from how the company organizes information on the Internet and elsewhere, trusting mechanisms of self-regulation and decentralization to counteract noise in the system.

As described above, the basic advantage that Google's algorithms provide in comparison to its competitors is the way they rank results. Noticing that some sites were "linked to" more often than others provided a key to weighing the importance of sites against each other. Sites with many incoming links were bound to be more important than others. Rather than being totally disorganized, there was a structure to the Internet and it was a structure that the users provided themselves. By observing the mechanisms of this self-regulation and making them explicit through their search technology, the company managed to build its successful technology. Work in Googleplex seems to be organized in the same way. By having several small teams working independently on projects they choose themselves and letting these teams attract other workers if they find these interesting, Google has devised a system for their workplace similar to that of their search engine.

Another device implemented to manage the relationship between the micro and the macro is the Top 100 list, presenting the best projects currently being worked on. This way of organizing things at an Internet company with a strong belief in the democratic power of technology is not surprising either. In a way, this is how the Internet architecture as a whole balances the different demands placed on it by competing forces of decentralization and hierarchization (cf. Galloway 2004).

While the TCP/IP protocol places the entire Internet structure on a flat surface with equal connectivity between each and every node, the DNS structure (.org, .com, etc.) provides the Internet with its well-known hierarchies. Overall, Google relies on the kind of soft control Terranova (2004) described earlier: self-motivation in combination with self-regulation is seen to be the key to success. It would, however, be difficult to imagine that this kind of organization could hold together without any overarching structure. One such structure, which, in the words of Bruno Latour, can be called "the missing masses" (Latour 1992) of decentralized management, and which supplies the needed gravitational pull of Google is the architecture of its headquarters.

Architect Clive Wilkinson explains the idea of using the "average American city" as a template for the architecture of Googleplex: "People like variety. They need places to congregate. Casual interaction fosters teamwork and creativity" (quoted in Chen 2006). The solution the architect offered Google is evidently based on the belief that communication and interaction result in innovations as well as a feeling of community, echoing Wiener's words that the community stretches only as far as its effectual communications (Wiener 1948). At the core of Googleplex is a miniature city of tinted glass rooms, padded pavilions and Astroturf lawns, all anchored by a monumental stairway embedded with laptop ports. Keywords for the construction are openness and transparency, echoed in the use of glass and large open spaces in the building. The building also features a central spine, or in the words of the architect, a "main street," around which "neighborhoods" of activity are clustered (quoted in Chen 2006). The construction is meant to create a communicative autostrada ending in the stairway where the employees can gather and be able to keep their laptops running. The stairway underlines the rhizomatic ideal of Googleplex. It is a place for meetings and gatherings that at the same time seeks to keep and exploit the flexibility and connectivity of movement and fluidity, a place perpetually open to the formation of new connections or the re-formation of old ones, as people transport themselves through the building, pass by the stairway, join or leave, connecting or disconnecting in a self-organizing network of labor.

And in many ways the whole building organizes work through its communicative abilities. The "main street," a central nerve in the social life of many American towns and cities, is here understood as a channel for effectively and indiscriminately relaying information and people through the building, just like the glass and open spaces create an instantaneous awareness of what kind of work is going on in each part of the building. The keyword for how communication is understood here is transportation. As opposed to the business model of the Internet portals, which relied on the hope of keeping users within the main site while collecting valuable eyeballs, Google only directs users (and is paid per click) in the manner of a logistical company. Analogously, Googleplex offers no obstacles or boundaries for the free movement of information and in the end supplies a structure for the dissemination and transportation of information.

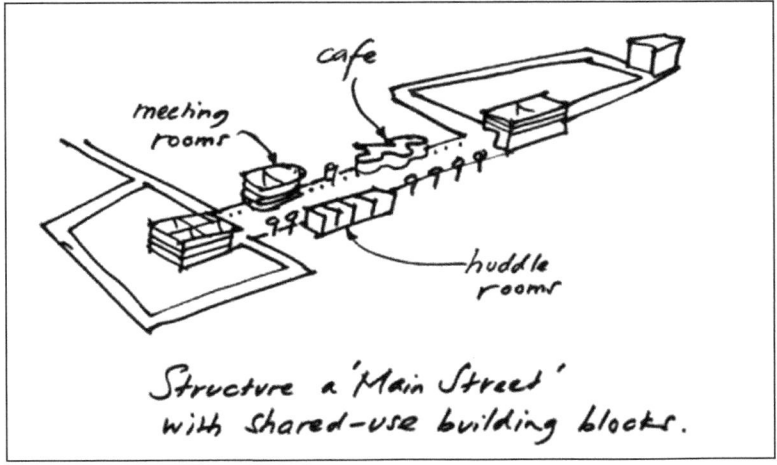

Fig. 3 Drawing of Googleplex. Courtesy of Clive Wilkinson.

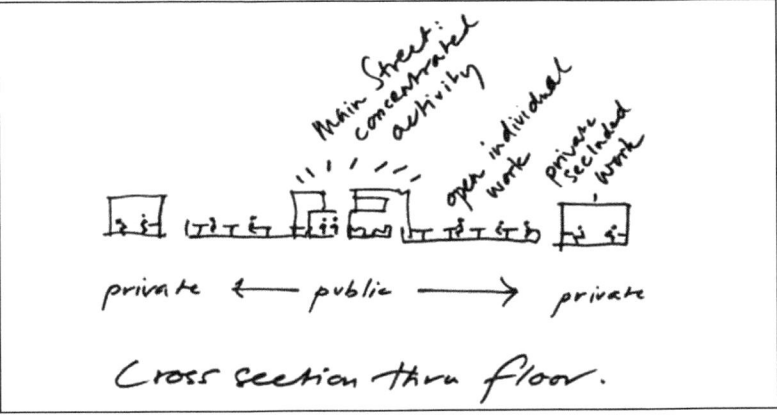

Fig. 4 Drawing of Googleplex. Courtesy of Clive Wilkinson.

Soft and Hard Architecture

The first thing that meets visitor and employee alike upon setting foot in one of the lobbies at Googleplex is a mediatization of the company's operations. As a reminder of what Google is about, monitors display search queries being entered into the company's search engine at all times, around the world. A constant stream of search strings pop up and fade away at a rate of dozens a second—of course, not nearly as many as are actually being processed by the system, and queries are also censored to avoid the possibly embarrassing truth of the actual use of the technology. Thus, while not an accurate representation of what is actually happening in the company's server halls, the flashing screens still speak plenty of Google's line of business and its function.

A perhaps more spectacular show, which can also be found on the premises, is provided by the visualization of Google searches, in the form of radiating light, on the projection of a spinning globe. As the globe spins, the spectator can witness light shooting off the surface of the earth, with different colors representing different quantities of data. In another viewing mode, the globe can show the way the data travel back and forth between users and Google's centers of computation. Apart from residing within the building itself, this globe is also something the founders use as a way of presenting their company in public settings (ted.com 2007).

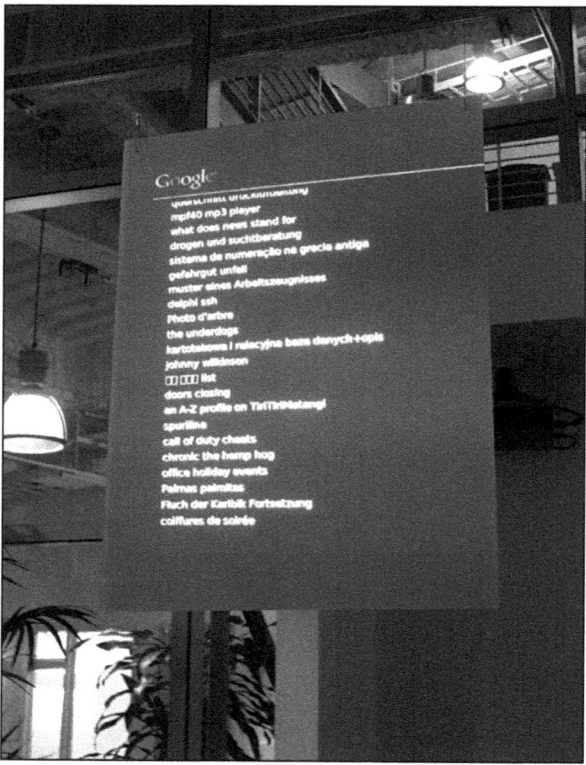

Fig. 5. Projection of search queries in Googleplex lobby. Photo courtesy of Yoz Grahame.

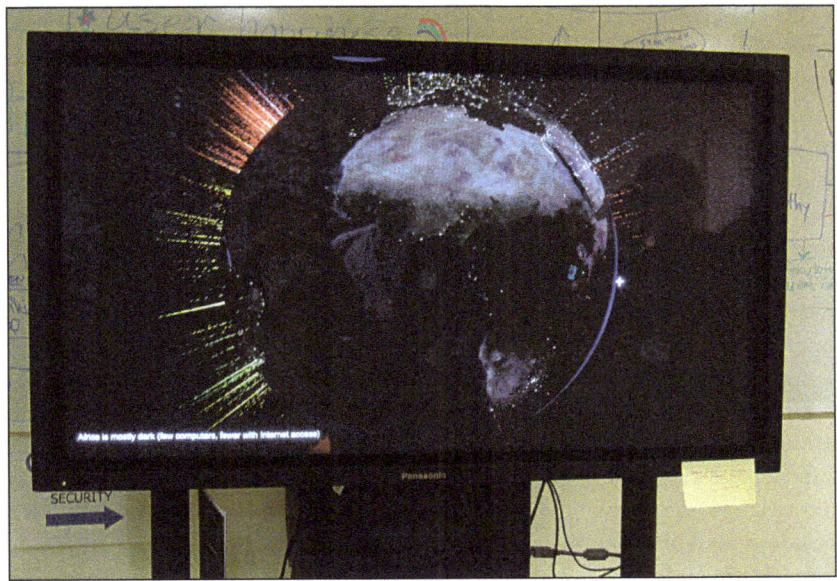

Fig. 6. Visualization of data handled by the search engine. Photo courtesy of Yoz Grahame.

What can we make of these representations of the company? For one thing, this is obviously a way for the company to represent its own operations to itself, its employees, and others. It provides an answer to the question "What do we do?", an obvious dilemma for companies that do not produce anything in the traditional meaning of the word. More than this, however, it makes visible the reversed logic of Google's operation as a media company. Whereas a traditional media building sends things out of the building, Google is instead the receiver of enormous amounts of information. In some sense, all media companies, as well as media houses, function as receivers. But for Google, not only is the very idea of being a media company alien to the company's self-perception, the business model as such is to receive, process, and create connections in an ever-increasing info-mass, constantly on the verge of entropic incalculableness. As light shoots out anywhere on the globe, information is rapidly being transported from sender to receiver and ends up somewhere in the company's databases, to be consumed and analyzed and finally converted into valuable knowledge for Google's engineers and companies looking for advertising space. Each search string and ray of light is simultaneously a user being served by the company as well as raw material for the search engine's and the advertising system's algorithms, waiting to be converted into productive knowledge for the company.

As Google represents its own operations through new media incorporated into the architecture, one aspect is missing. Search strings appear and fade away, light flashes and dies out, but the enormous amounts of information kept in the company's ever-expanding storage facilities and the facilities themselves are nowhere to be found. Search strings are not the only information the company gathers. In order to make the Web searchable, collecting and indexing each Web page is crucial. The quantity of Web pages is consequently one way search companies compete with each other. Apart from Web pages and search queries, the company also keeps and indexes large amounts of email traffic from its Gmail service. The private communication of millions of users is also to be found in the company's databases. Nowhere, however, are these aspects of Google's operations to be found in the public parts of Googleplex.

Indeed, the locations of the company's data storage facilities are shrouded in mystery. No one, outside the company, really knows where they are located, and no one knows how many of these data centers are there. This is partly because the establishment of new computing centers is subject to nondisclosure agreements with local authorities at the places chosen by the company (Markoff & Hansell 2006). According to Miller (2009), there are at least 12 major server halls within the United States and five more in Europe. There have been rumors of new data centers to open in Asia, for example, in Taiwan, as well as speculations of new data centers in Lithuania (ibid.). Although an amount of secrecy is not in any way unusual in this line of business, there is something about Google's self-presentation regarding this matter that overplays the decentralizing tendencies while downplaying the centralizing aspects of its business strategies.

From the beginning, Google has relied on off-the-shelf consumer electronics when constructing their computational and storage facilities. By connecting large numbers of relatively cheap computers, they have bested the computational capacities of most supercomputers. This is a sometimes forgotten, but crucial, part of Google's strategy (Vise 2005). This unique system architecture has occasionally been called "Googleware" (ibid.) or "distributed computing" (Battelle 2005, p. 129). A great advantage Google has over its competitors lies in the huge investments in hardware it has made over the years, about which it is still rather secretive, but it has been approximated that Google maintains as many as one million servers. It has also been estimated that Google spent about $2.4 billion on four new data centers in 2007 and that as much as one-third of all servers shipped by the entire computer industry go into the data centers of Google, Amazon, Yahoo, eBay, and Microsoft, and a few others. As search terms swoosh by on the monitors in Googleplex, this material basis for its operations is hidden from view.

If software seems malleable, portable and often provisional (e.g., Manovich 2001), hardware implies the opposite. The representation of Google's operations within Googleplex suggests that Google is a software company based on the power of its search algorithms, making the company appear less traditional, less intimidating, and less enduring. But the material base for these representations is to be found in the traditional industrial geography in which the data centers are inscribed. Since, for example, the single most important factor for the placement of a data center is the availability of large volumes of cheap electricity and vast amounts of water for cooling,[2] they often come to inherit facilities used as paper mills or aluminum smelters (Strand 2008). The immaterial architecture of Googleplex (for example, the screens with search strings) displays an ideological version of software as a decentralizing force: "among postmodern strategies of appearance, none is as effective as the simulation that there really is software" (Kittler 1997, p. 156). As long as we are led to believe that Google bases its operations on the benevolent PageRank algorithms and forget the massive computational powers and storage facilities of the company, Google can continue to portray itself as a "personal" and empowering medium fit for a globalized order: totally decentered, effectuating total community.

Monumental Architecture of Googleplex

One general feature of media headquarters seems to be their monumentality. This at least appears to be the case for national and state-regulated media such as those discussed in the other chapters of this book, as well as other large media organizations like the *Chicago Tribune* or the *New York Times* and its tower in Times Square. The very centrality of their positioning in the cityscapes, as well as their size, contributes to inscribing them in the esthetic regime of the monument. The homes of "old" media, at least in their exteriors, resonate with times past (in the way that the BBC Broadcasting House resembles a medieval fortress) or history in the making (like the space race replica rocket that makes up the 1960s Ostankino television tower in Moscow). In a similar fashion, the interiors at Googleplex are filled with elements that could be labeled as monumental: large-scale installations, metaphors and materializations of Google's place in space and time.

The monumentality of Google, however, is different from the one we are familiar with from the media buildings of national television and radio, as well as the monumentality of churches, memorials, and official buildings from the modern era. First of all, the exteriors of Googleplex are anonymous, flat, and sprawling. The buildings are not organized according to a vertical and hierarchical scheme; instead, the facilities spread horizontally and the area is crossed by roads and open spaces. There is no master plan, the entirety of strength or collected, intended effect, which monumentality seems to require, is missing.

Instead, the monumental features of Googleplex are to be found in the interiors of the building. Here we will briefly discuss two of the largest and most spectacular features of the design of Googleplex, explicitly connected to questions of time and space. The first is the full-scale replica skeleton of a T. rex displayed in an aggressive mode, frozen in a roar toward passers-by (Figure 7). The skeleton was left when the previous tenant, Silicon Graphics, moved out of the building. Silicon Graphics was the company behind the special effects of the movie *Jurassic Park*, famous for its extensive and, at the time, original use of computer animation (Takahashistaff 2007).

Fig. 7. T. rex. Photo courtesy of Bryan Green.

The second monumental feature we will discuss here is a replica of *SpaceShipOne* (Figure 8)—the first space plane to complete a privately funded human space flight—hanging from the ceiling in the lobby at the main entrance. To get it there, the wall of the main building had to be torn down and then rebuilt after the installation of the space plane inside. These installations could be understood as "geek-chic" manifestations of the nerdy fascination with the "coolness" of spaceships and predators. Certainly, the monumental features of Googleplex could be understood as monuments over Silicon Valley itself and the developments in space technology and special effects that have been created there. But as interior design these features also work to "reinvent and communicate the values of the company," in the words of architect Clive Wilkinson.

Fig. 8. A replica of *SpaceShipOne*. Photo courtesy of Nan Palmero.

The dinosaur and the space plane as artifacts, as objects of interior design, are *readymades*. As opposed to what one would spontaneously think of a monument, they are not constructed as site-specific buildings or parts of buildings. Instead, they are objects lifted out of specific contexts (places, times) and put together in Googleplex. This fact underlines the tendency of Googleplex in general to express the difference between Google and other media companies. Googleplex is not a building whose location is adapted to a situation of transmission, but an object of architecture that underlines Google as being on the receiving end in the communicative relationship or as being a mediator, a connective hub, facilitating the connection instead of the content. At least this is how Google wants to be perceived, as a media company that does not transmit or produce content—hence the anonymous character of the exterior—and accordingly the building lets objects with symbolic historical force enter the premises and be assembled in order to make the building speak, in the first place, to those inhabiting it. But soon, pictures and texts, representations of these features, are disseminated—not by Google itself but by visitors photographing, filming, writing, and publishing online, creating a decentralized and distributed, omnipresent and immaterial monumentality of sorts.

The objects obviously handle questions of time and history. They contribute to telling the story of Google as something radically new, a new phase or era of human existence (or of the world). Through the integration of these rather arbitrary, but highly symbolic, "quotations" of historical events—the rise and fall of giant predators during the late Triassic and Cretaceous periods and the human conquering of outer space in the twentieth century—into the building, Google is represented as transcending these phases. To put the previous periods in the building is to seal them off as "historical," in the same way as a museum functions to create history through periodization of its displays. But even more than that, since Googleplex is not a museum, these monuments serve to tell a very particular history. Just like the dinosaurs became extinct, the Space Age is now transcended by the digital era, whereby the new frontier is not the conquering of foreign worlds, solar systems, or planets but the organization of all knowledge and information. The Space Age sought to cross the frontiers to realities beyond human experience and expand the world as we know it, in making outer space visible (and audible) through modern technologies of representation and transmission (such as the camera, microphone, and satellite). Google, on the other hand—as represented in Googleplex—inherits a world that is fully visible (a world "after the orgy" [Baudrillard 1986/1993, p. 46]). What remains is to map and systematize this already conquered space, as well as the digital space, and not least the interiors of human minds and bodies. This is clear in the Google DNA project, in which Google is making the entire human DNA code searchable and visible (understandable) for everyone.[3] This is also manifested through the moon project in which Google is charting and making visible to all—not only for astronauts and their cameras—the surface of the moon (Google 2008b). This is equally visible in the ways Google Gmail indexes and makes searchable (and commodifies) every single word written in one-to-one, interpersonal communication and customizes the advertisements in Gmail according to what a user's correspondence is about. And most evidently, this can be seen in the ways our queries are indexed and made into knowledge; the inner longings and passions, the everyday curiosities and the cognitive abilities of billions of people all become visible and are turned into information through the Google algorithms and hardware.[4] The technology translates our vernacular into computer code, and back again—making it possible to systematize and hence anticipate not only the answers we are looking for but also the questions we ask: "'The ultimate search engine,' says Larry Page, 'would understand exactly what you mean and give you back exactly what you want'" (Vise 2005, p. 282). This understanding of search implies that relevant search results require not only massive indexes but also an understanding of whoever is looking for information. Google aims to construct a search engine that not only is good at taking commands but that with the help of the sheer mass of information lets Google understand its users from within and make their desires visible and transparent. Informational culture ultimately turns not only everything but *everyone* into information, thereby overcoming the noise constituted by the modern "superstitions" of subjectivity, humanity, and the individual.

The monuments of Googleplex thus tell us what Google wants to be or how it would like to be perceived. But these features of the building, around which the majority of the on-line commentaries and photographs of Googleplex circulates, also contribute to a masking of what Google is truly about. The most common interpretation of the dinosaur is that it represents the era of the hardware giants.[5] This is also the ideological triumph of Googleplex, as hinted at earlier. Software *appears* to be more democratic than hardware. Not everyone can write software, of course, but still, since the whole idea of a participatory culture rests on the ability of everyone to write, instead of just read (and according to this ideology there is only a gradual difference between assembler code, high-level programming languages, and human languages), the idea of a decentralized media landscape rests on the promise of software. The so-called gift economy of the Internet always stops at software, since information is nonrivalrous and affords copying. Google sees itself as a forerunner in this software economy and, as such, as surpassing the slowly evolving dinosaurs of hardware. But as previously mentioned, the extreme dominance of Google is based not on its algorithms but on its computing power, its hardware. It is also the computing power of the company that allows it to reach inwards as well as outwards to access and organize evermore kinds of information. Whereas Googleplex embodies and represents the soft power of decentralization, we have in this chapter shown how informational organization, in the case of Googleplex, relies on the mediating functions of a very material and tangible "machine for working" and, in the case of the Web, their veritable centers of computation. Put together these act as a more centralizing force than any of the old mass media companies could ever hope to do.

References

Barbrook, R. & Cameron, A. (1995). "The Californian Ideology." In *Mute*, no. 3, 1995. Available on-line: http://www.alamut.com/subj/ideologies/pessimism/califIdeo_I.html

Battelle, J. (2005). *The Search: How Google and Its Rivals Rewrote the Rules of Business and Transformed Our Culture*. New York: Portfolio.

Baudrillard, J. (1986/1993). *America*. London & New York: Verso.

Brin, S & Page, L. (1998). The Anatomy of a Large-scale Hypertextual Web Search Engine. In *Computer Networks and ISDN Systems*. Vol. 30, Issue 1–7. pp. 107–117.

Buisson, E. & Billard, T. (2004). *The Presence of the Case Study Houses*. Basel: Birkhäuser.

Chang, J. (2006). "Behind the Glass Curtain." Metropolismag.com. July 2006. Available on-line: http://www.metropolismag.com/cda/story.php?artid=2123[Accessed: 081027]

Chen, A. (2006). "The Builder." Fastcompany.com. Issue 109. Available on-line: http://www.fastcompany.com/magazine/109/open_design-builder.html (081027)

Colomina, B. (1996). *Privacy and Publicity: Modern Architecture as Mass Media.* Cambridge, MA: MIT Press.
Entenza, J. (1945). "Announcement. Case Study House Program." *Arts & Architecture,* January 1945. Available on-line: http://www.artsandarchitecture.com/case.houses/pdf/csh_announcement.pdf [Accessed: 081027]
Galloway, A. (2004). *Protocol: How Control Exists after Decentralization.* Cambridge, MA: MIT Press.
Google (2008a). "Corporate information." Google.com. Available on-line: http://www.google.com/corporate/ [Accessed: 081027]
Google (2008b). "Google moon." Google.com. Available on-line: www.google.com/moon [Accessed: 081027]
Graham & Guy (2002). "Digital Space Meets Urban Place: Sociotechnologies of Urban Restructuring in Downtown San Francisco." In *City,* Vol. 6, No. 3. pp. 369–382.
Halavais, A. (2009). *Search Engine Society.* Cambridge: Polity Press.
Johnson, S. (2001). *Emergence: The Connected Lives of Ants, Brains, Cities and Software.* London: Allen Lane.
Kittler, F. (1997). "Protected Mode." In *Literature, Media, Information Systems: Essays.* (Ed.) J. Johnston. Amsterdam: G+B Arts International.
Latour, B. (1992). "Where Are the Missing Masses? The Sociology of a Few Mundane Artifacts," In *Shaping Technology/Building Society: Studies in Sociotechnical Change.* (Eds.) W. E. & Law Bijker, J. Cambridge, MA: MIT Press, pp. 225–258.
Lécuyer, C. (2006). *Making Silicon Valley: Innovation and the Growth of High Tech, 1930–1970.* Cambridge, MA: MIT Press.
Manovich, L. (2001). *The Language of New Media.* Cambridge, MA: MIT Press.
Markoff, J. & Hansell, S. (2006). "Hiding in Plain Sight, Google Seeks More Power." *The New York Times.* June 14, 2006. Available on-line: http://www.nytimes.com/2006/06/14/technology/14/technology/14search.html [Accessed: 081027]
Martin, R. (2005). *The Organizational Complex. Architecture, Media, and Corporate Space.* Cambridge, MA: MIT Press.
Miller, R. (2009). Data center knowledge.com (090316). http://www.datacenterknowledge.com/archives / category/google
Page, L. & Brin, S. (2001). Method for node ranking in a linked database. US Patent 6285999. Available online: http://patft.uspto.gov/netacgi/nphParser?Sect1=PTO1&Sect2=HITOFF&d=PALL&p=1&u=%2Fnetahtml%2FPTO%2Fsrchnum.htm&r=1&f=G&l=50&s1=6285999.PN.&OS=PN/6285999&RS=PN/6285999 [Accessed: 081027]
Ross, A. (2004). *No-Collar: the Human Workplace and Its Hidden Costs: Behind the Myth of the New Office Utopia.* Philadelphia, PA: Temple University Press.
Saxenian, A. (1994). *Regional Advantage: Culture and Competition in Silicon Valley and Route 128.* Cambridge, MA: Harvard University Press.
Shannon, C. & Weaver, W. (1949). *The Mathematical Theory of Communication.* Urbana: University of Illinois Press.
Sheff, D. (2004). "Google guys." In *Playboy,* September 2004.
Soja, E. (1989). *Postmodern Geographies: The Reassertion of Space in Critical Social Theory.* London: Verso.
Strand, G. (2008) "Keyword: Evil." *Harpers Magazine,* March 2008.
Takahashistaff, D. (2007). "Grasping the Googleplex." In *Oakland Tribune,* August 6, 2007. Available on-line: http://findarticles.com/p/articles/mi_qn4176/is_/ai_n19443559 (081027)

Ted.com. (2007). "Sergey. Brin and Larry Page: Inside the Google machine." Ted.com. Video available on-line: http://www.ted.com/index.php/talks/sergey_brin_and_larry_page_on_google.html (081027)
Terranova, T. (2004). *Network Culture: Politics for the Information Age.* London: Pluto Press.
Thrift, N. (2004). "Remembering the Technological Unconscious by Foregrounding Knowledges of Position." In *Environment and Planning D: Society and Space.* Vol. 22. pp. 175–190.
Vaidhyanathan, S. (2007). "The Googlization of Everything: How One Company Is Shaking up Culture, Commerce and Community." Paper presented at New Network Theory. Amsterdam, June 28–30, 2007.
Valleywag.com (2007). "25 Things to See at the Googleplex before You Die." http://valleywag.com/tech/google/25-things-to-see-at-the-googleplex-before-you-die-234103.php (081027)
van Couvering, E. (2008). "The History of the Internet Search Engine: Navigational Media and the Traffic Commodity." In Spink, A. & M. Zimmer (eds.) (2009). *Web Search. Multidisciplinary Perspectives.* Berlin: Springer Verlag.
Vise, D. A. (2005). *The Google Story: Inside the Hottest Business, Media and Technology Success of Our Time.* New York: Random House.
Wiener, N. (1948). *Cybernetics or Control and Communication in the Animal and the Machine.* Cambridge, MA: Kessinger Publishing, LLC.
Wiener, N. (1950). *The Human Use of Human Beings: Cybernetics and Society.* Boston, MA: Houghton Mifflin.

Notes

1. The patent describes the so-called PageRank algorithm, also described in Brin & Page (1998).
2. It has been estimated that every single server farm demands about 103 megawatts of electricity (enough to power 82,000 homes).
3. There is of course also a connection here between the dinosaur and the DNA project since it can be argued that it was the film *Jurassic Park* that for the first time brought the implications of biotechnology into popular culture.
4. This is best exemplified in the Google Zeitgeist project (www.google.com/intl/en/press/zeitgeist/index.html), which tracks trends in search queries over time.
5. Or perhaps also the large, bureaucratic, and nonuser-friendly software developers such as Microsoft.

CHAPTER SIX

Edge Blending: Light, Crystalline Fluidity, and the Materiality of New Media at Gehry's IAC Headquarters

SHANNON MATTERN

Barry Diller's original plan was to build his company's new headquarters on a pier extending into the Hudson River. Admitting that city planning officials would never approve such a proposal, he settled for a river *view*. Now, on the site of a former truck garage, between 18th and 19th streets on the far west side of New York's Chelsea neighborhood, is the new headquarters for Diller's InterActiveCorp (IAC).

The building is hard to miss. Driving south on the West Side Highway, where the road curves at 23rd Street and the massive Chelsea Piers sports complex looms to the right, one cannot help but notice the glowing iceberg a few blocks ahead. This is Frank Gehry's first free-standing building in New York—and his first all-glass structure. Its western façade zigzags around angled structural columns, creating five distinct bays. Five floors up those five bays fold into three, which extend up to the tenth floor. The folds here are gentle creases rather than razor-sharp pleats, thanks to a slight curve in the glass. The building's 1,500 glass panels were "cold warped," torqued several inches to fit the façade's curves, on site (Iovine 2007). The waves are fewer and gentler on the north and south façades, and a portion of the eastern façade, which faces more traditionally rectilinear neighbors, is straight.

Fig. 1. IAC's glowing iceberg, or "glass schooner." (c) Albert Vecerka / Esto.

At some point during the design phase, Gehry showed Diller a model with a white material standing in for the windows, and Diller "got hung up on the building being all white, which, of course, you can't do with glass," the architect said (cited in Lieberman 2007). The solution was to use "frits," ceramic dots applied to the glass. The dot pattern is dense near the top and bottom of each panel and transparent at the middle—at occupants' eye level—thus framing their city views with a blurred edge. The fritting also serves to reflect light and reduce glare, thereby increasing the building's energy efficiency.

Some have likened the building to a ship—more precisely, a glass schooner with billowing white sails (Hockenberry 2007b). "The shape made sense," design writer Jade Chang (2007) says, since "several of Gehry's previous projects have incorporated sail shapes, and Diller was in the midst of building a gigantic boat." Architecture critic Paul Goldberger (2007) argues that "Gehry's buildings aren't usually based on analogies, and this one can be understood without resorting to comparisons." *Architectural Record*'s Clifford Pearson (2007) agrees that Gehry's approach to form is more sculptural than symbolic: "Gehry emphasizes the purely formal aspects of the building and underscores its role as an *object* in the landscape" (italics mine). At the time of its opening, in early 2007, this was the most intricate object in the vicinity. Yet architecture critic Robert Campbell (2007) disagrees: "Whatever it is," he writes, "this is the architecture of metaphor. You're supposed to read meanings into it." Whether they saw an iceberg or a schooner, or simply an intriguing sculptural form, *Business Week* and *Architectural Record* chose to name the building a 2008 Award of Excellence winner.

Could this building also represent, as Innis (1991) might have it, the new shape of space in a new media landscape? Might it also be a metaphor for the next phase of the symbolic economy, the "scapes" of Appadurai's (1996) global cultural economy? In answering these questions, I will look first at the IAC building's historical context—particularly New York's existing media headquarters—and highlight its departure from the traditional corporate architectural form, which could be explained in part by IAC's departure from the traditional corporate media model. So, in the next section, I recount IAC's company history and describe its continuing struggles to define itself. I then situate the building within its contemporary local context, and, drawing on Venturi, Scott Brown, and Izenour's (1972) model of architectural communication, explain how the building functions within that local context as an advertisement for the company. Turning inward, I then build on the work of Ross (2003) to address the IAC as a new media workspace. Finally, in the last two sections, I examine the continuities and breaks between the building's exterior and interior identities; I argue that IAC's attempts to blur the edges between outside and inside, old and new media, materiality and immateriality, instead reveal the awkward tension between old and new political economies.

Historical Context: Media Headquarters in Twentieth and Twenty-first Century New York

Scanning the western Manhattan skyline periodically over the past decade, one might have gotten the impression that American media are booming. First, the mammoth Time Warner Center, two 80-story towers atop a curved glass base, opened on Columbus Circle in 2003. By 2006, The Hearst Corporation had added a 42-story glass tower supported by an exoskeleton of "diagridded" steel beams, set inside and atop its existing headquarters, a 6-story Art Deco building on 8th Avenue between 56th and 57th streets. Just down the avenue, at 41st, the *New York Times* Company moved in 2007 to its new Renzo Piano-designed 52-story glass tower sheathed in rows of ceramic rods. Their billion-dollar budgets, brand-name architects, and prominent sites, and their visibility from across the river and throughout the city suggest that these buildings and the institutions they house are thriving, that they hold a central place in New York's—and the nation's—economic and public life.

Many of these recently constructed media headquarters have adopted the modern city's quintessential architectural form: the skyscraper. The skyscraper's rise in the latter half of the nineteenth century can be attributed to the convergence of a number of engineering technologies and increasing land values (Domosh 1988, pp. 320–321). By the twentieth century, the skyscraper had become

> [the] paradigmatic statement, not only of American architecture and urbanism, but of the economic ideology, mode of production and ethos from which it was largely (if not entirely) produced: capitalist land values, speculative office development and big business materialism.... (King 2004, p. 11; see also van Leeuwen 1990)[1]

But as the towers "exceeded the limits of functional efficiency"—once they grew past 10 or 20 stories, and had to devote a large proportion of their floorplates to the elevators needed for vertical transportation—"their market becomes increasingly based in symbolic capital" (Dovey 2001, p. 107).

Geographer Mona Domosh argues that "the earliest industry to translate its promotional needs and notions of corporate imagery"—its symbolic capital—"into tall structures was the newspaper industry" (p. 327). The area around Park Place in Lower Manhattan was home to the first collection of tall buildings in nineteenth-century New York. Here were the headquarters for the *New York Tribune*, the *New York World*, and the *New York Times*. These nineteenth-century newspaper buildings, media historian Aurora Wallace (2006) writes,

> attempted to communicate the supremacy of the press generally and their own paper specifically.... Deliberate and precise plans were made for these buildings that gave citizens a recognizable and unambiguous sign that commercial media were thriving in America (p. 178).

Their "thriving" contributed not only to public life, but also, as the skyscraper form with its attendant ideologies would have us believe, to New York's economic life.

Domosh similarly describes the *World* building's symbolic function: it served as an "advertisement to the mass market, as a monument to Pulitzer's success, and as a sign of the paper's legitimacy as a public institution" (p. 331). Wallace (2006) explains how George Browne Post's design for the *New York Times* building represented its occupant in form, material, and ornament:

> [The building] was an architectural translation of the Aristotelian principle that all forms should have a beginning, middle, and end. The base was clearly differentiated from the middle shaft, and the capital was an ornamental and climactic finish, typically of classical buildings of the period . . . For a newspaper building, this conscious adaptation of narrative structure added yet more layers of meaning to the design, a play on the words "story" and "storey." (p. 184)

She also acknowledges the *Times*' "serious exterior of olive granite that paralleled the somber grey pages of the newspaper" (ibid).

The *Times*, the *World*, and the *Tribune* adopted different approaches to journalism, Wallace (ibid.) concludes, yet they all . . .

> chose locations next to each other and architectural styles that would differentiate them from one another, and most importantly, built taller than their neighbors in order to declare their supremacy. . . . Despite the sensationalism of the *World* and the sobriety of the *Times*, all of the newspapers adopted architecture which was reminiscent of classical styles. This appropriation suggested a desire to convey social and cultural legitimacy on the part of businesses for whom such legitimacy was not easily won. (pp. 186–8)

These nineteenth-century media companies chose their downtown location not only to be close to their competitors, but also because of the concentration of news-making and distribution resources in this area. When the railroad terminals, theaters, and banks headed uptown in the early twentieth century, the newspapers soon followed (Turner 1999). Most big media companies today are still concentrated in Midtown, which makes notable IAC's choice to settle on the fringes of Chelsea.

Perhaps our contemporary media buildings are, like their nineteenth-century counterparts, attempting to "communicate their supremacy"—or at least the continued relevance—of their specific sectors of the media industry, and to collectively demonstrate that "commercial media [are still] thriving in America" (Wallace 2006). But rather than choosing neoclassical architectural styles to convince the public of their legitimacy, today's media companies have chosen a variety of styles to communicate a variety of new values. Height, however, is still in. The skyscraper—though not the same skyscraper we saw on Park Row or at Rockefeller Center—is still a structure, and symbol, of choice (see Koolhaas 1994).

Time Warner Center sits on the circumference of Columbus Circle. From below, its twin towers appear to bend backward, pushed by the centripetal force of the circle's swing. There is no unified front here; the building has always embodied a split—a split that will become ever more real when Time Warner was broken into two parts in December 2009. Regardless of any corporate fracture, these twin towers will have to stand awkwardly in one another's company in perpetuity. Meanwhile, Hearst's construction required the gutting of Joseph Urban's 1928 International Magazine Building; all that remains is the landmarked façade. The new composite structure has been likened to a "jack-in-the-box without the Jack"—a spring with nothing to elevate (Amelar 2006). And in the age of newspapers' precipitous decline, some doubt the Times Tower's "proposition that insists that a building can symbolize a vision for a venerable cultural institution, [and] can project the confidence of a reformulated business model for an aging product" (Hockenberry 2007a).

While the skyscraper might still suggest cultural legitimacy and financial strength, as it did on Park Row in the nineteenth century, the reality of today's media industries is quite different: hemorrhaging budgets, massive layoffs, divestments, and closures. "Rome is definitely burning while these guys are building," Michael Wolff, *Vanity Fair* media columnist, told "I Want Media," a media news Web site, in 2001. He continues: "This partly has to do with the fact that these real estate deals were begun in better times, but it also reflects the bigger-is-always-better, consolidate-or-die, fortress mentality of the media business" ("Media" 2002). These fortresses may project strength and stability, but their occupants are increasingly unstable.

Yet even their projected images, the designs' symbolism—a split tower, an eviscerated box—carries an unintended double message: these media fortresses are crumbling; their centers cannot hold. Perhaps IAC, which diversified to expand beyond the purview of a traditional "media" business, and whose identity as a digital company continues to evolve, has chosen to house itself, appropriately, in a building that is decidedly *not* a skyscraper—a building with no easily discernable structure and a shifting center of gravity. Does this new prefractured, decentered media space represent a viable alternative to the mass media monoliths? Is it a more appropriate symbol for an industry undergoing rapid change?

As we examine the IAC building, we must keep in mind Wallace's (2006) reminder that "investigating only the buildings does not tell the whole story" (p. 188):

> [T]here can be little doubt that newspapers in the nineteenth century used architecture as a way of branding their businesses, but a formal analysis of their structures is not sufficient to explain their style. The conflation between the character of a newspaper and the character of its building was made clear through the particular way in which a new building and its construction were *reported* rather than being the natural interpretation of the characteristics of the chosen style. (ibid., italics mine)

Addressing how architecture is *reported*—or represented in a variety of media—becomes even more essential when considering modern architecture, which, according to architectural historian Beatriz Colomina (1994), *becomes* modern "with its engagement with the media" (p. 14). She writes:

> [It will be necessary to think of architecture as a . . . series of overlapping systems of representation. This does not mean abandoning the traditional architectural object, the building. In the end, it means looking at it much more closely than before, but also in a different way. The building should be understood in the same terms as drawings, photographs, writing, films, and advertisements; not only because these are the media in which more often we encounter it, but because the building is a mechanism of representation in its own right. The building is, after all, a "construction." (pp. 13–14)

The same is true, even more so, with contemporary architecture. Thus we will look at the entire "construction" of the IAC building: how the building constructs the company's identity; how the company, its spokespeople, and the designers represent the building and the company in various media; and how amateur critics respond to the building. We will consider how the building, as a mechanism of representation, combines with, flows into, other means of representation, to provide a composite identity of InterActiveCorp.[2]

IAC, of course, shares some of New York's early newspapers' ambitions. Several critics have already placed the building within the "promotional" architectural context that Domosh writes about. Sara Silver (2006) draws parallels between Gehry's schooner and two of New York's modern and postmodern architectural icons: "The building is expected to give Mr. Diller a place on the Manhattan architectural map of buildings that stand for the corporations that built them—like the Seagram Building, Lever House and Philip Johnson's AT&T Building, now the Sony Building." Reinhold Martin (2007/2008) also mentions Mies van der Rohe's Seagram Building, "to which Gehry's IAC will inevitably be compared." Goldberger (2007) reinforces the analogy:

> [Gehry and Diller] wanted to create something that would embody the dynamism of the new, Internet economy as powerfully as the Woolworth Building represented the democratic idealism of the five-and-dime store in the early 20th century, and the Seagram Building captured the sophistication of liquor 50 years ago.

"Even as the [media] industry grapples with a nebulous, digital future," critic Justin Davidson (2004) argues, "it is still reckoning with its masonry-and-paper past." Hearst, Time Warner, *The New York Times*, IAC, Condé Nast, Bloomberg, and other media companies that have recently constructed new media headquarters "have bet not just on real estate and location but on the galvanizing power of architecture" (ibid.). Yet IAC—the design project, if not the building form or IAC's business model—is, in a way, the most traditional of all. It "represents something . . . almost old fashioned," Goldberger (2007) says: "a corporate headquarters born out of the partnership of a strong-willed executive and a strong-willed architect."

Corporate History: IAC's Search for a Coherent Identity

Diller famously started off in the mailroom of the William Morris Agency, then moved on to join ABC's programming department in 1966. By 1974, he was chairman and CEO of Paramount Pictures, then moved to Fox, Inc., where he launched Fox Broadcasting in 1987. In the early 1990s, he left Fox and purchased a stake in shopping channel QVC. By the late 1990s, he had acquired Silver King Communications, along with the Home Shopping Network, and bought rights to the USA Network, which he later sold. Over the next few years, his company incorporated Ticketmaster, the Hotels Reservation Network, Match.com, Sidewalk city guides, Expedia, and TV Travel Group, and, in 2003, became InterActiveCorp (see Balio; IAC n.d.a). The new company then added TripAdvisor, Service Magic, Home Loan Cutter, and AskJeeves; and, in 2005, spun off its travel businesses as Expedia, Inc.

At this point, IAC's offices were scattered around midtown Manhattan. The new building was intended to bring everyone together under one roof—and to impart some "physical coherence" to the company (Silver, January 11, 2006). Yet, as the *New York Times'* Joe Nocera (2007) argues, simply bringing together the various businesses in "an open, airy building does not necessarily mean that [Diller's] somewhat hodgepodge collection of Internet businesses will automatically turn into a seamless, integrated company." He continues: "Ever since he started IAC 12 years ago, the rap on Mr. Diller has been that he lacks a clear, consistent vision for his company." Diller himself, eventually recognizing that "internal complexity makes for superficiality," sought to make IAC less complex (Ovide 2008a).

> . . . Diller claimed that he . . . was no longer interested in wheeling and dealing so frantically, and that his goal was [to] make the whole more than the sum of the parts. "There is no question that two years ago we were a holding company," he said. "But we decided strategically that we had enough mass, and we didn't need to be in on the deal of the day."
>
> Instead, he said, he wants to transform IAC into a true operating company—the kind of company that shares resources, takes advantage of the expertise of the different companies to help other companies, and so on. (Nocera 2007)

According to its Web site, IAC "began looking for and finding natural synergies across many of its existing businesses" (IAC n.d.b). AskJeeves was relaunched as Ask.com; and a new site, AskCity, combined the services of Citysearch, ServiceMagic, ReserveAmerica, Ticketmaster, and Ticketweb. "To get these companies to relate to each other is very hard to do," Diller admitted (quoted in Nocera 2007). Shareholders noticed the strain and, despite Diller's best efforts, still did not know how to make sense of IAC's collection of old and new media properties (see Fung 2008). Diller admitted: "What I've learned over the years is that focus and singular purpose is the best approach for business. How can you function across 12 different businesses from financial services to dating?" (Ovide 2008a). In November 2007, IAC announced a major change: Ticketmaster, the Home Shopping Network, LendingTree.com, and Interval Leisure Group, a timeshare company, would become separate, publicly traded companies, and what remained would become the "new IAC."

With the divestiture completed in August 2008, the newly thinned company attempted again to explain the coherence among this motley collection of remainders.[3] The new IAC, its Web site explains, is an "internet company mastering expertise in online advertising, content distribution and monetization across the web" (IAC n.d.b). Despite their efforts to impose a business logic on a suite of properties that ranges from an emoticon library to a camping reservation site, the company reported a loss of $14.8 million in the third quarter of 2008. They managed to turn profitable in the fourth quarter.

"We're making it up as we go along in the interactive [commerce] area, and because of the nature of interactive revenue, there are few rules," Diller told the *Wall Street Journal* (Silver 2006). IAC has to set its own boundaries: "We won't get out of the parameters we have set for ourselves, which is pure Internet whose drive wheel is this distribution and marketing machine," Diller said (Ovide 2008a). "To me that is focused enough, and we may get even more focused as we go." Diller suggests that the volatile field of interactive media requires that companies continually redefine themselves. Yet he also acknowledges that this need for continual self-evaluation and redefinition is not exclusive to new media; Diller, who is on the board of directors of the *Washington Post*, says of the future of newspaper companies: "If they call themselves newspaper companies they are probably going to be toast. It will depend absolutely on what the product is" (Ovide 2008a). What is IAC's "product"? What kind of business is it in? What does it call itself? Depending on whom one asks, IAC works in online advertising and marketing, interactive commerce, content distribution, and "monetization across the web." Rather than focusing on content creation, as many of its uptown neighbors do, IAC is concerned with distributing and "monetizing" content that it may or may not have created itself.

How the company labels itself and how it houses itself are both mechanisms for representation and sources of power. Diller reportedly said to his staff, in "trying to pull together all these disparate businesses" into a shared space, "We can build a box, but why should that be our inspiration?" (quoted in Nocera). "We were trying to do something new with this company, and I wanted a different kind of place" (quoted in Goldberger 2007). What is that "something new," and what makes its new headquarters different?

Local Context: Architectural Pioneers on Manhattan's Western Frontier

According to IAC's real estate coordinator Shannon Johnson (November 19, 2008), Diller and Joseph Rose of the Georgetown Group, the project's developer, scoped out the West Chelsea location around 2000. Right down the street from the building site was The Kitchen, an experimental art space that has been in the neighborhood since the mid-1980s—around the same time that the Dia Art Foundation moved here and precipitated the move of Manhattan's art center from Soho to Chelsea. The old Nabisco factory on 9th Avenue between 15th and 16th streets was transformed in the late 1990s into the Chelsea Market, a ground-floor collection of restaurants and food shops, with upper-level office space for several media companies. And cutting between the West Side Highway and 10th Avenue was the

High Line, an elevated railway unused since 1980 but which, shortly before Diller chose his site, inspired local supporters to advocate for its preservation and reuse. Directly across the highway from IAC's site is a set of four historic piers that, in the mid-1990s, was transformed into the 28-acre Chelsea Piers Sports and Entertainment Complex.

Diller "envisioned his new headquarters as a catalyst for transforming a part of town he has long championed," writes Pearson (2007). "An early and generous supporter of the High Line, Diller—along with his wife, fashion designer Diane von Furstenberg . . . prides himself on being an urban pioneer." The local context has indeed changed tremendously since Diller's early "pioneer" days and even since IAC's groundbreaking in 2004. Diller's $130+ million project was financed in part by $80 million in tax-exempt Liberty Bonds, intended to aid the revitalization of Lower Manhattan after 9/11. While Chelsea is about four miles north of Ground Zero, it is indeed in the middle of its own major construction zone. The High Line park is now under development; the project has drawn celebrity supporters and developers with plans for new restaurants, clubs, and hotels. Rising next door to the IAC building are Shigeru Ban's Metal Shutter Houses, an 11-story condominium with "garage doors" on each duplex unit; and just across 19th Street is Jean Nouvel's 23-story "vision machine" apartment tower. "No other block in America will have such a concentration of high-end architecture," writes Davidson (2007a).[4]

Some critics and bloggers have noted how the local context provides inspiration for the building's form. The nautical metaphors are of course appropriate for a building so close to the river. Martin (2007/2008) also acknowledges the building's compliance with "the contextualist ideology built into the New York zoning code by reproducing a zoning envelope that holds the street edge and steps back above" (p. 3). He find parallels between the IAC Building and the "streamlined, horizontal fenestration of the comparably nautical *Starrett-Lehigh Building*," a 2.2 million-square-foot former freight distribution building on 26th Street that is now home to companies like Martha Stewart, Palm Pictures, and Hugo Boss. The IAC building's references to its context, its Web site's acknowledgment of Chelsea's assets—and Diller's casting of himself as an "urban pioneer"—suggest that IAC is rooted in its local context. "It is an embryonic neighborhood," Diller said, "where we could be a participant instead of just tacking onto the Rockefellers' legacy"; in other words, what the old money of the RCA era was to Midtown, Diller and other entrepreneurial developers could be to the city's western frontier (Silver 2006).[5]

Still, Pearson (2007) says, "you might expect the IAC to reach out and engage its neighbors more directly than it does." Instead, the building "seals itself off from its neighborhood"; a more appropriate visual metaphor for the building might be a "cocoon." Its object-quality makes it feel unrooted; it has "no base to sit on, so you get the impression it could be lifted up and taken away as easily as it was placed here" (ibid.). Martin (2007/2008) also notes its "tentative encounter with the ground plane" (p. 4). Furthermore, the glass fritting pattern, while conducive to exterior views from the inside, makes the building appear opaque to those walking or driving by at ground level; they have a hazy view into the ground floor, but no higher. The main entrances on 18th and 19th streets do not reach out to meet the sidewalk, and on West Street, there are only a few inconspicuous emergency-egress doors. Diller agrees that "the entrance to the building is in the wrong place.... It really should be on ... [West] street," although pedestrian traffic on the highway is typically light (cited in Hockenberry 2007b). Moreover, when the building first opened, there was no signage to introduce it to the neighborhood; Iovine (2007) reports that Diller was "adamant that no signs should mar the structure's monolithic It-ness." Now, there are large—apparently none-too-popular—blue and yellow signs, at "driving-by-at-high-speed"-scale, on the highway side of both the 18th and 19th street entrances.

Architectural Billboards: Spaces of Projection and Display

It is telling that the "tall-ships-at-full-sail metaphor ... that inspired the building's form is experienced most immediately and effectively by the cars whizzing by [on West Side Highway], making the IAC the city's first LA building" (Iovine). This is spatial design and experience at the scale and speed of the highway. We might wonder if this is the same "antispatial" architecture Venturi, Scott Brown, and Izenour wrote about in 1972, in *Learning from Las Vegas*:

> [It is] an architecture of communication over space; communication dominates space as an element in the architecture and in the landscape ... But is it for a new scale of landscape. The philosophical associations of the old eclecticism evoked subtle and complex meanings to be savored in the docile spaces of a traditional landscape. The commercial persuasion of roadside eclecticism provokes bold impact in the vast and complex setting of a new landscape of big spaces, high speeds, and complex programs. (p. 8)[6]

In Venturi et al.'s terms, there are two primary ways to construct communicative structures: a "duck" is a building that, through its sculptural form, is a symbol, while the "decorated shed" is a shelter with *applied* symbols. Along the West Side Highway, we have exemplars of both types situated directly across the street from one another: the IAC building is a "duck," a sculptural object whose form reveals itself fully only to drivers-by, and Chelsea Piers is the "decorated shed," a huge box with mega-signage. The IAC's exterior, Davidson (2007b) says, "is an advertisement for itself," an "office building wrapped in a gimmick." Gehry and his persona were brought on board "so the building would function as a cryptic billboard for a company that hides behind more-public brands" (Match.com and Ask.com are more recognizable names than IAC) (ibid.).

Light and projection are the organizing principles of the building's lobby, which is purportedly open to the public—although Johnson told me that visitors are typically not permitted to wander far beyond the reception area. The expansive, concrete-floored ground level is divided into a large gallery and a smaller reception lobby. A few sinuous Gehry-designed benches, resembling driftwood, are scattered throughout the floor—but two video walls are the centerpieces.[7] The wall behind the reception desk features a globe displaying current worldwide use of IAC's sites; visitors can use a touch screen on the reception desk to select a particular property, then spin a blue trackball to rotate the globe and see where people are using, say, Match.com anywhere in the world at that moment. Inside IAC's west lobby and facing the highway is an 11-foot high, 120-foot long video wall—upon installation, the largest high definition video wall in the world. Bruce Mau Design, the building's graphics consultant, proposed a "giant presentation device for large audiences"; it just so happens that those audiences are zipping by in automobiles (Hall 2007). According to the building's official Web site, "an average of 75,000 cars pass by the IAC building daily, all with a clear view of the West Wall"—"clear" through the un-fritted middle portion of the ground-floor panes of glass, at eye-level for drivers-by, but hazy around the edges (IAC n.d.c). "This unique video wall provides a powerful marketing tool," the Web site reports, and plays "a communications role for the community"—presumably a community of drivers, since few people walk along West Side Highway. The screen offers performances that "blur the boundaries between video art and commercial communications"; its programming ranges from promotional videos, to video art created by NYU students, to LED light shows (ibid.).

And all the machinery that makes it work—dozens of computers, eighteen 12,000-lumen projectors and 36 mirrors—is hidden in a sealed six-foot-deep closet immediately behind the screen. "We didn't want lots of bells and whistles," said IAC's chief administrative officer Jason Stewart; "We wanted the technology throughout the building to be seamless with the architecture" (quoted in Pearson 2007).[8] Architect Todd DeGarmo agrees that Diller prefers an understated currency: "Barry . . . doesn't like things techie or iconic," so, in most places, the technology is integrated into the architecture (quoted in Hockenberry 2007b). Video *is* the wall, and vice versa.

Gehry seems an odd match for a nontechnophilic anti-iconicist. The architect is, after all, known for designing signature buildings that would not be possible without advanced computer modeling systems that facilitate the translation of design to fabrication and construction.[9] As it turns out, however, Gehry's trademark curves translate much more easily to titanium and steel—his usual building materials—than glass. So, although the IAC building's glass, unlike the blindingly reflective steel of his Walt Disney Concert Hall in LA, seems to "erase" itself and downplays the engineering heroics that made it possible, the building required significant technical and structural innovation. We will return to this theme of "invisible" innovation.

Fig. 2. The IAC building's media wall, visible through the West façade. (c) Albert Vecerka / Esto.

Inside the Screen: Spaces of Media Labor

Johnson said that IAC could not afford to have a top-to-bottom, inside-and-out Gehry design, so they asked Gehry to focus on the ground floor and floors six and nine and to recommend another architect to design the other interiors. STUDIOS architecture was brought on board late in the design process, according to DeGarmo, to "find a way to mute the overwhelming gestures of Gehry's exterior"—to "deliver a Barry Diller, not a Frank Gehry, interior"—and won a 2008 Interior Architecture Merit Award for its work from the American Institute of Architects' New York chapter (cited in Hockenberry 2007b). Yet Gehry is the star inside the building, too. *Metropolis* magazine's John Hockenberry writes:

[E]verywhere you go in this glass house of offices the exterior is on display. The workers inside get the best view of IAC's lines and surfaces. There are the odd angles of glass that curve tantalizingly back into view of work spaces, surfaces that easily and deliberately mix the building's silhouette with reflected images of the city. There's the nighttime view, which is already pretty spectacular from outside; but from inside, the mixing of the pointillist lights of Manhattan with the color brilliance of the interior puts each worker inside an ever-changing sculpture of glass and light.

The building thus forms its own viewfinder, framing images of the Hudson River, the Statue of Liberty, and the palimpsest of Chelsea and Midtown to the north and east. It is its own screen, reflecting and refracting those vistas and *its own image* for its inhabitants. And it is its own projector, glowing for cars zipping by and gallery-goers wandering through the streets of Chelsea (although denying them interior views above the ground floor).

Fig. 3. The building frames both exterior and interior views. (c) Albert Vecerka / Esto.

The structure frames interior vistas, too, in a way that constructs IAC's corporate identity for its inhabitants. Many design writers comment on the vibrant, invigoratingly chaotic, interiors. The private offices on nonexecutive floors feature glass dividers and doors in "Tropical Fruit Lifesavers" colors, Julie Iovine (2007) writes. She continues:

> Austin Powers orange seating pods dot the floor, and supergraphics by Mau cover the elevator landing walls. Gehry installed a rug with a tiger-striped pattern in Diller's executive suite. It all screams "Youth! Creativity! Energy!" which could become tiresome in the long run.

The choice of materials "creates a certain amount of visual chaos," Pearson admits, "but seems appropriate for the kinds of employees IAC attracts," which, judging from appearances, are twenty- and thirty-somethings in dress ranging from jeans and button-downs to Ann Taylor suits. Pearson finds the interior spaces "energized without being wacky or contrived."

Fig. 4. The IAC building's "Tropical Fruit" corporate interiors. (c) Albert Vecerka / Esto.

The IAC Building's official Web site offers a virtual tour that previews different kinds of space within the building and also, notably, addresses the quality of light in these spaces. The tour highlights places for gathering (e.g., the ninth floor snack commissary), for interacting (e.g., kitchens in each elevator lobby), for collaboration (e.g., conference rooms with smartboards and high-definition teleconferencing equipment), and for work (e.g., "workstations [that achieve] . . . a balance of style, functionality and flexibility"), and addresses the central role that natural and artificial illumination plays in supporting this program. The frits on the exterior walls impart a distinctive quality to the interior light, Campbell (2007) explains:

> [The] office spaces are utterly delightful, filled with a light that seems almost palpable, bright and white but shadowless. . . . It always seems to be lightly snowing outside. Walking around these spaces is like walking among your unopened Christmas presents.

Yet, when I visited, the neutral carpets and uniform warm light seemed to mute the "Tropical Fruit" colors into a general aura of "pleasant"—nothing especially kinetic, nothing warranting Iovine's exclamation marks ("Creativity! Energy!").

Uptown, in Times Square, Gehry's 2000 design for the cafeteria at Condé Nast, philosopher Mark C. Taylor (2003) suggests, goes beyond "delightful" by offering visitors an especially invigorating visual and kinesthetic experience:

> Rippled surfaces of undulated glass shapes reflect the reflections of the titanium panels. Along a mirrored corridor, reflections of reflections create figures that flow, torque, morph, and liquefy only to reform and return to circulation. In this virtually aqueous environment, the surging currents of network culture pulsate through mind and body. As forms swirl and images flicker, everything drifts far from equilibrium and rapidly approaches the edge of chaos, where it becomes clear that this moment of complexity is where the action is. (p. 46)

Even though now, nine years after the cafeteria's opening, magazine publishing certainly is *not* "where the action is," the IAC building still cannot match Condé Nast's verve. The iceberg's eccentric exterior form creates a number of oddly shaped interiors, including boat-shaped conference rooms christened "Prow" and "Wheelhouse" and a board room known as the "Bridge." Wave shapes continue through to IAC's furniture design; the arcing and radiating workspaces on most floors accommodate six or eight people and, architecture critic James S. Russell (2007) notes, leave "eddies of space that encourage on-the-spot collaboration." But in a world that stopped "surfing" the web years ago, such seafaring metaphors and nautical forms fail to conjure up the sense of urgency and excitement that Taylor experiences at Condé Nast. The currents of network culture do not "surge" through IAC's corridors.

But is the new media workplace necessarily as fantastically dynamic (and psychedelic) as Taylor might lead us to believe? In an interview with the *Wall Street Journal*, Diller said that one of the major differences between running a movie studio or a broadcast network—both of which he has done—and running an internet company, is that in "traditional" media, power is hierarchical, whereas in interactive media, the "value" is in the "distributed middle"—among the mid-level employees (Ovide 2008b). We look to see how this new social system might be embodied in the building: Wood and metal dividers between individual work stations are just high enough to offer privacy to workers who are seated at their computers, but low enough to allow "over-the-fence" conversation. Most work stations have translucent curving "back gates," in lieu of a back wall, that provide workers with a sense of security while not sealing them in. Almost all interior walls—including those to closed offices and conference rooms—are translucent glass, supporting the visual continuity and communal feeling and permitting natural light to flow throughout each floor. Ultimately, though, one finds these same tropes in any twenty-first-century open workspace. There are no "forms swirl[ing] or images flicker[ing]" here—in large part because IAC is not in the same business as other content-creating media companies.[10] There is no need for the cacophony of a newsroom or the fervor of a production facility when IAC's primary "productions" are schemes for extracting profit from online content created, for the most part, off-site.

Similarly, while the morphing and liquefying forms in the Condé Nast cafeteria supposedly create an invigorating sense of possibility and energy, IAC's similar shapes create confusion. Because of the 150,000-square-foot IAC building's irregular shape, none of its ten floor plates is the same; consequently, Johnson explained, many of IAC's divisions are imperfectly matched to their office spaces. During my visit, it was apparent that Mergers & Acquisitions, on the seventh floor, had plenty of space to spread out, while Tina Brown's *Daily Beast* staff, on Four, had outnumbered its workstations. Ikea tables were brought in to serve as temporary desks. The *Beast*, which, Johnson informed me, is the division that operates "most like a newsroom," needed access to news in multiple formats and to different equipment, so concessions were made to allow them to use Mac computers, while everyone else got PCs, and to mount a few flat-screen televisions on the walls. There is no room for the *Beast*'s "production facility" on the fourth floor, so we found down on Three, in a windowless private office, a trio of headphoned young workers laboring on laptops.

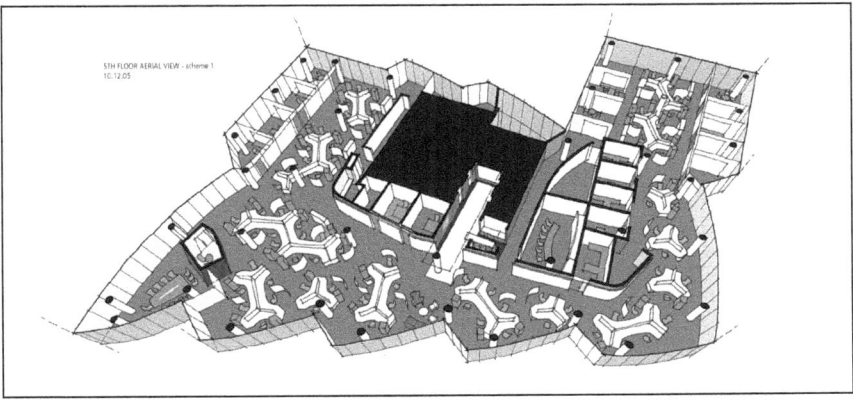

Fig. 5. The building's oddly shaped floorplans—here, the 5th floor. Created by STUDIOS architecture.

The building's finishings do not help to clarify the program. The brown and blue carpet tile patterns alternate by floor, which, according to Hockenberry (2007b), "gives each floor a distinct identity," yet fails to clarify "what IAC businesses are grouped together [on each floor] or why." Bruce Mau Design created wall collages of IAC businesses' logos that are placed outside the elevators and that were purportedly to assist with wayfinding. The collages make for vibrant public art—yet their layered type, in different typefaces and sizes, compromises legibility. The fact that these collages include logos for companies that are no longer a part of IAC further diminishes their utility in providing spatial order. These finishings thus offer little assistance in transforming Diller's "somewhat hodgepodge collection of Internet businesses . . . into a seamless, integrated company" (Nocera 2007).

That that new spatial order was to reflect a new *social* order in online media—the distributed middle—is negated by the completely incongruous sixth floor, the executive floor, with six traditional closed offices, linked by a two-story atrium to more corporate offices on the seventh floor. Diller requested this arrangement so that he and other executives could be "in the center of things," said IAC's Stewart (cited in Pearson 2007). Yet, after moving into the building, Diller admitted, "I actually think the sixth floor is totally counterpoint to the rest of the building" (cited in Hockenberry 2007b). The new media workplace, Ross (2003) writes, is to represent a "revolt against . . . rigid office design and its formulaic expression of hierarchy" (p. 110). But here we have the same cubicles and sterile corporate offices. "The translucent glass partitions that surround the atrium are stiff and flat," the *New York Times*' Nicolai Ouroussoff (2007) writes. "A curved staircase, in pretentious tigerwood with brushed stainless steel handrails, looks imported from a Park Avenue office building"—which, given the difference in character between uptown and downtown, old money and new economy, is precisely the architectural type to which the IAC building should be defining itself in opposition (ibid.).

Crystalline Liquidity: Where Old and New Media, Old and New Economies Meet

Here we witness a clashing of cultures: Diller's studio background vs. his new media present; the centralized authority of the studio system vs. the "distributed middle" of the new media workplace; the "masonry-and-paper past" vs. the digital future; the Midtown of the Rockefellers vs. the West Chelsea of the symbolic economy entrepreneurs; tigerwood vs. trampolines (Davidson 2004). In the building, Martin (2007/2008) writes,

> [W]e find a new-economy office landscape dedicated to intra-office social life (snack bars on every office floor, cafeteria above, etc.). The plans demonstrate the difficulty of squeezing this system of social systems—quasi-modular, loose, but still systematic—into Gehry's

undulating shell and core. STUDIOS accomplishes this with a certain finesse, though the two architectures grate against one another at their many points of contact. (p. 2)

The building, ostensibly transparent and immaterial, provides a physical workspace for embodied labor dedicated to the production of immaterial media products. It is both, in Martin's words, "crystalline"—like the Seagram Building, which "evinces a sense of brute mechanical construction"—and "liquid":

> Liquidity, juice: the very definition of capital, and therefore appropriate enough to describe this instance of corporate architecture. Anything more solid—geological rather than fluid or atmospheric—implies indifference (or resistance?) to capital's inexorable, circulatory pulse and therefore might seem behind the times, out of sync. But that still may be the most advantageous position from which to consider this building. Formal dynamism in architecture may or may not be related to the suppleness of today's corporations and the economic flows they channel. (p. 1)

It seems as if walls, cubicles, even *glass* are made to bend to accommodate the flows, the "scapes," of the new global cultural economy. Interior features were supposedly designed to be adaptable. Mau's collages of company logos, for instance, were designed with significant affordances for change. "[T]he beauty of the design," according to a Mau designer, "is that it's not just about the logos—it's also a gorgeous pattern. If one company comes or goes, there isn't an immediate need to replace the graphic" (cited in Cameron 2007). Corporate change is thus absorbed by indeterminate signage whose value is more esthetic than semantic. The floors and walls are not quite as adaptable, though. As Johnson pointed out to me, the oddly shaped floorplates, which wrap around the elevator core, leave variably sized and shaped "wings" or "branches" that may or may not fit the size and culture of the IAC business that are asked to occupy them. So, as companies come and go, or grow and shrink, they are occasionally asked to move, to find a floor zone that is a better fit. This rhizomatic interior space perhaps is not as smooth and fluid as it seems to be.[11]

Diller himself acknowledges the difficulty of balancing the competing spatial demands, forms, ideologies, and ontologies of old and new media, materiality and immateriality. "A building is a narrative," he says, "but it's more complex than a traditional narrative form. . . . Most good narrative comes from rewriting. But when they actually start digging [at a building site], you can't erase" (cited in Hockenberry 2007b). Physical architecture is not as mutable as digital code.

Hockenberry (2007b) notes that, during his visit to the new building, he was struck by the ubiquity of cups containing black no. 2 pencils featuring IAC's logo. The pencils' presence perhaps reflects Diller's ties to his "old media" past; they might also suggest that, even if the building cannot be rewritten, the work taking place inside—the work of defining a business plan for the new economy—involves revision. How does one embody an evolving corporate narrative—one that Diller and company are "making . . . up as [they] go along"—in a physical form that, despite its *formal* fluidity, still resists easy renovation? How does one reconcile the need for spatial flexibility with the fact that architecture has limits—imposed by material affordances, budget, zoning—to how much rewriting it can withstand?

As Martin (2007/2008) suggests, however, "formal dynamism in architecture" might not even be related to the "suppleness of today's corporations" and global economic flows. The IAC building's foregrounding of form and surface—and its effective service as an advertisement for the company—seems an appropriate use of architecture in a symbolic economy. Yet we might wonder what connection IAC's external skin and form have to the interior program and the spatial experience of IAC's employees. "The workers inside get the best view of the IAC's [exterior] lines and surfaces"—but interior life is not only about looking out (cited in Hockenberry 2007b). Behind those fritted glass sails, between those pleats, is an interior that people must inhabit, and where work must get done.

Goldhagen (2008) addresses the occasional lack of *internal* critical work in Gehry's design:

> His overall approach to design suggests nothing about how to make a plan that resolves or stimulatingly interprets the building's program, makes spatial sequences, or folds into or works with its site. Gehry has often finessed these architectural challenges by using the building's skin as a figurative textile that he drapes, or drops, on top of the spaces that his buildings' users inhabit in all the usual and time-honored ways, spaces which are themselves at best ordinary and at worst incoherent and oppressively residual. (p. 33)

All skins—even "smart" or "smooth" ones—have inside them skeletons, infrastructures, functional programs that must be accommodated. Beneath all codes, architectural and digital, is a protocol, Galloway (2004) reminds us, that determines the limits of its flexibility. When we look behind the giant media wall, we find a room full of projectors that generate heat, suck up electricity, and wear out light bulbs. This equipment lives in a controlled environment custom designed to support the backstage operations. Similarly, behind the IAC building's skin are the workers who produce the company's 30+ Web sites. Yet they do so in spaces that, aside from the Life Savers-colored translucent panels and the organically shaped work stations, are the same open office plans implemented in insurance offices and ad agencies across the globe. IAC's form may be more rhizomatic than Euclidean, but its underlying architectural and social "protocols" are like the corporate "box's" in their compartmentalization of work functions and reinforcement of hierarchy. The power structures and working conditions at IAC thus end up being the same they are at any other "modernist" corporation—which may be fitting, since a media company focused on "monetizing" content tends to regard media as just another consumer product.

Edge Blending

Yet that product, unlike those created by IAC's "old media" counterparts in their skyscraping architectural embodiments, is born digital and lives its entire life in the virtual realm. It seems fitting, then, that much writing about IAC and its building highlights their apparent immateriality. Unlike the *Times* building on Park Row, whose "serious exterior of olive granite ... paralleled the somber grey pages of the newspaper," the IAC's "white glass palazzo," Goldberger (2006) says, "looks less like a building than like a computer-generated image of one" (Wallace 2007). Davidson (2007b) particularly appreciates when "[f]og and snow haze its edges and bleach its white skin whiter, so that it seems to be constantly evanescing and rematerializing." The building wavers between the material and immaterial.

Some who look closely notice slight imperfections that reveal the materiality—the physical constructedness—of this alternatively crystalline and fluid structure. In some spots, one can see the "code" behind the architectural interface. Ouroussoff (2007) notices that on the upper floors, where the "faceted [glass] geometry is more extreme," the "[j]oints don't line up perfectly; corners look patched together." In some places, where the fold of a window opening requires more than one piece of glass, "the additional mullion creates an odd, patchwork pattern. The effect," he says, "bristles with energy, as if the building were beginning to crack at the seams. It brings to mind early Gehry projects. . . . What you feel is someone struggling to make sense of something he has yet to fully grasp—the incompleteness of the creative struggle." We have seen Diller grappling with similar questions about the new media business.

Perhaps we could think of the building as a resonance structure or hologram, slipping between images of the ephemeral and material, the fluid and splintered. Inside is the world of the weightless and placeless product, but outside, the velocity and roar of passing cars on the highway and the river wind make one particularly conscious of gravity and physicality. The incongruity between the frictionless movement of information taking place inside IAC and the friction of distance—cars, boats, smog, clamor—outside might explain the building's "tentative encounter with the ground plane," its unrootedness.

The media wall in the lobby also reflects, literally, this slippage. "Those flat image walls," Davidson (2007b) writes, "are the company's *raison d'être*, since all that matters in the IAC world happens on a computer screen." McCann Systems programmed the wall's 18 sequential projectors for "edge-blending," so as to eliminate the visible bands that typically appear where adjacent projections overlap; the "point at which one projected image starts and the next takes over is barely discernible" (Hall 2007). At least that was the idea. Hall and Johnson report that there have been problems with jagged edges and glare and the cost of replacing the projector bulbs—and occasional complications in their collaborations with local universities to provide content for the wall. "The idea that IAC had indulged in this project without fully considering the conditions of the site," Hall says, "is, perhaps, an indication of the seductive power of multimedia as an architectural element." Hall is here referring to the media walls—but we might also take "this project" to mean the building itself, for, as we have seen, architecture has tremendous seductive power as an element of corporate branding or a management tool (see Martin 2005).

In attempting to "blend the edges" of old and new media and business models—and to represent that blending in architectural form—IAC calls attention to the friction between two seemingly incompatible systems and the extreme difficulty of identifying new symbols for a new political economy. New media firms of the late 1990s, Ross (2003) writes, often found themselves borrowing ill-fitting business models from other industries, including traditional media and technology, and "figuring things out as [they went]" (p. 240). While this improvisatory "pastiching" approach led to many "no collar" firms' demise, a very similar approach seems to define Diller's management of IAC. No-collar firms likewise had difficulty creating workplaces that embodied their business cultures and supported the kinds of work their employees performed; many ended up recreating the exploitative corporate working conditions that they defined themselves in opposition to. Since the dot-com bust in 2000, few new media firms have had the audacity to attempt to redefine the media workspace. The media headquarters constructed since then—Midtown's monuments for dying media behemoths—offer little in the way of spatial innovation. IAC at least exemplifies the struggle to define the identity of the new media corporation and the nature of labor in a new media economy, and to seek out their architectural embodiment.

What, Innis might ask, is the shape of this new media landscape? It seems not to be the skyscraper of the Park Row newspapers or Rockefeller Center broadcasters. Perhaps the IAC headquarters, despite—or perhaps *because of*—the incompatibility of its interior and exterior, is in fact a fitting representative of the contemporary American media company. Both crystalline and fluid, it is stuck between old and new models, unable to blend the edges between them.

References

Amelar, S. (2006), "For Its Manhattan Debut, Foster and Partners Creates the new Hearst Tower...," *Architectural Record*, August, p. 74.

Appadurai, A. (1996), *Modernity At Large: Cultural Dimensions of Globalization*, Minneapolis: University of Minnesota Press.

Balio, T. (n.d.), "Diller, Barry," Museum of Broadcast Communications. Available from: http://www.museum.tv/archives/etv/D/htmlD/dillerbarry/dillerbarry.htm [November 20, 2008].

Cameron, K. (2007), "Floor Graphics," *Metropolis*, June, p. 138.
Campbell, R. (2007), "Now for Something Completely Different," *Boston Globe*, April 29. Available from: http://www.boston.com [November 20, 2008].
Chang, J (2007), "Model timeline," *Metropolis*, June 20. Available from: http://www.metropolismag.com/cda/story.php?artid=2836 [November 20, 2008].
Colomina, B. (1994), *Privacy and Publicity: Architecture as Mass Media*, Cambridge, MA: MIT Press.
Davidson, J. (2007), "Because a Single Block in Chelsea Is Becoming an Architectural Wonderland," *New York Magazine*, December 17. Available from: http://nymag.com/news/articles/reasonstoloveny/2007/42071/ [November 20, 2008].
———(2007), "The Glass Menagerie," *Newsday*, April 15. Available from www.newsday.com [November 20, 2008].
———(2004), "Jewels on the Horizon," *Newsday*, May 2; reprinted in Wired New York Forum: Available from http://wirednewyork.com/~edward/forum/showthread.php?p=26906#post26906 [November 20, 2008].
Domosh, M. (1988), "The Symbolism of the Skyscraper: Case Studies of New York's First Tall Buildings," *Journal of Urban History*, vol. 14, no. 3, pp. 320–45.
Dovey, K. (2001), *Framing Places: Mediating Power in Built Form*, New York: Routledge.
Fung, A. (2008), "For IAC/InterActiveCorp, Breaking up Is Easy to Do," *Crain's New York Business*, August 18, p. 4.
Galloway, A. (2004), *Protocol: How Control Exists After Decentralization*, Cambridge, MA: MIT Press.
Goldberger, P (2007), "diller@gehry.nyc," *VanityFair*, June. Available from: http://www.vanityfair.com/culture/features/2007/06/diller200706 [November 20, 2008].
———(2006), "Gehry-rigged," *New Yorker,* October 16. Available from: http://www.newyorker.com/archive/2006/10/16/061016crsk_skyline [November 20, 2008].
Goldhagen, S. W. (2008), "Making Waves," *The New Republic*, February 13, pp. 32–6.
Hall, P. (2007), "Media Wall," *Metropolis*, June 20. Available from: http://www.metropolismag.com/cda/story.php?artid=2800 [November 20, 2008].
Hockenberry, J. (2007), "The 100-year Home," *Metropolis*, November 21. Available from: http://www.metropolismag.com/cda/story.php?artid=3044 [November 20, 2008].
———(2007), "Diller, Gehry, and the Glass Schooner on 18th Street," *Metropolis*, June 20. Available from http://www.metropolismag.com/cda/story.php?artid=2835 [November 20, 2008].
IAC (n.d.), "Acquisition and Divestitures Timeline." Available from: http://www.iac.com/About-IAC/Timeline [November 20, 2008].
———(n.d.), "History." Available from: http://www.iac.com/About-IAC/History/ [November 20, 2008].
———(n.d.), *The IAC Building*. Available from: http://www.iacbuilding.com/interactive/content.html [November 20, 2008].
Innis, H. A. (1991)[SM2], *The Bias of Communication*, Toronto: University of Toronto Press.
IIovine, J. (2007), "He'll Take Manhattan," *Architect's Newspaper*, April 4. Available from: http://www.archpaper.com [20 November 2008].
King, A. D. (2004), *Spaces of Global Cultures*, New York: Routledge.
Koolhaas, R. (1994/1978), *Delirious New York: A Retroactive Manifesto for Manhattan*, New York: Monacelli Press.
Lieberman, P. (2007), "Where the Wind Led Them," *Los Angeles Times*, April 25, p. E1.
Martin, R. (2007/2008), "The Crystal World" *Harvard Design Magazine* 27. Available from: http://www.gsd.harvard.edu/research/publications/hdm/back/27_Martin.html [November 20, 2008].

———(2005), *The Organizational Complex: Architecture, Media, and Corporate Space,* Cambridge, MA: MIT Press.

"Media Companies Build New Headquarters" (2002), *I Want Media,* January 2. Available from: http://www.iwantmedia.com/topmediastories2001.html [November 20, 2008].

Nocera, J. (2007), "Can Company Be as Visionary as Its Building?" *New York Times,* April 14, p. 1.

Ouroussoff, N. (2007), "Gehry's New York Debut: Subdued Tower of Light," *New York Times,* March 22. Available from: http://www.nytimes.com [November 20, 2008].

Ovide, S. (2008), "Barry Diller's Breakup," *Wall Street Journal,* October 7, p. B4.

———(2008), "Boss Talk: IAC's Barry Diller," *The Wall Street Journal Online,* October 7. Video interview. Available from: http://online.wsj.com/video/boss-talk-iac-barry-diller/ADBAEF9B-DD17-4C77-ABF3-8A1FC5DD9629.html [November 20, 2008].

Pearson, C. (2007), "IAC Headquarters" *Architectural Record,* October, pp. 112–19. Available from: Lexis Nexis.

Ross, A. (2003), *No-Collar: The Humane Workplace and Its Hidden Costs,* New York: Basic Books.

Russell, J.S. (2007), "Gehry bakes glass confection for Barry Diller's IAC in Chelsea," Bloomberg.com, April 5. Available from: http://www.bloomberg.com/apps/news?pid=email_en&refer=muse&sid=aCqCjp543Jbw [November 20, 2008].

Silver, S. (2006), "Gehry New York Debut," *Wall Street Journal,* January 11, p. B1.

Taylor, M. C. (2003), *The Moment of Complexity: Emerging Network Culture,* Chicago: University of Chicago Press.

———(2008), "Turning Forty," *Log,* vol. 13/14, pp. 7–16.

Turner, H. B. (1999), *When Giants Ruled: The Story of Park Row,* New York: Fordham University Press.

van Leeuwen, T. A. P. (1990), *The Skyward Trend of Thought: The Metaphysics of the American Skyscraper,* Cambridge, MA: MIT Press.

Venturi, R., Scott Brown, D. & Izenour, S. (1972/1998), *Learning from Las Vegas,* rev ed., Cambridge, MA: MIT Press.

Wallace, A. (2006), "A Height Deemed Appalling: Nineteenth-century New York Newspaper Buildings," *Journalism History,* vol. 31, no. 4, pp. 178–89.

———(2000), "The Architecture of News: Nineteenth Century Newspaper Buildings in New York." Ph.D. dissertation, McGill University.

Wolff, M. (2006), "Panic on 43rd Street," *Vanity Fair,* September. Available from: http://www.vanityfair.com [November 20, 2008].

Zaera-Polo, A. (2008), "The Politics of the Envelope," *Log,* vol. 13/14, pp. 191–207.

Zaloom, C. (2006), *Out of the Pits: Traders and Technology from Chicago to London,* Chicago: University of Chicago Press. .

Notes

1. Of course, throughout history, architecture has been used to exercise control and symbolize political power, authority, and economic might.
2. At the same time, we cannot reduce the building-particularly its outer shell, or "envelope"-to a representational system. In contemporary architecture, architect Alejandro Zaera-Polo (2008) argues, "the envelope has become a field where identity, security, and environmental performances interact" (p. 199). We cannot assume that the façade's only politics reside in its ability to represent its inhabitants.

3. See "Our Businesses" at www.iac.com for a current list of the company's properties.
4. The official IAC Building website presents this busy context as an asset. "Neighborhood," one of the four key sections of the Flash site, describes spaces to "inspire" (e.g., the Chelsea art galleries), "dwell" (e.g., new residential development), "walk" (e.g., the High Line), "dine" (e.g., Chelsea Market), and "play" (e.g., Chelsea Piers). The site also contains a static link for "Events," which tells one how to reserve the IAC building's lobbies for private events; we can assume that potential event hosts and the press are key audiences for this site.
5. In a small early victory, IAC successfully lobbied the Metropolitan Transit Authority to have the #14 bus stop directly across from the building on 18th Street; Johnson (November 29, 2008) said this was a great victory for workers who had to schlep three long, cold blocks from the subway when the building opened in early 2007.
6. We might also wonder if a model designed to explain a car-centric 1960s Las Vegas can be translated to explain a spatial phenomenon in twenty first-century New York. Taylor (2008) writes: "While Venturi recognized the importance of telecommunications technologies for postmodernism, he did not appreciate the significance of emerging information and networking technologies. His focus on images and superficial phenomena rather than systems and networks is more characteristic of consumer capitalism than [the] financial capitalism" of the early twenty first-century (p. 14).
7. These walls have served not only to market the company, but also to sell the building as a popular event space; the website makes it clear that event planners are a target audience.
8. On the day of my visit, however, technicians were changing some of the wall's projector bulbs (which, I was told, burn out frequently and are quite expensive to replace), and the screen's guts were spilling out into the lobby.
9. Gehry Technologies uses CATIA—Computer Aided Three Dimensional Interactive Application—a custom modification of the software used to design fighter jets, cars, and ships (another explanation for the building's nautical form?), to design its buildings.
10. The most daring elements are Pronto.com's ping pong table and Ticketweb's trampoline—both examples of "dotcom gimmicks" (Ross 2003, p. 14). The bathrooms, with their Skittles-colored tiles, are among the most vibrant spaces in the building.
11. Some reports, which note the building-wide wireless access and the "voice-over-Internet phone connections [that] follow employees wherever they are," suggest that workers would migrate fluidly throughout the building, untethered to any particular space; Johnson informed me that this is not the reality (Hockenberry 2007b; see also Ross 2003, p. 114).

CHAPTER SEVEN

Looping Ideology: The CCTV Center in Beijing

SVEN-OLOV WALLENSTEIN

Architecture, Media, and Materiality

How should we conceptualize the relation between architecture and media—between the built environment and the kind of spatial qualities that pertain to the electronic age, but also the history of media as technologies and bearers of ideology as they have evolved throughout the century, and undoubtedly in an even longer time span? The challenge would be not just to investigate the way in which architecture symbolizes the development of media on the iconic level, but also how it integrates media logics into its very tectonic and organizational structure, as well as branches out to include an urban environment that increasingly can be characterized as a mediascape.[1]

The present essay addresses this general question through a discussion of the work of Rem Koolhaas and the Office of Metropolitan Architecture (OMA), and in particular the new television center in Beijing, codesigned with Ole Scheeren, which is still under construction, and may, or may not, open at the end of 2009.[2] Writing about a work that currently only exists in part obviously poses acute methodological problems, but in this case it also highlights the issue of media and architecture: the material that will be examined consists largely of texts, statements, and images, and in this sense, it is an architectural work that for most people still exists only in a mediated form.

The imbrication of architecture and media—in the widest sense of the term that includes images and the transmission of information in general, which is a recurrent theme in Koolhaas—calls for a type of questioning and critical analysis that transcends traditional approaches that focus primarily on the formal aspects of buildings. In fact, as we will see, the criticism of such a formal perspective on architecture, both with respect to production and analysis, is a constant theme in Koolhaas's writings and projects, from the earliest texts on "Manhattanism," through the ideas of "bigness" and the "generic city," and up to the present work. As an "incubator" of new social forms, he suggests, architecture must actively approach a positive condition of formlessness that displaces perceptual wholeness and integration, and attain an intractability to formal decoding that does away with traditional legibility and esthetic analysis—although it is equally true that such a refusal of legibility in itself produces a new type of "image" quality, projected in publications and exhibitions, which is undoubtedly one of the reasons why the work of Koolhaas and the OMA has become so frequently cited also outside of architectural circles. This condition of non- or aformality, on the one hand rejecting traditional ideas of form, on the other hand approaching a kind of formal extreme, seems to be able to tell us something about our present cultural condition, not just about a particular stage in the development of design discourse, but also about our desire for an architecture that will articulate the contemporary moment in its very illegibility and contradictory qualities.

From the point of view of theoretical analysis of media structures, it has become evident that media are a way of organizing our perception of space, both in the sense that they produce a global order of the near and the far, the relevant and irrelevant, etc., into which the subject and its agency is inscribed, and that they exert a profound influence on our understanding of everyday space. The "spatial turn" within media studies (for more on this term, see the introduction to this volume) thus emphasizes location as an active creation of place, as a production of centrality by which differences in the social order (political-public vs. individual-private, corporate vs. public, public vs. restricted access, etc.) are negotiated, ranging from the individual experience in front of the television or computer screen to the way in which society as a whole is experienced and organized in terms of spectacle and participation, enjoyment and repulsion, identification and alienation.

The introduction of the architectural object into this more extended form of spatial analysis implies that it too be understood not just as an inert physical object, but as a part of a flow of information that it both reflects and attempts to control. Inserting the building into a network structure, where it is no longer solely a form that can be characterized by morphologically based concepts drawn from the history of art or architecture (is it still modernist? is it postmodernist, or something else?), nor simply a reflection of external functions, but a conduit for information, behavior, actions, and perceptions that works both by way of its material structure and the image quality that it projects, thus requires a different kind of theoretical approach. The "materiality" of architecture is in this sense only to a limited extent—sometimes approaching zero—equivalent to the matter that it contains, and the technological framing that enables matter to hold together in a certain configuration.[3]

This, I think, is the idea behind Beatriz Colomina's highly influential analysis of architecture as a "mass medium" (Colomina 1994). Drawing on close readings of buildings and plans, texts and statements, but also a rich material of images from the archives of Le Corbusier and Adolf Loos that by far surpasses the normal sources of architectural history, she theorizes the architectural object as only one part of an entire cycle of representation that aims to generate a global effect on the perceiving subject. The look of "modernity" achieved by Le Corbusier, which is also a desire, an affective response, and a structure of fantasy that mobilizes a series of unconscious investments, is a construct that requires a sophisticated rhetoric of text-image assemblages (of which Le Corbusier's books provide such striking examples, and in this they are obvious predecessors to the massive books produced by a firm like OMA). This type of access to the historical archive has considerably renewed the writing of architectural history, as can be seen in the pioneering works of Reinhold Martin (2003) and Mark Wigley (1995), the first of which addresses, the impact of cybernetics and information theory on the formation of the "organizational complex" in the postwar development of a U.S. corporate International Style, and the second how the discourse of fashion and clothing became decisive for the emergence of the white surface as the preeminently modern look in the early twentieth century.

In a certain way, this dissolution of the autonomy of the object—understood along the lines of the late modern theory of autonomy that we find in, for instance, Adorno—into an open set of cultural determinations may seem to deprive it of its status as work, and thus of its capacity to negate, resist, and make a difference in the world. Some theorists and architects, no longer arguing from the point of view of historical research, but from a standpoint closely associated with certain strands in contemporary image production in media and publicity, have suggested that this means we must take leave of an older model of critique and theory, even that the very idea of "criticality" is obsolete, and that we have to move into what is variously called the "post-critical," the "projective," the "performative," or the "instrumental."[4] The perspective outlined here will be an argument for the continued relevance of the "critical," although it surely needs to rethink many of its traditional parameters.

Such a "post-critical" stance could arguably also be derived from the fact that we—to use Edward Soja's expression (Soja 2000)—have entered into a kind of "postmetropolitan" condition where old urban forms only remain as an estheticized scenography. Here material forms are increasingly defined in relation to their communicative potentials, which are interiorized into their very fabric, and "architecture" becomes "electrotecture," as has been suggested (ANY 1993; Taylor and Saarinen 1994), a process which could be traced into the minute details of architectural production, from building materials to designer software and the virtual ubiquity of the computer, not only as a tool, but as a generative instrument in its own right. Given this type of implication of the architectural object into a larger set of parameters, which introduce themselves at the most basic physical level, what sense could there be in talking of autonomy, let alone resistance?

Today, more than a decade after these initial statements, the development seems to follow two tracks: in the first, the structure of electronic capital is interiorized into the design process itself and becomes a type of generative esthetic, and in this it is no doubt analogous to the industrial look, the machine esthetic, of early modernism, which is now being relocated on another technological plateau.[5] This is still an *esthetic*, however, with all the limitations that this implies. The second option, which I think is the proposal by Rem Koolhaas (even though he also uses metaphors and tropes from the first version, I find this less important), is to address the new form of capital on the level of urbanism. In this version, esthetics is usually repudiated in favor of politics—which, of course, is not in itself a guarantee that this does not amount to just another "estheticized" version of politics, this time transferred to the levels of infrastructures and urban systems, or that it avoids the risk of becoming another version of the technological sublime, where the marvels of engineering and computational power foreclose all critical questions. The unique quality of Koolhaas's work, I would argue, is that it indeed runs those risks, reflects upon them, and to the extent that it is successful allows us to understand why they can be neither simply avoided nor embraced. The "critical" in this sense has to do with the production of *divisions* (which is indeed the Greek root of all crisis, critique, and criticism) and conflicts in the real itself, rather than with assuming an external stance outside of the system.

The possibility of future urban forms seems to release a vast array of both utopian and dystopian energies. The most interesting cases of this are those that manage to include both of these positions, play them off against each other and generate a profound insecurity that allows us to enter into a "beyond-good-and-evil" experience—not in order to remain there, but to use this leveling or willing suspension of previous esthetic and sociocultural hierarchies as a means to grasp what is emergent instead of residual in our present. In a series of books and projects from the mid-1970s onwards, Koolhaas has ceaselessly asked the question, which to some may seem to border on the senseless, since this stance is what appears to define any intellectual responsibility *as such*, why we perceive our present, our cities and architectures, as lacking something, as imperfect. The purely affirmative option—"the Strip is almost all right," as Robert Venturi said some forty years ago at the inception of Pop Art, which indeed was another moment when a culture of media and electronic images came to disrupt the common sense of the fine arts, including architecture—seems difficult to digest, and it would be wrong to say that Koolhaas simply embraces it.[6] What he *is* saying is that we should attempt to think differently, if only for a short while, in order to see whether this could release new energies. From his ideas about "Generic Cities" to the recent work on shopping, and Asian and African urban forms, he seems obsessed with the idea of the urban as a wholly new type of experience (and in this sense he is surely pursuing a classic modernist legacy), liberated from traditional humanist, moral, and esthetic values. This does not, as I see it, constitute a simple affirmative stance, or an outright acceptance of the powers that be, but an attempt to insert a prismatic wedge into the light of the present, so that it becomes split up in several possible directions and paths; it makes it possible to think the present as an intersection of many times, pasts, and futures, and it releases an unmistakable critical and *reflexive* potentiality in the reader, precisely by suspending the kind of judgments that we normally make.

Program and Image

The CCTV center in Beijing in many ways constitutes one of the nodal works in most contemporary discussions of media and architecture: it combines a superb visibility and an iconic status with a highly complex architectural treatment of the program, and it claims to integrate the development of digital media into the structure itself, which then is assumed to project a different mode of behavior. There is no doubt a split here between the marvels of technology and engineering and a more outspoken political agenda: OMA themselves sometimes take pride in describing it as "the world's most advanced postmodern building," and on other occasions they stress the political intent, presenting the building as a possible blueprint for a more democratic and transparent society.[7]

The complex is set on a 10-hectare site in the new Central Business District (CBD) in Beijing and comprises two high-rise buildings and a service center. The main headquarters is 230 meters high, with a floor space of approximately 400,000 square meters (which makes it into the world's second largest office building, and no doubt also the most complex: all the 55 stories have individual floor plans), and is intended to house more than 10,000 employees. It contains administration, broadcasting, and various production facilities, with the intent of integrating the whole production process in a "single loop of interconnected activity" (a concept that will return in various guises throughout our discussion).[8] OMA describes it as two structures arising from a common production platform partly located underground: one dedicated to broadcasting, the other to research and education, both of which merge at the top to create a cantilevered headquarters for the management. In this sense, the building forms a loop not just in terms of program, but also in a physical sense, comprising horizontal and vertical sections whose aim is to "establish an urban site rather than point to the sky," eschewing the two-dimensionality of the "soaring tower" for a "truly 3-dimensional experience."

Fig. 1. CCTV Headquarters, Beijing. Photo by Helena Mattsson.

The loop structure is also assumed to have a behavioral impact on the employees: the adjacency of different functions produces an awareness of the coworker's activities, and it is supposed to foster a spirit of collaboration materialized in the structure of the building, inwardly as well as outwardly. The third dimension of the loop is that the building, although a high-security complex, will still allow for a path of public access that circles through the entire structure, and offers views not only of Beijing CBD, but also of the production process itself. Through glass partitions the visitors will be able to inspect the making of television, at least ideally speaking in all of its details, which will increase the sense of transparency, both in a visual and literal, and a social and metaphorical sense. As we will see, this loop is what brings together, in a contradictory unity, the program and the (still conjectural, it must be remembered) reality of the building's modus operandi: it projects the idea of transparency and openness while at the same time making legible and visible the current constraints on this idea in a double movement that I will refer to as "allegorical."[9]

The second major building, the Television Cultural Center (TVCC), is a more traditional 115,000 square meter high-rise (although designed to comprise a number of variations, ranging from the irregular façade to the hotel rooms, which all have an individual layout), and includes a five-star hotel, a visitor's center, a large public theater, and exhibition spaces. Unlike the CCTV, this second building is meant to be freely accessible to the public and has a more conventional layout. These two buildings, together with the third low-rise structure containing technical facilities, are set in the Media Park, which is intended as a landscape for public entertainment and outdoor filming areas that will form an extension of the central green axis of the CBD, all of which indicates the extent to which the complex is itself understood as a spectacle or amusement park, and forms part of a kind of "spectacularization" of media production itself (for more on this, cf. Helena Mattsson's contribution in this volume).

Fig 2. The TVCC building, partly destroyed by fire. Photo by Håkan Nilsson.

The location of the CCTV in the urban fabric of Beijing is also meant to be a decisive factor in the production of a new image of centrality. From the point of view of the symbolical geography of Beijing, it is an efficient way to forge a different Chinese identity, more oriented toward economic growth than party power, or, more precisely, a projection of the new kind of state-run capitalism that has come to characterize China today. Located on the West–East axis defined by the Chang'an avenue, and not the North–South axis of imperial power, where we find the Forbidden City and Tienanmen Men Square, the building symbolically redraws the map of Chinese power, by opposing itself to the old television center located close to the centers of political administration; built in a Soviet style in the early 1980s, the old building is a fairly anonymous high-rise, heavily guarded and allowing for no public access, and it can be taken as an epitome of all the image qualities that new leadership in China is attempting to move away from.

Fig. 3. Earthquake test model of the CCTV main building. Photo by Helena Mattsson.

On the level of imagery, the new CCTV building has a clearly iconic status (the idea of an "icon" is also embraced by OMA, who regularly use the term in their publicity), but it also functions as a political "brand" that must unite several contradictory features: the emphasis on openness and communication flows must coexist with an image of centrality and authority, above all because of the role played by CCTV as a unifying mechanism in Chinese media culture, but also as a shop window to the outside world. The iconic function also comes across in the way in which the building has already long since been used in advertising, as a symbol for a new

Chinese modernity, and for the opening up toward a global mediascape. It is often featured in cartoons and has come to form part of common jokes, where it is compared to a pair of trousers. This iconic quality can obviously also meet with negative reactions, even a sense of fear, since the building is sometimes understood as a direct image of governmental power and repression.

The role of CCTV headquarters as a window to the world is, however, just as insecure as its status in the quickly changing domestic Chinese mediascape.[10] There is at present only one English-language channel being broadcast by CCTV, and one may wonder to whom this test probe is in fact directed: not to the Chinese population, but just as little to the foreigners, who would undoubtedly choose other means to acquire information. The Chinese-language channels are mostly perceived as mouthpieces of the government and have little credibility, and especially so since the dominance of CCTV goes hand in hand with many recent attempts to thwart local media, and to integrate them in a system of central command.

Furthermore, an additional question posed to any centralized media system, and CCTV in particular, is how to enter the digital age. The current phase of growth may be seen as a way to meet the challenge of new media through expansion and diversification. This attempt is, however, not unlikely to fail, which would mean that CCTV is doomed—and that the creation of a symbolical and highly prestigious architectural gem may in fact be read as an act of desperation. Given the insecurity of the current media situation, and the role of central television in an increasingly digitalized media environment, there is a fatally ironic sense in which the building may be understood as a way of embalming the future—and in this sense it would, in a curious twist, corroborate Adolf Loos's claim, made at the beginning of the media age, and by an architect who in fact refused to partake in the modernist culture of images and representation, that the only authentic architecture is the *tomb*.

The Work of Allegory

The CCTV project picks up many formal characteristics from Koolhaas's previous works, some of which can be traced back to his earliest ideas, for instance, the degree projects at the AA, Exodus, or the Voluntary Prisoners of Architecture, and The Berlin Wall as architecture. The first and architecturally more ambitious project comprised a megastructure to be placed over the whole of central London, whose residents would then have to decide whether they would choose to live inside the structure, in a life of luxury, lacking nothing, but without the possibility of ever leaving, or outside, in a life of misery and deprivation, but with the freedom of movement. The work on the Berlin Wall, while staying within the limits of an interpretation of an already existing structure, in a similar fashion pushes us into a beyond-good-and-evil territory, in proposing a reading of the wall as a piece of sculpture.

Already in these early works we encounter a latent idea of "bigness," maybe combined with a grandiose Nietzschean immoralism,[11] a fascination for architecture as a "projective" practice, and perhaps also, at least in a germinating form, the idea of a loop or Moebius strip: a figure with two sides that run in parallel and never intersect, two separate worlds in an infinite division: inside and outside, East and West, affluent and poor, freedom and restriction. The theme of an inside and an outside that are both autonomous and joined together to form a contradictory whole has continued to be operative in Koolhaas's subsequent work, and we will see its both structural and metaphorical, or, as our term will be, "allegorical," implications for the CCTV center.

Fig. 4. Exodus, or the Voluntary Prisoners of Architecture, 1974. Courtesy of OMA.

The work that first gained Koolhaas notoriety was the book *Delirious New York*, where many of the ideas that still influence his work were first developed. Here we find a radical farewell to any ideas of a natural and "proper" urban form in the guise of a celebration of a "culture of congestion" that radically accepts and even attempts to intensify those traits in modern urban culture, which in so many of the postwar recantations of modernism appeared as its disastrous results. In an inversion of the classical idea of the manifesto, which attempts to program, project, and control a not yet existing future, Koolhaas proposes a "retroactive manifesto for Manhattan": Given that "to exist in a world totally fabricated by man, i.e. to live *inside* fantasy" is what we secretly desire, and that what fuels our imagination is a vision of a "hyperdensity" and the city as a "paradigm for the exploitation of congestion" (Koolhaas 1978, p. 10), what *would* a manifesto have looked like, which would have produced exactly this result? In this he obviously opposes, but also inverts, Le Corbusier's famous criticism of Manhattan for lacking a generating idea: the point is to find this idea *post factum*, a "*theoretical* Manhattan, a *Manhattan as conjecture*" (p. 11).

One of the founding principles of Manhattanism that Koolhaas formulates develops the inside–outside split in terms of a radical discontinuity between buildings that all negate each other and their context. This division is made possible by the grid structure, and then by a similar discontinuity inside the building itself, where an act of "lobotomy" disconnects the outside from the inside, so that the skyscraper comes to form a universe of its own in a "schizophrenic" fashion: "From now on each metropolitan lot accommodates—in theory at least—an unforeseeable and unstable combination of simultaneous activities, which makes architecture less an act of foresight than before and planning an act of only limited prediction" (p. 85). Or: "fuck the context," as he would later and somewhat graphically refer to this principle.[12]

These and many other similar early statements were at first seen as provocations, and to some extent they were; but on another level we can read them as attempts to rethink the basis of architecture, above all, the idea of the city, which has more and more become predominant in the work of Koolhaas and OMA. The grid structure of "Manhattanism" was only a transitory phenomenon—and in fact, as Koolhaas suggests, the subject of *Delirious New York* "passed into premature senility before its 'life' was completed" (Koolhaas 1978, p. 11)—or a first step in the emancipation of urbanism from the Greek *polis*, whose foundational power still haunts the imaginary of most urban planners.

In a later essay like "Generic City," which can be understood almost as a kind of cinematic fantasy,[13] a more decentered form of urbanism appears, beyond any question of historical identity, made up of simulated history, without distinctions between center and periphery, always ready to be reconstructed according to current needs, also on the level of its self-understanding. Those values that once pertained to the European city, and then to its various extensions and dialectical reversals in the United States, have here mutated into a posthistorical state: "the generic city is a city liberated from the captivity of center, from the straitjacket of identity. The Generic City breaks with this destructive cycle of dependency: it is nothing but a reflection of present need and present ability. It is a city without history" (Koolhaas 1995, p. 1251f).

In its fascination with grand scale mutations, the idea of the Generic City testifies to a profound kinship with the planning visions of the modernism of the 1920s and 1930s, from avant-garde urban theories of Russian urbanism[14] to Le Corbusier's *Ville radieuse*, although with the decisive difference that it wants to dislodge the Planner in favor of a process that integrates chance and contingency. Already in the book on New York, hyperdensity and the lobotomy of the skyscraper were meant to ensure "perpetual programmatic instability" (Koolhaas 1978, p. 87), and later, in relation to the project for the Eurolille terminal, Koolhaas speaks of a "dynamique d'enfer"[15] that replaces overview with a process that inevitably links parts together into a new kind of aleatory unity that can only be surveyed and controlled at a meta-level.

The brief programmatic statements on planning and the generic city from the mid-1990s then coalesced into major research projects at Harvard, which have resulted in several publications dealing with emerging urban forms in Asia and Africa, as well as forays into the world of shopping. These investigations may seem unrelated and even opposed, and yet they should no doubt be understood as derived from a central issue, which is the question of how we should conceptualize the urban form of the future without nostalgia.

The point here is that these theoretical investigations into large-scale urban structures have their parallel in singular projects that attempt to articulate them in individual objects, and one way to approach the CCTV project would be to see it as such a point of crystallization between different lines of research. Here I will just briefly mention two earlier projects, both from 1989, where we can see the ideas germinating that would eventually come to the fore in the CCTV headquarters.

In the project for the new National Library in Paris, Koolhaas addresses the issue of how to conceive of a building whose main role is to contain and transmit information, and which in a certain way encloses a whole world within itself. The concrete question of how we can rethink the idea of a library in the present of course resounds with the CCTV project, and the technological transformations since 1989 have indeed only sharpened the problem.[16]

The first answer in the Paris library was to understand the rooms in the building as empty spaces hollowed out of a dense cube comprised of information, and then to work with a high degree of "cross-programming" that would render the traditional divisions of labor within the library insecure and unstable. The rooms hang like suspended organs within the translucent cube, while they at the same time may be described as voids: "In this block," Koolhaas says, "the major public spaces are defined as absences of building, voids carved out from the information solid.

Floating in memory, they are like multiple embryos, each with their own technological placenta" (Koolhaas 1995, p. 616).

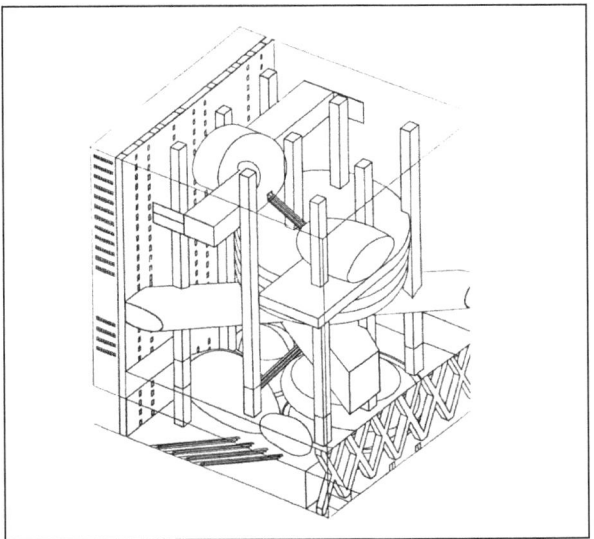

Fig. 5. National Library of France, Paris, axonometric. Courtesy of OMA.

As Fredric Jameson suggests, the emphasis on formal nonlegibility (the "block" that contains all the interior organs seems to lack specificity) may be seen as a typical attempt to evade esthetic perception, just as it opposes Le Corbusier's idea of the outside as an expression of an inner organization and instead proposes an idea of "incommensurability."[17] But the condition of "non-" or "aformality" here also results from the program itself, or rather from the impossibility of defining and circumscribing the program: the information solid (the image of the network was here only on the horizon, and it would undoubtedly have modified the spatial schema: depicting information as a "solid" today appears counterintuitive) only allows for embryonic spaces that do not come together into a structural totality.

Something similar takes place in the Seebrügge Sea Terminal project, which, as Jameson notes, even further highlights the quality of a "container" and the coexistence of radically discontinuous activities. Heterogeneity may be too weak a word to capture what is happening here, Jameson suggests, since the coexistence created here implies a "radical absence of ground" (Jameson 1994, p. 139), a new groundlessness that begins to produce a category of its own, opposed to the schema of totality vs. part, and instead must be understood in terms of "replication" (p. 140), i.e., a way to interiorize the split between object and urban fabric that was characteristic of modernism.

The CCTV project inserts these themes—producing and maintaining divisions and yet allowing for an overlap of previously compartmentalized functions—into a new and highly charged ideological context, where the formal layout of the building constitutes a complex allegory of the role of media in contemporary China, but also, and on a more general level, the role of media in the culture of current capitalism.

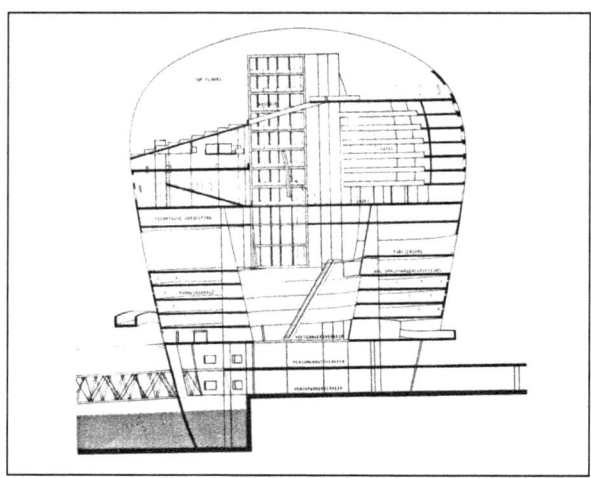

Fig. 6. Sea Trade Center, Seebrügge, section through the terminal building. Courtesy of OMA.

The headquarters under construction at present is in fact the second of two proposals: the first, a traditional *hudong* structure, was rejected, and the second one claims to incorporate the first, and to project the traditional labyrinthine low-rise building into a new spatial configuration. Both of these proposals were directed against the idea of the skyscraper, which, as we have noted, was a recurrent typological idea in Koolhaas's and OMA's previous theories, from the "lobotomy" and "culture of congestion" celebrated in the late 1970s, to the idea of the high-rise as the "only remaining typology" in the mid-1990s, as is claimed in the essay on the Generic City. Instead, we are now faced with what OMA on their official Web site baptize the "tragedy of the skyscraper"—today, they suggest, this typology is caught up in a pointless "race for ultimate height" that can only be lost as time goes on, and although it claims to mark the place as significant, it produces repetitive banality, and is unable to act as "incubators of new cultures, programs, and ways of life." The location of the CCTV center at the heart of new Beijing CBD, replete with highrise buildings, makes this statement more significant; many comments, also critical ones, have been made about the grand scale of the building, which is probably an effect of the way it is presented on Web sites and in publicity, as a kind of luminous icon dominating its surroundings. Seen in its actual urban context, it appears neither overbearing nor grandiose—it actively challenges and attempts to deal with the chaotic surroundings of the CBD, but does not attempt to exercise any power of domination.

But if the earlier praise of the skyscraper is now rejected, the idea of the container-building as a city of its own remains, as a transformed "bigness" and a renewed emphasis on iconicity. This iconic quality is longer achieved through phallic erection, but through a pliant form, which we might understand as a collapsed skyscraper, or a structure that refers back to traditional *hudong* typologies, although it must in the end obviously be seen as something new, also in the sense in which it organizes what I here have called an allegorical operation.

The essential structure of the building, and that which establishes both its outer form as well as the organizational structure, is the loop. As we have seen, this loop has three senses: the *first* is the physical layout of the building itself, which loops around itself or forms a kind of knot; the *second* is the production process as a "loop of interconnected activity"; the *third*, and for my proposal most essential aspect, is the loop as a continuous transparency implemented in the structure of the building, a Moebius strip that allows one public trajectory through the edifice to coexist with a closed and sealed-off trajectory for the employees, thus creating a continual sense of public space and communication while at the same time marking the division by impenetrable glass partitions.

In this way, production and consumption of media remain separate, and yet they are united in the structure of a building that itself claims to constitute a common space as a kind of "spectacle," or a viewing machine that produces the sense of a political unity while at the same time prohibiting it at every level.

My proposal is that the CCTV project can be read as an allegory of this imbrication of openness and closure, and in this way it can be said to already display and unmask its own ideological operation. The work of Koolhaas is in this sense not so much *beyond* good or evil (a position that he, as we have seen, often seems to assume, as in his oft-cited statements about the necessity for architecture to ride the crest of the wave, the necessarily "uncritical" stance that must be assumed for there to be any architectural creation at all, or the creation of a "dynamique d'enfer" that empties out the subjectivity of the architect) as it is *both* good and evil in an inextricable double-bind: it carries out the task of projecting an image of openness while at the same time rendering physically legible the current constraints on this promise; it displays its own symptom in its very structure, and perhaps it can even be said to "enjoy" its symptom, in the sense that the particular joy that it produces is always and necessarily entwined with fear, violence, and repression, also in a political sense.[18]

We should also note a difference in communicative strategy. In their various public appearances, OMA tends to emphasize different things in the West and in China, in the sense that the idea of openness may be directed to Western intellectuals, whereas in China the technical complexity and the sophisticated engineering solutions are highlighted. While undoubtedly an effect of the different intellectual and ideological contexts of Chinese politics and a Western audience of architecture critics and intellectuals, this can also be taken as symptomatic of a split in the role of the architect, of which Koolhaas can be taken as the paradigmatic case at the present moment: is he a provider of high-tech solutions that in the end must accommodate themselves to the political order,[19] or a producer of political or social visions that may have the capacity to challenge this very order? On the one hand, the complex publicity maneuvers of the OMA testify to the delicacy of these issues and to the limitations of architectural work. But on the other hand, the materialization of ideology is also the becoming-physical of its contradictions, which allow us to read the work precisely as a *work* in the emphatic sense, in the same way that we read other works of art not just as passive reflections of an existing order, but also as interventions, resistance, and transformation.

The work of Koolhaas has been labeled as "postcontemporary" (Jameson 1994), and maybe this term (which in Jameson's case seems to displace the idea of the "postmodern" in a somewhat obscure manner) can provide us with a clue to the reading of this strange work that is the CCTV headquarters. In a certain sense, it remains sealed in the contradictions of the present moment, but it also points to a future that it projects, but also *embalms* already in advance, and in this sense it constitutes a point of intersection between different times and histories, between ideological masking and unmasking, which is what I have here attempted to grasp in the term "allegory." It makes our present readable precisely by staging the conflicts inherent in any attempt to grasp it.

Fig. 7. CCTV Headquarters, detail. Photo by Helena Mattsson.

References

Althusser, L. (1997), *Sur la reproduction*, Paris: PUF.
ANY (1993), Theme Issue: Electrotecture: Architecture and the Electronic Future. No. 3.
Baird, G. (2005), "Criticality and Its Discontents," *Harvard Design Magazine*, No. 21.
Calderón, O., Calderón, C., and Dorsey, P., (eds.) (2004), *Beyond Form: Architecture and Art in the Space of Media*, New York: Lusitania Press.
Colomina, B. (1994), *Privacy and Publicity: Modern Architecture as Mass Media*, Cambridge, MA: MIT Press.
Foucault, M. (1970), *L'ordre du discours*, Paris: Gallimard.
Jameson, F. (1994), *The Seeds of Time*, New York: Columbia University Press.
Koolhaas, R., and Oorthuys, G. (1974), "Ivan Leonidov's Dom Narkomtjazjprom, Moscow," *Oppositions* 2.
Koolhaas, R., and Whiting, S. (1997), "Spot Check: A Conversation Between Rem Koolhaas and Sara Whiting," *Assemblage*, No. 40.
Koolhaas, R. 1994 (1978), *Delirious New York: A Retroactive Manifesto for Manhattan*, New York: Monacelli Press.
Koolhaas, R. (2000), *Mutations: Rem Koolhaas Harvard Project on the City*, Barcelona: Actar.
Koolhaas, R. (2001), *Harvard Design School Guide to Shopping*, Cologne: Taschen.
Koolhaas, R. OMA (1995), *S, M, L, XL*, New York: Monacelli.
Koolhaas, R. (2004), *Content*, Cologne: Taschen.
Kostka, A., and Wolfarth, I. (eds.) (1990), *Nietzsche and "An Architecture of Our Minds,"* Santa Monica: Getty Institute.
Lootsma, B., and Rijken, D. (1999), *Media and Architecture*, Amsterdam: Berlage Institute.
Lucan, Jacques (ed.) (1991), *Rem Koolhaas—OMA: Architecture 1970–1990*, New York: Princeton Architectural Press. .
Lynn, G. (1998), *Folds, Bodies & Blobs*, Brussels: La lettre volée.
Lynn, G. (1995), "Forms of Expression: The Proto-Functional Potential of Diagrams in Architectural Design," *El Croquis* 72.
Mattern, S (2008), "Broadcasting Space," *International Journal of Communication* 2.
Martin, R. (2003), The Organizational Complex: Architecture, Media, and Corporate Space, Cambridge, MA: MIT Press.
McQuire, S. (2008), *Media City: Media, Architecture and Urban Space*, Thousand Oaks: Sage. .
Nesbitt, K. (ed.) (1996), *Theorizing a New Agenda for Architecture: An Anthology of Architectural Theory, 1965–1995*, New York: Princeton Architectural Press.
Neumeyer, F. (2001), *Der Klang der Steine. Nietzsches Architekturen*, Berlin: Gebr. Mann.
Rajchman, J. (1994), "Thinking Big," interview with Rem Koolhaas, Artforum, December.
Rattenbury, K. (ed.) (2002), *This Is Not Architecture: Media Constructions*, New York: Routledge.
Saunders, W. S. (1997), "Rem Koolhaas's Writings on Cities: Poetic Perception and Gnomic Fantasy," *Journal of Architectural Education*, Vol. 51, No. 1.
Schwarzer, M. (2004), *Zoomscape: Architecture in Motion and Media*, New York: Princeton Architectural Press.
Scott-Brown, D. (1971), "Learning from Pop," *Casabella* December, 359-360.
Somol, R., and Whiting, S. (2002), "Notes Around the Doppler Effect and Other Moods of Modernism," *Perspecta 33: The Yale Architectural Journal*.
Speaks, M. (2002), "Design Intelligence and the New Economy," *Architectural Record*, January 2002.

Taylor, M., and Saarinen, E. (1994), *Imagologies: Media Philosophy*, London and New York: Routledge.
Vidler, A. (1993), "Books in Space: Tradition and Transparency in the Bibliothèque de France," *Representations* 42.
Wallenstein, S-O. (2008), *The Silences of Mies*. Stockholm: Axl Books.
Wigley, M. (1995), *White Walls, Designer Dresses, The Fashioning of Modern Architecture*, Cambridge, MA: MIT Press.
Zhengrong, H. (2005), "Towards the Public? The Dilemma in Chinese Media Policy Change and Its Influential Factors," Research Paper, John F. Kennedy School of Government, Harvard University.
Žižek, S. (1992), *Enjoy Your Symptom!: Jacques Lacan in Hollywood and Out*, New York: Routledge.

Notes

1. Pioneering efforts in this area have been in the last decade and a half by, among others, Colomina (1994), Mitchell (1995), Lootsma and Rijken (1999), Martin (2002), Rattenbury (ed. 2002), Schwarzer (2004), Calderón, Calderón, and Peter Dorsey (eds. 2004), McQuire (2008), to name but a few.
2. During a visit in Beijing in November 2008, the author and the author of chapter 8, Helena Mattsson, were generously granted access to the building site. The outer shells of the buildings were at the time in principle ready, while the floors and interiors, i.e., most of those aspects belonging to the organizational logic that the present essay addresses, were still under construction. Since then the one of the three buildings in the complex, the TVCC, has been partly devastated by fire, which undoubtedly means the official opening will be even further postponed.
3. The idea of "materialism" introduced here is derived from Althusser and Foucault, who I think converge at least on this point. See Althusser (1995) and Foucault (1970). I am fully aware that this use of "materialism" would require a much more elaborate philosophical argument, which I hope to be able to develop elsewhere.
4. The idea of a "post-critical" turn has recently been advocated by Michael Speaks in several essays, see, for instance, Speaks (2002). For the idea of a "projective" practice, see Somol and Whiting (2002). For a general survey of the discussion, see George Baird (2005). The reference to Koolhaas is explicit in Somol and Whiting, who discuss his Downtown Athletic Club, New York, in terms of a "projective architecture." The argument developed in the present essay may be read as continuation of my discussion of the possibility of a transformed critical theory in Wallenstein (2008).
5. The key theorist in this development was for a long time Greg Lynn, whose writings and projects were instrumental in developing a new kind of morphogenetic aesthetic. Lynn was also significantly enough the first, at least to my knowledge, to introduce Deleuze in a more productive fashion in the debate on architecture (see Lynn 1998). To some extent this was also an emphasis on form as non-semantic, and as expression of a kind of technological design expertise; for Koolhaas's response to this, see Koolhaas and Whiting 1997.
6 . For Koolhaas's relation to Venturi, see Koolhaas (2001, pp. 590-617). The impact of a new medium like video on architecture was noted early on by Denise Scott-Brown (see Scott-Brown (1971, in Nesbitt 1996), one of the coauthors (together with Venturi and Steven Izenour) of the path-breaking *Learning from Las Vegas* (1972), which has been called the "manifesto for the newly emerging 'cultural studies'" (Jameson 1994, p. 141), but which is also a book that in a certain way begins to register a cinematic impact on architecture in terms of moving images: Las Vegas

should ideally speaking be seen from a car window, and almost all of the photographs in the book are produced in this fashion.
7. "We are engaged," Koolhaas says, "with an effort to support within [China's] current situation the forces that we think are progressive and well-intentioned . . . We've given them a building that will allow them to mutate." *Time Asia*, May 2, 2204: http://www.time.com/time/asia/covers/501040503/story2.html. To some extent the split between these two agendas is due to the context of presentation, as we will see, but it also corresponds to a deeper problem lodged within architectural practice and theory as such. This problem is obviously not particular to Koolhaas, although his projects tend to make it acutely visible in a reflexive form, which is why he becomes an easy target for criticism, but also the reason why, as the present essay argues, his work indeed constitutes works in a qualified sense, and calls upon, even demands, a response not just from within the architectural profession.
8. These and the following quotes relating to the CCTV project are all taken from one of OMA's official Websites: http://www.oma.eu/index.php?option=com_projects&view=portal&id=55&Itemid=10, last accessed January 22, 2009. The same text, with small variations, can be found in Koolhaas (2004).
9. My proposal here intersects with the analysis already developed in Mattern (2008), from which I have drawn many valuable insights. My accent, however, falls slightly differently; for Mattern, the fact that the building embodies contradictions runs "contrary to the designer's claims" (p. 869); in my reading, the point is that the embodiment, even exacerbation, of such contradictions has been part of Koolhaas's different projects from the outset. The strategically planned introjection of social conflicts is, I would argue, what makes it possible for them to achieve the status of "works" in a qualified sense, and this is what warrants my understanding of them as allegorical.
10. On the current politics of the Chinese media system, see Zhengrong Hu (2005).
11. The beyond-good-and-evil perspective often adopted by Koolhaas may have a background in Nietzsche, although he is to my knowledge never mentioned in Koolhaas's writings. This connection may seem tenuous, but in fact Nietzsche's writings had a profound influence on many of the early modernists (Le Corbusier, Behrens, Mies, etc.), for whose large-scale projects Koolhaas shows a great sympathy; he may even be said to be one of the few to continue modernism with other means, in the transformed sociopolitical space of a globalized postmodern capitalism. For Nietzsche's influence on early modernism, see Kostka and Wolfarth (1999) and Neumeyer (2001). For a critical discussion of Koolhaas's writings on urbanism as an attempt to retrieve a Nietzschean position, see Saunders (1997).
12. See the chapter on "Bigness" in Koolhaas (1995), and the interview with John Rajchman (1994).
13. See, for instance, the final sections in "Generic City," which are shot through with sexual imagery (Koolhaas 1995, pp. 1263-64). It is perhaps not entirely coincidental that Koolhaas, before embarking on a career as an architect, attended film school and co-wrote *The White Slave*, a 1969 Dutch film noir, and subsequently wrote a script for legendary soft-porn director Russ Meyer.
14. The project that first took Koolhaas to New York in the 1970s and the Institute of Architecture and Urban Studies led by Peter Eisenman, and eventually led to the publication of *Delirious New York*, was the writing of a thesis on Russian constructivism and Ivan Leonidov. Parts of this material were eventually published as an essay in *Oppositions* (Koolhaas 1974).
15. The phrase was coined in a lecture entitled "Beyond Delirious," where Koolhaas reflects on different ways to organize the planning process, and proposes "a dynamic from hell, which is so relentlessly complex that all the partners are involved in it like prisoners chained to each other so that nobody would be able to escape" (reprinted in Nesbit 1995, p. 336).

16. Already in 1989, Koolhaas writes: "At the moment when the electronics revolution seems about to melt all that is solid—to eliminate all necessity for concentration and physical embodiment—it seems absurd to imagine the ultimate library" (Koolhaas 1995, p. 606). For a discussion of the other entries in the competition (which was won by Dominique Perrault), see Vidler (1993). As Vidler notes, "Koolhaas' mistake was to configure information under the sign of translucency and shadowy obscurity; the politics of the moment insisted, and still insist, on the illusion that light and enlightenment, transparency and openness, permeability and social democracy are not only symbolized but also effected by glass" (p. 131f). As we will see, the play with transparency in the CCTV center takes this idea one step further, and shows how transparency as such can be a means of hiding, and how visibility can become a means of obscuring.
17. In his discussion of Koolhaas, Fredric Jameson (1994, p. 135) points to the analogy between Le Corbusier's idea and what Althusser in a rather different context called "expressive causality," i.e., the conception of society as a totality that expresses itself in all of its minute details and all of its levels, against which Althusser pits the theory of a "structural causality" that allows each level to have a semi-independence, while still hanging on to the idea of a determination in the final instance.
18. My appropriation of Žižek's (1992) book title does not imply that I here would attempt to establish any more precise correlation between his Lacanian theory of cinematic visuality and the reading of Koolhaas, although there are undoubtedly points of contact.
19. A significant amount of criticism has been leveled against the building from the point of view of engineering, most vocally in a speech at Harvard University in March 2008 by Alfred Peng, who can be seen as representative of a more traditionally "official" view of architecture. This stress on technological efficiency also comes across in Peng's statement that the architect has no responsibility for the organization of the building in terms of social structures (interview conducted by Helena Mattsson and the author in Beijing in November, 2008). The source of this conflict is obviously two wholly different ideals of the architect, where Peng and OMA can be located at the extremes of the spectrum.

CHAPTER EIGHT

Real TV: Architecture as Social Media

HELENA MATTSSON

Two months after the Olympic Games, I found myself in the Beijing Central Business District (CBD), where one of today's most spectacular buildings is being completed—the headquarters of China Central Television (CCTV), designed by Rem Koolhaas and Ole Scheeren of Office for Metropolitan Architecture (OMA). Together with one of the engineers from CCTV, Liu Ning, I strolled across the building site in the direction of what will become the entrance to a building that in the local vernacular has been nicknamed as "the trouser legs." This icon was to have been completed by the time of the Beijing 2008 Olympic Games, which meant that its silhouette would have been shown on television screens throughout the world. Walking through the construction site four months later, that time line seemed to be only a utopian possibility. We passed through what is planned to be a media park—both an urban public space and a non–public production facility, described by the architects as a "landscape of public entertainment." On the right hand side there was what the architect's drawings call the "Service Building," at present the only part completed, but in fact more or less ignored in OMA's descriptions of the facility. This building was in fact used for broadcasting during the Olympics, although at the time, it too remained invisible.

The gap between the media images of the project and its physical reality becomes obvious on location. I was overcome by a sense of emptiness but also a feeling of euphoria in the presence of a site where image and reality are combined to form an "impossible" world. This impossible correlation between two worlds, the physical and the mediated, is a central issue in architecture, and a crucial tool in the way it is practiced. The mediated image is not a "true representation" of material structure; instead it most often seeks to convey a particular message of atmosphere that transcends the facts—it is more like a fantasy of a world that never was, and never will be. It is a mediated dream tapping into the power of collective desires.

Fig. 1. The CCTV building site. Photo: Helena Mattsson.

That which our current situation appears to dismiss or at least render doubtful is in a certain way resuscitated in architecture, which could be seen as compensation for the gaps and losses in the real world. When media become increasingly fragmented and compartmentalized in a global culture industry, media organizations like CCTV or the BBC construct media edifices that project the idea of a focused and centralized organism. When public space shrinks and loses its status, it is restaged with architecture and reemerges "inside" new projects. In direct proportion to the increasing invisibility and opacity of the process of production and consumption in a global economy, a process that applies to other forms of "manufacturing" as well, production is opened up and becomes a spectacle through techniques of architectural transparency. And finally, when the boundary between fiction and reality becomes more and more blurred, the architecture of these new media centers appeals to the audience to establish them once again.

We turned to the left on Road 8, presently under construction. This street will align with the Ceremonial Plaza, the public space in front of the spectacular central headquarters. The CCTV building's exterior is completed, and already it is a significant landmark in the Beijing cityscape. I had hoped to enter the building, but when I approached the entrance and looked into a maze of scaffolding and welding flames, sheets, and concrete steel, I realized that this was not possible. I asked Liu Ning about one of the most spectacular and, at least in the West, most talked about features of the building, the public loop. In OMA's own descriptions, the audience will have access to this high-security building through "the 'loop', a dedicated path circulating through the building and connecting to all elements of the program..." (OMA 2004, p. 489). When I tried to locate the beginning of the loop according to the plans, Ning looked at me in disbelief, and said that he knew of no such thing. To him, it was highly unlikely that CCTV would be open to the public, with the exception of the recording of the occasional entertainment program or talk show. Later on, I would acknowledge that Liu Ning is by no means the only one who is unaware of this part of the plan.[1]

Fig. 2. The CCTV building site, Ceremonial Plaza, and the beginning of the loop.
Photo: Helena Mattsson.

The insecure status of the CCTV public loop points to the ambiguous and controversial sense of concepts like *publicity* and *transparency*, on the one hand, as energizing fantasies of a more open society, and on the other hand, of a society of increasing control. By introducing a public space into what is normally a closed structure, the organization is opened up and the internal parts of the machinery are laid out for public inspection. This is almost an exhibitionist display that estheticizes everyday life and work by "exhibiting" it as entertainment in a fictitious public space. Through this process of exposure the work itself becomes a commodity to be consumed. This *commodification of the production process* can also be found in other media complexes as well, for instance, in the BBC's new London headquarters, Broadcasting House.

Just as my personal experience of CCTV "live," "on location," was formed by the merging of image and reality, fact and fiction, into a new reality, so the public spaces created by media institutions will generate a similar experience in the audience. My proposal is that the experience of media production "on location" will intensify and render the exchange between fiction and reality even more complex, in a way that could be understood in terms of double bind (cf. Bateson 1965), or a place where limits are established at the same time as they are crossed (Couldry 2003, pp. 76–77).

The two cases compared here will be the CCTV headquarters in Beijing (OMA/Rem Koolhaas/Ole Scheeren) and the BBC headquarters (MacCormac, Jamieson Pritchard Architects). Both of these buildings—or rather their representations as images, drawings, and texts—display a desire to expose their own machinery that could almost be called "exhibitionistic." The questions addressed in this essay are: What kind of power relations are set up in these transparent spaces and how do they construe the relation between audience and media? How is transparency used as a marketing technique and as a way to generate public experience? I will attempt to chart these spaces by looking at them from five different angles (that indeed also overlap): the idea of a staged public space, the experience economy and brandscapes, the commodification of the production process, the exchange between fiction and reality, and finally how architecture can be said to function as a medium.[2]

Staged Public Space: The BBC

At the same time as the idea of the media as a transparent public space and as a "center" of society is increasingly questioned (Couldry 2003), both CCTV and the BBC are investing large amounts of capital in architectures that project the idea of transparent public spaces where audiences can participate. These spaces could be likened to experience zones, where events and activities are programmed and staged in different ways. The two-dimensional sign of the facade is replaced by the three-dimensional space of events. What is at stake is not so much a visual communication as the possibility to experience media. In an analogy to the dissolution of the boundary between fact and fiction—between documentary and drama documentary, and between news and reality TV—different types of physical boundaries are set up that renegotiate the relation between broadcasting and nonbroadcasting.

The original BBC Broadcasting House from 1932 (designed by Colonel G. Val Myer) was built for radio transmissions. The building is a closed monument with a decorated shell that provides an outside screen. The division between the street outside and the interior of the institution is clearly marked, and the massive door at the entrance sets up a threshold between producers and consumers. In the film *Death at Broadcasting House* we see one of the radio celebrities from the 1930s opening the gates and entering the closed world of the BBC.[3] After having been on air, he leaves the building through the same gate and plunges into an ocean of autograph hunters, as if to highlight the duality between the two worlds.

Fig. 3. The BBC Broadcasting House shortly after completion in 1932. Photo: BBC Photo Library.

The new BBC complex consists of the main bodies connected to each other and the old building by transparent façade screens. (See Fig. 20 in Chapter 2, p. 46.)

Instead of being a screened-off facility for production, the new structure is open, and by setting up a new exterior space, Langham Place, which flows into the building, it creates an in-between *event zone* with activities like restaurants and shops, but one which is also intended to house temporary events.

> For the public, the focus of MJP's development will be the public space in Langham Street, the area scooped out between the prow of the original BH and its new counterpart on the Egton House site. Plans are afoot to use this outdoor arena for public events, such as theatre and dance, as well as debates and concerts. There are ambitious ideas for a public art programme at BH, much of which will focus on this arena and will attract the public and give them another reason to walk up Oxford Circus. (Jackson 2003, p. 58)

This public space is meant to serve as a stage for the BBC, with a display of "public art" to attract audiences and a way to broadcast "live" on stage. From within the organization, the hope is that BBC and Langham Place will become an important part in city life, similar to the Regent Street Festival, "and also become the focus for the street's famous Christmas lights" (Jackson 2003, p. 58). Via programs like The Radio Theatre Café and the BBC shop on Langham Place, different commercial activities are to become part of an expanding space of experiences.

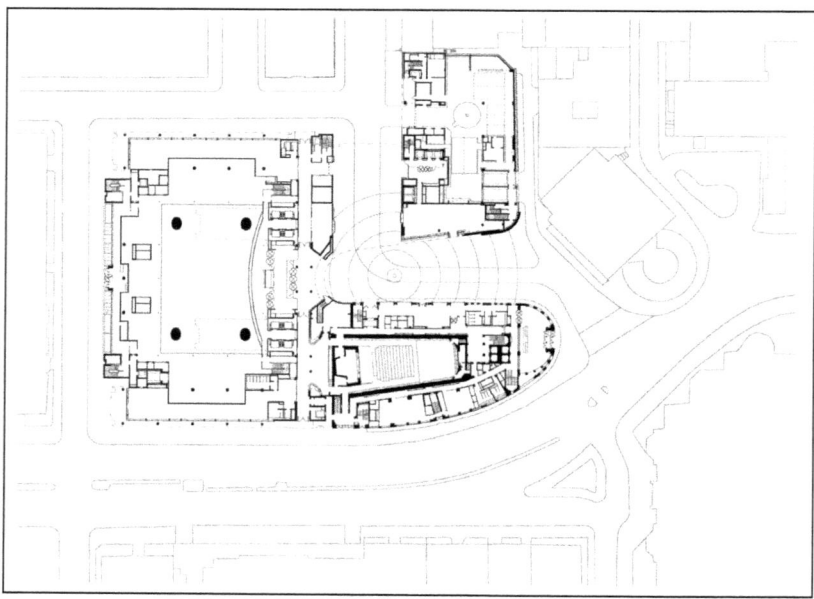

Fig. 4. The new BBC site plan. Drawing courtesy by MacCormac Jamieson Prichard.

The public space will be enhanced through an arcade that runs from Portland Place to Hallam Street and provides an opportunity for the public to gain access to the building without passing security controls. The public arcade will serve as a foyer for the Radio Theatre and other public facilities such as cafés, exhibition venues, and shops. In mixing functions and allowing public space to enter into the space of media production, the earlier clear demarcations between city space and interior, private, and public are rendered more fluent. At the same time as the BBC connects closer to its audiences by techniques such as entertainment, information, do-it-yourself activities, and shopping, a space is set up in the city with certain public qualities, seemingly open for all. This satisfies two parties: the BBC acquires a platform for the production of an audience and the city gets a new public space. As the architects claim:

> We are working with the BBC to contribute to this part of London by creating a major new public space outside the building that will open the organization's relationship with its audiences. (www.mjparchitects.co.uk)

The BBC not only offers an exterior public space and a public arcade to the city, but they also want a unique opportunity to display their products in the making. Langham Place is connected to the arcade, which in turn is visually connected to the production facilities via transparent surfaces. The public may enter the newsroom visually, if not physically.

> The BBC is a creative organization, the product of which is television and radio programmes. But unlike conventional "manufacturers", it is not usually possible to see the process by which the product is made. Efforts are being made in all the new buildings to show visitors studio spaces and dispel much of the mystery of the BBC. What it will never be able to show is the thinking process—the hours of debate and discussion that go into each episode of every television or radio series. (Jackson 2003, p. 64)

The boundary between audience and production is transgressed through architectural means, while it is simultaneously made clear that certain partitions remain inviolable—just as the process of thought itself can never be made transparent. This creates a kind of architectural double bind: on the one hand, crossing the line is permitted, even encouraged; on the other hand, it remains only an ideal possibility and never a real option, all of which produces an entangled constellation of fiction and reality.

Staged Public Space: CCTV

A similar strategic use of public space as a link between audiences and media, and a technique for generating a spatially and ideologically tense concept of "public relations," can be found in the CCTV. The current headquarters has separated broadcasting from production, and the tower dedicated to the former is a public access building marketed as tourist attraction:

As a whole, the Central Television Tower is a modern and advanced structure with comprehensive functions like transmitting radio signals and TV programs, tourism, restaurant and recreation. (www.ctvt.com.cn/english/about.asp)

Production, takes places in this case in the closed environment of an anonymous high-rise surrounded by fences and guards, and the public is prevented from even entering into physical contact with the building.[4] Displaying a generic façade, this high-rise building communicates its presence to the city as an object (landmark) and not as an ornamented surface, as in the case of the BBC. What we encounter is more like a security zone, and it is only at a distance that the building conveys a message different than the mere prohibition of close contact.

Fig. 5. A guard in front of the existing CCTV. Photo by Helena Mattsson.

The city of Beijing is traditionally seen as comprising two axes, the east–west axis of the "people" and the north–south axis of "power." The new CCTV headquarters is located at the far end of the popular axis; far from the centers of political administration to the CBD, which obviously can be taken as a sign of a new orientation toward the market economy. The new site originally comprised four lots with two intersecting main roads.

REAL TV: ARCHITECTURE AS SOCIAL MEDIA | 191

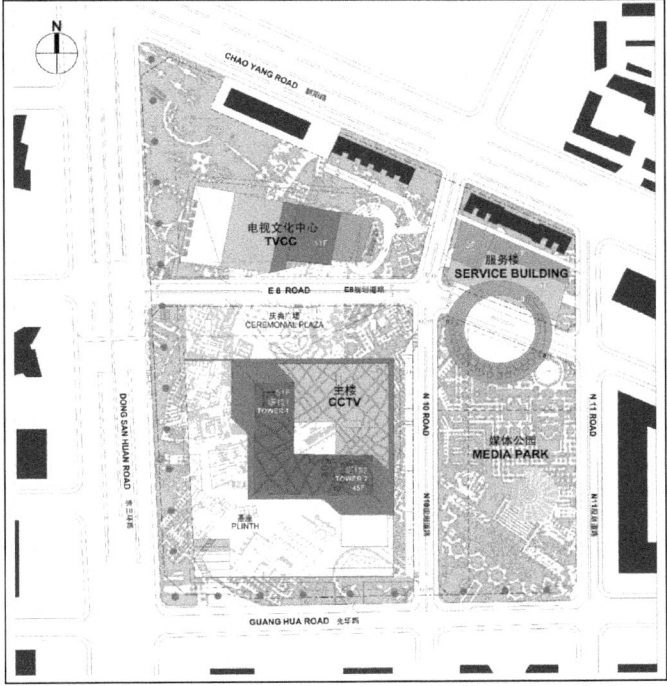

Fig. 6. The new CCTV site plan. Drawing courtesy of OMA.

The new CCTV complex will contain all the facets of television production, while the opposite tower (TVCC) is a wholly public building with restaurants, a hotel, and a theater; the third structure is the rather anonymous service building.[5] The site will be open to the public, with a media park conceived as an extension of the green areas planned in the CBD:

> ... the Media Park is conceived as an extension of the proposed green axes of the CBD. It is open to the public for events and entertainment, or closed, so that it can be used for outdoor filming. (OMA 2004, p. 486)

This public space can, however, at the discretion of CCTV and at any time, be shut off and turned into private property, disconnecting the roads formerly integrated into the urban grid from the rest of the city. In this way, we can speak of a temporary staging of public space on private land. The space connecting the CCTV and TVCC, "Ceremonial Plaza," could be described as a staged public space and is marked by an intricately worked paved area. From here the public can move either into the foyer of TVCC or into the CCTV loop, both of which cut through the media production and expose CCTV as a workplace.

> CCTV combines administration and offices, news and broadcasting, program production and services—the entire process of TV-making—in a loop of interconnected activities. Two structures rise from a common production platform that is underground. Each has a different character: one is dedicated to broadcasting, the second to service, research and education: they join at the top to create a cantilevered penthouse for the management. A new icon is formed ... not the predictable 2-dimensional tower "soaring" skyward, but truly 3-dimensional experience, a canopy that symbolically embraces the entire population ... an instant icon that proclaims a new phase in Chinese confidence. (OMA 2004, p. 289)

The building is not so much a two-dimensional visual sign, but, as OMA proposes, should be approached as a three-dimensional experience that addresses the audience in a manifold number of ways. The idea of public access is perhaps the most efficient way to achieve this type of multisensorial address:

> Public visitors will be admitted to the "loop," a dedicated path circulating through the building and connecting to all elements of the program and offering spectacular views across the multiple facades towards the CBD, Beijing, and the Forbidden City. (OMA 2004, p. 489)

According to the plans, the core of the building will be a spatial setting that offers the audience a multitude of experiences, ranging from the sight of programs actually being produced, the purchasing of souvenirs and other paraphernalia, through to the stunning vistas of the surrounding CBD and Beijing cityscape. The activities in the loop are laid out sequentially as follows: ticket office, security gate, snack bar, studio viewing, media wall, merchandizing, studio viewing, information, merchandizing, studio viewing, panorama viewing, museum, restaurant, back to the snack bar and entrance.

Public space has become increasingly difficult to define, both as an immaterial entity and as a physical space, and together with this, the division between public and private seems less certain than ever. In a discussion with Sara Whiting, Rem Koolhaas suggested that today's cities are undergoing a revolution where public space is lost:

> The city used to be free; now we have to pay for it. We are witnessing the birth of the post-public; the private city ... What is stunning is the somnolence with which we have watched this revolution, how casually we have tolerated our good intentions about city life to be perverted. (Koolhaas & Whiting 1999, pp. 42–43)

When Rem Koolhaas in 1999 reformulated the brand strategy of Prada, he introduced a series of noncommercial typologies—the street, the square, the library—into the normally sealed-off world of shopping. Through this, OMA wanted to render the frontier between public and private spaces similar to the strategies we find in BBC and CCTV.

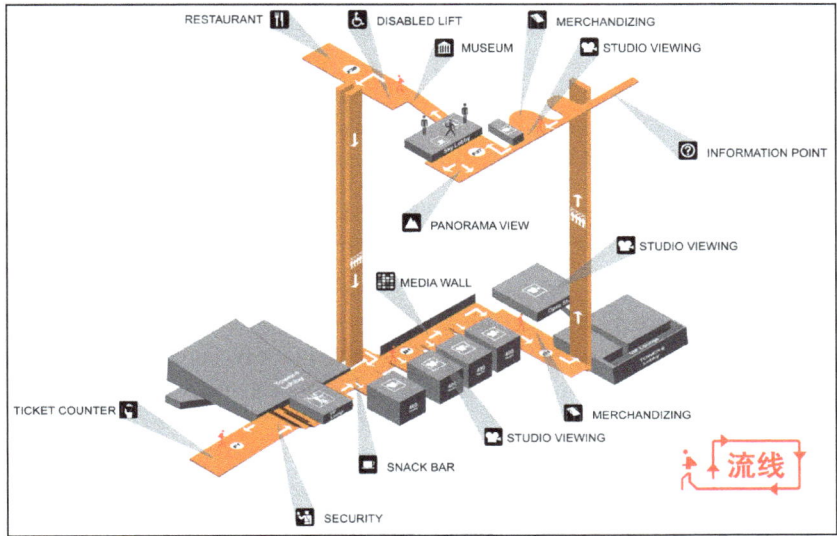

Fig. 7. Visitor loop diagram. Drawing courtesy of OMA.

Two major sources can be found for this strategy. The first is that the increasingly insecure status of urban public space has meant that the "staging" of such a space has been outsourced to consultants; companies and institutions create their own public spaces, this being a condition placed on them if they wish to build, as in the case of Nike in New York City (Kayden 2000).[6] The second is a kind of "becoming-amusement park" of public space, where companies brand themselves through the creation of spaces where everyone is a possible consumer, both in the form of exteriors and interiors, parks, playgrounds, and settings for sculpture. This is a way to produce personal experiences in the form of an entertainment that "connects" the potential customer to the brand. This may be seen as an extension of ideas that were formulated in the 1990s, when it was discovered that "goods and services are no longer enough," as Pine and Gilmore's claim in their *Experience Economy* (1999). These two tendencies seem to overlap in an efficient way: public space remains as a staging of private space, creating the possibility for consumption as an integral part of a fictitious public realm.

Experience Economy and Brandscapes

The relation between architecture and media is just as obvious as it is elusive. Beatriz Colomina (1994) has noted the extent to which architecture had positioned itself in relation to the mediascape already at the beginnings of modernism, where architecture too played the role of a media technique, or a "mechanism for representation" (p. 13). This has become a predominant feature in the marketing of nations, regions, and private companies, where architecture is increasingly called upon to fulfill the task of image production. According to Charles Jencks, a member of the jury for the CCTV competition, this is the reason why OMA finally won:

> The most important idea in the brief was that the building should be a "landmark," and the words clearly implied something approaching the stature of Gehry's Bilbao. (Jencks 2004, p. 107)

As a "mechanism for representation" architecture, however, need not limit itself to the domain of the image, but can also achieve its result through the way it organizes space. Architecture must be understood as a complex set of strategies for controlling a space that is both physical and mediatized, and as a way to generate a set of corresponding experiences in the subject. Like the image, architecture can convey knowledge, but it also adds something in the way that the individual uses the space. This is something that Benjamin stressed in his essay "The Work of Art in the Age of Mechanical Reproduction":

> For the tasks which face the human apparatus of perception at the turning points of history cannot be solved by optical means, that is, by contemplation, alone. They are mastered gradually by habit, under the guidance of tactile appropriation. (Benjamin 1936, p. 240)

In those media buildings that I have discussed above, transparency is used both as an image (translucent materials) and as a bodily experience (transparent organization). This double quality of architecture, as a two-dimensional visual image and a three-dimensional haptic experience, makes it into a technique for conveying messages that are distinct from most others. The use of transparency in architecture has, unlike in the case of painting, often been understood too literally, as is claimed by Rowe and Slutzky (1964). What they call "literal" transparency in painting, where the third dimension can only be implied, in architecture becomes a physical fact. Since this transparency is more difficult to achieve in architecture, it has come to be associated with a property of certain materials:

> Therefore, at the very beginning of any enquiry into transparency, a basic distinction must be established. Transparency may be an inherent quality of substance, as in a glass curtain wall; or it may be an inherent quality of organization. One can, for this reason, distinguish between a literal and a phenomenal transparency. (Rowe and Slutzky 1964, p. 23)

In contemporary theories of marketing, one often emphasizes the capacity of architecture to generate places, and the "brand" is understood as a combination of image and experience. The distinction between phenomenal and literal transparency proposed by Rowe and Slutzky may also help up us understand the significance of architectural transparency in environments like CCTV and the BBC.

Brandscape can be defined as an artificial landscape that produces personal experiences and that plays a crucial role in an experience economy (Klingmann 2007). In this "new economy" (Kelly 1998), consumers must be made active and entertained, and this occurs through the production of experiences—it is an "emotional or passionate economy" that enhances the process of estheticizing and the performative qualities (Löfgren & Willim, 2005).

> Sign-value and the brand are not qualities of products: they are qualities of *experiences*. This experience is situated at the interface—or surface—of communication of the consumer and the brand. It is part of events; it is eventive. (Lash & Lury 2007, p. 7)

Those zones that I have previously talked about in terms of an interface between audience and media could in the terminology of Lash and Lury be called a "brand," a space of events which has replaced the media buildings' communicative facades.

It is, however, not only within economy that a shift from object to experiences and social relations can be detected, but also in art. Since the late 1950s we find many examples of how ideas of the "social" become predominant in both art and architecture, from Harold Rosenberg's idea that the artist's choice is what defines art (Rosenberg 1960), and Alan Kaprow's introduction of the "happening," to Cedric Price's Fun Palace, where architecture is understood as a platform for events. In 1998, Nicolas Bourriaud coined the expression "esthétique relationnelle" (Bourriaud 1998), and the year after saw the publication of Pine and Gilmore's *Experience Economy*—both of which established a close link between art and marketing, so that both experiences, relations, and events could be understood as commodities in a new and expanded sense of the term. O'Dell and Billing (2005) suggest that experiences are highly subjective and elusive, but as things we can locate them to physical sites outside of individual consciousness. Even though the experience itself may be ephemeral, the process of reification has a material basis, and the experiences can be understood as spatially organized in what O'Dell and Billing call an *experiencescape*. In this way, architectonic spaces can be seen as physical nodes in an experience-based marketing. That power in a world shaped by a global economy and information technology still remains tied to centrality and materiality has been emphasized by Saskia Sassen (1992). According to Renée Delder, this is the quality that will be the most important aspect of OMA's CCTV project in the future:

> As CCTV's digital brain becomes ever more transparent and ubiquitous, it will be precisely the immaterial elusiveness of tomorrow's networked world that will give the new building's presence its greatest importance. (OMA 2004, p. 504)

In the media spaces that I have referred to above, a public space replaces the physical façade as an interface between production and consumption. The task of architecture, both as image and as physical organization, is to induce a set of personal experiences in the audience. This use of architecture as a marketing device is by no means new, as we can see in the shop windows from the beginning of the twentieth century, and car factories like the Ford Factory in Highland Park, Detroit (1913), or the Fiat Factory in Turin (1923). What appears to be a contemporary invention is, however, the increased use of transparency in the encounter between organization and audience, producer, and consumer.

Commodification of the Production Process

The limit separating the production of a commodity from its consumption seems today displaced in a way that integrates production into consumption. In industrialism and early capitalism, production was split off from the finished product. In Taylorism and Fordism, the link between work and product was severed and the product got transformed into a commodity with supernatural characteristics. This disrupted process could be understood in terms of Marx's concepts of alienation and fetishism. If mass production turned art into a commodity (Benjamin 1936), then the commodity itself was also transformed into an anesthetized object, as has been pointed out by Andreas Huyssen:

> Just when art works become commodities, the commodity itself in consumer society has become an image, representation, spectacle. Use value has been replaced by packaging and advertising. The commodification of art ends up in the aesthetization of the commodity. (Huyssen 1986, p. 21)

Displaying the commodity as a magic object in a shop window more or less like a work of art also meant to enhance its character as a fetish through estetization. The "dirty work" that preceded the finished product took place in factories closed to the consumer, and often located in the outskirts of urban space. Taylor's "army of gorillas" (workers) was hidden from the public, just as the unfinished products, for reasons both political and economic. Marketing meant to display the object, and the interface between commodity and consumer was the shop window and the image it procured.

Today it is the other way around. Factories are located inside cities, and the so-called production is open to the public. The commodity is on display throughout the production process. If production previously took place in Taylor-like factories, it is now assemblage that takes place in modern factories. In an experience economy, the division between production and consumption is not obliterated but redrawn. The process of production is global; much of it takes place in developing countries. Where previously the walls of factories made production invisible, it is now territorial distances that divide the consumer from the largest part of the production process.

The BBC describes itself as a "creative organization" whose product is television and radio programs. It proudly speaks of the energy and money spent on its new facilities, whose aim, as noted previously, is to "show visitors studio spaces and dispel much of the mystery of the BBC" (Jackson 2003, p. 64). The mystery of the BBC is its production—and by allowing audiences to penetrate far into the building, this creative organization can provide the public with an insight into the everyday life and work of its employees (although the thought processes remain concealed, it is asserted). The same thing applies to CCTV, where consumption, information, and the ability to get a glimpse of the studio work almost merge in the "public loop."

Similar phenomena can be found in other sectors of production. In the BMW factory in Leipzig, designed by the architect Zaha Hadid, the three central segments of the production chain—body shop, paint shop, assembly line—are opened up to each other, "showing each one of the workers how their roles at BMW are interrelated" (www.zaha-hadid.com). BMW also offers a public tour through the various stations: "Take a look behind the scenes and experience live how BMW are built."[7] Another major car manufacturer, Volkswagen, presents its *Transparent Factory* (*Die gläserne Manufaktur*) in Dresden designed by Henn Architekten, as "the only place in the world to turn production into a real experience." They also speak of a "new transparency" as a surface of communication:

> The new transparency. We stage what usually takes place behind closed doors as a place of communication and exchange.[8]

The work on display is clean, almost clinical, and the workers all wear white overalls—the factory has been estheticized to the point of appearing like an art gallery, and production is akin to art production. The artists Michael Singer and Linnea Glatt developed a similar project entitled Solid Waste Management Facility after having won an open competition for a waste sorting station in Phoenix, Arizona. Through large windows the public can watch garbage being sorted by a workforce drawn from the local prison, who themselves have become image-like and all wear the same clothes. Experiences, entertainment, and control here overlap in a performance that borders on the outright cynical.

Gilles Deleuze (1992) speaks of an emerging society of control that replaces Foucault's disciplinary societies and the carceral environments that reached their peak at the beginning of the last century. It would not be far-fetched to look at the contemporary deployment of transparency, which opens up closed organizations and reveals their inner functions and organs, as a kind of exhibitionist regime that locates the individual within a polarized desiring structure, "to be seen" and "to see," thus always also has "to be controlled" and to "control." The disciplinary matrix was to a large extent made up of architecture—in the central tower of the Panopticon, the presence of a guard was not needed, since the architecture allowed the inmates to be seen, but not to see, and visibility itself became a "trap," as Foucault says. The guard has now finally abdicated from his position in the tower, and what frightens us today seems to be the possibility of never being seen. A similar thought is expressed by Ursula Frohne who speaks of the "panopticon of the media" and the theatricalization of public life.

Fig. 8. In front of the Solid Waste Management Facility. Photo by Michael Dudley.

> In the age of globalization, the panopticon of the media becomes the new disciplining authority. In the context of this development, the theatricalization of all spheres of public and private life has proven one of the most striking features of our everyday experience in contemporary culture. (Frohne 2002, p. 255)

To expose the work process seems to respond to several needs: on the one hand, it is part of an expanded idea of economy, art, and advertising, and also of a public demand for a "fair trade marked" production process; on the other hand, there is an increasing demand on the part of the individual to be seen and to see, which also means a way to control and to be controlled. In these media buildings, such an exhibitionist desire expressed in the exposition of production seems to insert itself in an encounter between fiction and reality, which renders the process even more intricate. Here, not only the limits between production and consumption are transgressed but also between staged reality and real life.

Exchange between Fiction and Reality

In relation to the media buildings discussed above, both "literal" as well as "phenomenal" transparency are concepts that can be applied, although with caution. There is no way to directly transfer the analysis of phenomenal transparency in Le Corbusier's Villa Garches to either the BBC or CCTV, but still there is a certain point to be made if one looks at the aspect that Rowe and Slutzky borrow from Gyorgy Kepes (1944). Kepes describes how two figures overlap in a plane, and both of them claim the common part as their own. This places the viewer in front of a visual conundrum, "a contradiction of spatial dimensions." Rowe and Slutzky suggest that we have to imagine a new optical quality in order to resolve the contradiction: transparency, implying that the two figures can coexist without deforming each other's respective optical qualities.

> Transparency however implies more than an optical characteristic; it implies a broader spatial order. Transparency means a simultaneous perception of different spatial locations. Space not only recedes but fluctuates in a continuous activity. (Kepes 1944, p. 77)

Kepes' transparency results in the two figures continually shifting their location with respect to the picture plane, in an oscillation between "figure" and "ground." For Rowe and Slutzky, the Villa Garches becomes a paradigmatic case of such double reading of "shallow space" and "deep space," as different sections through the building imply spatial connections that appear to be opposed:

> There is a continuous dialectic between fact and implication. The reality of deep space is constantly opposed to the inference of shallow space; and by means of the resultant tension, reading after reading is enforced. (Slutzky & Rowe 1963, p. 41)

In a similar manner to Rowe and Slutzky's definition, we may understand the transparency in CCTV and the BBC as the coexistence of several spatial orders that impose themselves simultaneously. The public gets the opportunity to see the production process, but can never enter into the space physically, a boundary created through differences of level and the use of transparent as well as non-transparent surfaces. In some places you are invited to learn more, maybe interact, and perhaps try out some recording technique, and in other places there may be a "staged event" or an "exhibition." At the same time as all of these opportunities are opened up, the audience is cut off at every point through various material partitions—walls, glass sheets, fences, thresholds, and doors. This organizational transparency produces a double reading, spaces are at once open and closed, "and by means of resultant tension, reading after reading is enforced," as Rowe and Slutzky might say. This double quality also comes across in the meeting of fiction, recording, and reality. The audience is constantly trying to figure out what is real and what is not, what is "live" and what is rehearsal. And this "perpetual reading" is precisely what makes this spatial fix into such an efficient marketing tool: it binds the audience to a line of division between fiction and reality, broadcasting and non-broadcasting, which can never be defined.

In the BBC's publication *Building the BBC: A Return to Form* the old and the new building are described as dramatic spaces, which give rise to two different temporal fictions. The chapter entitled "The New Broadcasting House" ends with the question: If the old Broadcasting House inspired George Orwell to the frightening room 101 in *1984*, what kind of stories could the new Broadcasting House generate?

> Who knows which literary figures will draw inspiration from MJP's Broadcasting House? What is certain is that it will provide some of the most inspiring and dramatic spaces in London, for BBC employees and the public alike. Orwell would be lost for words, were he alive to see it. (Jackson 2003, p. 66)

The building here appears as a machine for the generation of fictions, both in the sense of a technical recording facility, and as a point of departure for those non-transparent thought processes that lie at the basis of these fictions. In spite of the fact that these buildings are opened up so as to reveal their inner core, they will always harbor a tantalizing mystery that eludes us—the more we attempt to gain clarity about the fiction, the more we become ensnared in it.

Architecture as Social Media

Even if OMA may claim that "in China, money does not have the last word (yet)" (OMA 2004, p. 486), Zhengrong Hu (2005) notes that Chinese media too are run by commercial interests.[9] The last thirty years brought tremendous changes to the media system despite the heavy-handed control of the one-party system. A history of commercialization, decentralization, and departmentalization began, from 1978 and onwards, when advertising was allowed for the first time, all of which has been troublesome from the government perspective. When China became a member of the World Trade Organization (WTO) in 2001, the media became increasingly dependent on the market, and further deregulation subsequently speeded up this centrifugal process even more.

In the case of the BBC, market dependency is even more accentuated. In 2000, the year after MacCormac won the competition, the BBC's real estate section, earlier an in-house section with its own architects, transferred most of the responsibility for the buildings to the private company Land Securities Trillium. By signing an agreement with Land Securities, the BBC was able to free money for production and transfer the economic risk involved in the building project to the private sector. One of the architects at MacCormac's company MJP claims: "But this is the norm now, you have to apply the market and rigid criteria to everything. So even if this was a once-in-a-hundred-years building, for arguably Britain's most important cultural institution, it still has to be procured as if it was just a commercial office block around the corner" (Rose 2005).

The impact of the market and the global economy on the role of culture has led Lash and Lury (2007) to speak of a shift, during the last thirty years, from a *culture industry* (Adorno & Horkheimer [1945]) to a *global culture industry*. Once a part of the superstructure, as ideology, representations, and symbols, culture now permeates everything, from production to economy and consumption, and it has become "*thing*ified" (Lash & Lury 2007, p. 4). In the new CCTV and BBC buildings, we can see how media communicate with the audience not through immaterial images, but through physical environments and architecture. Media have become "thingified" into architecture, and the building may be seen as a continuation of the docusoap drama, the drama-fiction, or reality TV. Also the process of production has been "thingified" into a commodity, as discussed earlier. The physical television building becomes a place for experiencing TV "live, on location," a place for interaction—or for an imagined interaction. Zhengrong Hu (2005) predicted that a "quasi-public media system" would arise in China, where the idea of public life and participation would be cornerstones:

> It should provide more open access and public sphere so as to empower the public to participate and represent their interests. It would be conducive to consolidate the legitimacy of the political power. Efficiency, good administration and a certain concept of public service can be the hallmark of the system. (Hu 2005, p. 24)

What I have attempted to show here, is how "the public" has been made into a brand, just as experiences and relations have become commodities. It has often been pointed out that so-called "social media"—blogs, Facebook, Second Life—have become increasingly important in a global "network society," while traditional media—TV, newspapers, cinema—may seem slow, less interactive, even nonsocial.

Through producing human relations and networks, these social media are often considered to open up new public spaces where critical thinking and resistance can be formed as well as consensus created. I have argued that media buildings too may be considered as a social medium, in a global culture industry where relations and interactivity are highly valued commodities.

So far I have discussed the BBC and CCTV without going into their specific differences, the most obvious of which is the fact that one of the buildings is located in a European democracy, the other in a communist one-party state. In this respect, the difference between Beijing and London is vast. The situation of media in a one-party state is clearly something else than in the European context; and yet, in spite of these differences, there are common denominators that I have chosen to highlight: the way in which these facilities are presented as "experience centers," where the difference between audience and organization is enacted "live," indicates that both these projects, just as the organizations that support them, are part of a global cultural industry, characterized by, on the one hand, the "thingification" of representations, on the other, by the physical building playing the role of a social medium.

This description of the buildings is wholly based on projects that are not realized, and the objects under scrutiny are in this sense discursive rather than material. Earlier I pointed to the different roles played by the representation of a building in relation to the concrete object. Anyone who today can get a glimpse of the gradual materialization of this discursive object in Beijing CBD will be brought back to the materiality of everyday life and the gap between fiction and reality. As shown in this chapter there are many similarities between these two projects as representations of media buildings in a global cultural industry. It is certain, however, that there will be as many substantial differences between them when they become materialized through local politics.

References

Adorno, T. & Horkheimer, M. (1972), "Culture Industry" [1945] in Adorno, T. & Horkheimer, M., *Dialectic of Enlightenment*, New York: Seabury Press Co.
Benjamin, W. (1968), "The Work of Art in the Age of Mechanical Reproduction" [1936] in Benjamin, W., *Illuminations*, New York: Harcourt, Brace & World.
Bateson, G. (1972), *Steps to an Ecology of Mind*, New York: Ballantine.
Bourriaud, N. (1998), *Esthétique relationnelle*, Paris: Les presses du réel.
Jackson, N. (2003), *Building the BBC: A Return to Form*, London: BBC.
Couldry, N. (2003), *Media Rituals. A Critical Approach*, New York: Routledge.
Deleuze, G. (1992), "Postscript on the Societies of Control", *October* no. 59, pp. 3–7.
Frohne, U. (2002, "'Screen Tests': Media Narcissism, Theatricality, and the Internalized Observer" in *CTRL [SPACE]*, eds. T. Y. Levin, U. Frohne, P. Weibel, Cambridge, MA: MIT Press.
Hartley, J. (2007), "'Reality' and the Plebiscite" in *Politicotainment. Television's Take on the Real*, ed. K. Riegert, New York: Peter Lang.
Holzner, B. & Holzner, L. (2006), *Transparency in Global Change. The Vanguard of the Open*, Pittsburgh: University of Pittsburgh Press.
Hu, Z. (2005), "Towards the Public?," Joan Shorenstein Center, Harvard University, Boston, MA.
Jencks, C. (2005), *Iconic Building: The Power of Enigma*, London: Frances Lincoln.
Kayden, J. S. (2000), *Privately Owned Public Space: The New York City Experience*, New York: Department of City Planning, Municipal Art Society of New York Edition.

Kelly, K. (1998), *New Rules for the New Economy: 10 Ways the Network Economy. Is Changing Everything*, London: Fourth Estate.
Kepes, G. (1944), *Language of Vision*, Chicago: Paul Theobald.
Koolhaas, R. & Whiting S. (1999), "Spot Check: A Conversation between Rem Koolhaas and Sarah Whiting" *Assemblage* no. 40, pp. 36–55.
Klingmann, A. (2007), *Brandscapes. Architecture in the Experience Economy*, Cambridge, MA: MIT Press.
Lash, S. & Lury, C. (2007), *Global Culture Industry: The Mediation of Things*, Cambridge, MA: Polity.
Löfgren, O. & Willim, R. (2005), *Magic Culture and the New Economy*, New York: Berg.
Mattern, S. (2008), "Broadcasting Space: China Central Television's New Headquarters," *International Journal of Communication 2*, pp. 869–908.
O'Dell, T. & Billing, P. (2005), *Experiencescape: Tourism, Culture and Economy*, Copenhagen: Copenhagen Business School.
OMA–AMO/Koolhaas, R. (2004), *Content*, Köln: Taschen.
OMA (2006), "CCTV&TVCC", *El Croquis* no 3/4, pp. 270–311.
Peng, A. (2008), interview 081030, Beijing.
Pine II, J. B. & Gilmore, J. H. (1999), *The Experience Economy*, Boston: Harvard Business School Press.
Rose, S. (2005) "Did the Beep Bottle up?," *Guardian*, December 20.
Rosenberg, H. (1960), *The Tradition of the New*, New York: Da Capo Press.
Rowe, C. & Slutzky, R. (1997), "Transparency" [1964] in *Transparency*, Basel: Birkhäuser.
Sassen, S. (1992), *The Global Cities: New York, Tokyo, London*, Princeton: Princeton University Press.
Vattimo, G. (1992), *The Transparent Society*, Oxford: Blackwell.
Willim, R. (2008), *Industrial Cool. Om postindustriella fabriker*, Lund: Lunds Universitet.
www.ctvt.com.cn/english/about.asp
www.mjparchitects.co.uk
www.bmw-werk-leipzig.de/leipzig/deutsch/lowband/com/en/index.html
www.glaesernemanufaktur.de/gmd.jsp?dok=&lang=&docid=&ap=

Notes

1. This became clear after discussions with Alfred Peng, Professor of Architecture at Beijing University and the Head of Great Earth Architecture, and Shi Zengzhi, Associate Professor at the School of Journalism and Communication, Beijing University.
2. This text is based on interviews and visits on location: BBC October 5, 2008, and CCTV October 29, 2008.
3. The feeling of coming into another world when opening the door and entering the BBC was described by several employees in the discussion after showing *Death at Broadcasting House* (directed by Reginald Denham 1934) at the BBC's Arts and Music Festival, London, October 2008. For a discussion on the relation between *Death at Broadcasting House* and the physical building Broadcasting House, see Staffan Ericson's chapter in this volume.
4. To separate production from broadcasting, and let the broadcasting tower become the place for an interaction between media and its public, is also the case in the tower in Moscow, Ostankino. See Patrik Åker in this volume.
5. For a more extensive description and analyses of CCTV's new headquarters, see Mattern (2008). The project has been published extensively, for example, in *A&U* no. 7, 2005; El Croquis no. 3-4, 2006; *LOTUS* no. 123, 2004.

6. In New York, the history of privately owned public spaces started with the zoning regulations in 1961. Through the creation of public spaces permission was given to build higher buildings (Kayden 2000, 11ff).
7. See www.bmw-werkleipzig.de/leipzig/deutsch/lowband/com/en/index.html. (Accessed June 8, 2009).
8. See http://www.glaesernemanufaktur.de/gmd.jsp?dok=&lang=&docid=&ap. (Accessed June 8, 2009).
9. The tension between the state channel CCTV and the local satellite channels produced by commercialization was played out in the national restrictions that were set up after the singing contest "Mongolian Cow Sour Yogurt Super Girl Contest." The contest got more viewers than the most popular CCTV program, which threatened both CCTV's economy (with a loss of advertising) and its role as opinion-maker. See Hartley (2007).

Contributors

Patrik Åker— is Senior Lecturer in Media and Communication at Södertörn University College, and a co-leader of the project Media Houses. He has written about journalism, visual communication, and the medialization of places. His publications include *Vår bostad i folkhemmet* (1998) [The Visual Representation of the Home in the Tenant Organization's Magazine 'Our Dwelling'], "Newspapers' Picture of the World: The Domestic Family of Man" (2003), *Symboliska platser i kunskapssamhället. Internet, högre lärosäten och den gynnade geografin* [Symbolic Places in the Knowledge Society: Internet, Higher Education and the Preferred Geography](2008). He is co-editor of *Storylines: Media, Power and Identity in Modern Europe* (2002).

Staffan Ericson— is Associate Professor and Head of Department in Media and Communication at Södertörn University and head of the research project Media Houses. His dissertation *Två drömspel. Från Strindbergs modernism till Potters television* [Two Dreamplays–from Strindbergs's Modernism to Potter's Television] was published by Symposion in 2004. He has previously edited and co-authored a number of anthologies on the media: *Fjernsyn mellom høy og lav kultur.* [Television between High and Low Culture] and *Hello Europe! Tallinn Calling! Eurovision Song Contest 2002 som mediehändelse* [ESC 2002 as a Media Event]. He recently contributed to the anthology *Strange Spaces: Explorations into Mediated Obscurity* (Ashgate, 2008).

Peter Jakobsson— is a Phd candidate at Södertörn University, Sweden. His thesis work tracks the development of copyright in relation to new media in a

Swedish context. Currently he is working on a project together with Fredrik Stiernstedt regarding the material side of the information economy, through the search company Google, including visits to server farms and computing centers in rural America. He has previously published articles on game studies in, for example, *European Journal of Cultural Studies* and *Interactions*.

Shannon Mattern— is Assistant Professor and former Director of Graduate Studies in the Department of Media Studies and Film at The New School, New York. Her teaching and research address relationships between media and spatial theory and practice–particularly the links between mass media and architecture and urban planning–and connections between media and contemporary art. She has taught at New York University, the Parsons School of Design, and Rutgers University, and she was a Mellon Postdoctoral Fellow in the History of Art at the University of Pennsylvania. She is the author of *The New Downtown Library: Designing with Communities* (University of Minnesota Press 2007), which was supported by a grant from the Graham Foundation for Advanced Studies in the Fine Arts. Other work has appeared in the *Journal of Architectural Education, Invisible Culture, The Senses & Society, In the Place of Sound*, and *Public Culture*.

Helena Mattsson— is an architect and a researcher based in Stockholm, Sweden. Her thesis, *Arkitektur och konsumtion: Reyner Banham och utbytbarhetens estetik* [Architecture and Consumption: Reyner Banham and the Aesthetic of Expendability], was published by Symposion in 2004. She has written extensively on architecture, art and culture, and is the editor for *Kalmar Stortorg* (Stockholm: The National Public Art Council, 2005) and *1%* (Gothenburg: Glänta, 2006). Mattsson was in charge of the research project, "Architecture and Consumption in Sweden 1930–1970." She is an Associate Professor in History and Theory of Architecture at the Royal Institute of Technology in Stockholm, and a partner in the architectural office Testbedstudio Stockholm, as well as editor for the cultural periodical *Site*.

Kristina Riegert— is Associate Professor in Media and Communication at Södertörn University and Stockholm University. She is editor of *Politicotainment: Television's Take on the Real* (Peter Lang, 2007) and *News of the Other: Tracing Identity in Scandinavian Constructions of the Eastern Baltic Region* (Nordicom, 2004) and head author of *Transnational and National Media in Global Crisis* (Hampton Press, forthcoming), and *The Image War: NATO's Battle for Kosovo in the British Media* (Örebro University Press, 2003). She has contributed to the *European Journal of Communication, Journalism Practice*, and *Journal of Information Warfare*.

Fredrik Stiernstedt— is a PhD student and Junior Lecturer at Södertörn University. His dissertation research is on surveillance and audience commodification in the context of new media. Together with Peter Jakobsson he is currently working on a project about the material aspects of informational culture, including work on the Google server farms and the role of digital archives in the information economy.

Sven-Olov Wallenstein— teaches philosophy and aesthetics at Södertörn University, and is the editor-in-chief of *Site*. He is the translator of works by Winckelmann, Kant, Hegel, Frege, Husserl, Heidegger, Levinas, Derrida, Foucualt, Deleuze, and Agamben, as well as the author of numerous books on contemporary philosophy, art, and architecture. Recent publications include *Essays, Lectures* (2007), *Thinking Worlds: The Moscow Conference on Philosophy, Politics, and Art* (co-edited with Joseph Backstein and Daniel Birnbaum, 2008), *The Silences of Mies* (2008), *Biopolitics and the Emergence of Modern Architecture* (2009), and *1930/31: Swedish Modernism at The Crossroads* (with Helena Mattsson, 2009).

Index

Adorno, Theodor W., 165
Allon, Fiona, 73
All-Russian Exhibition Center, 90, 91
Amazon, 128
American Institute of Architects, 149
Appadurai, Arjun, 15, 139
Arcades Project (Benjamin), 100, 101
    Das Passagen-Werk
Architectural Association School, 30
architectural communication, model of, 139
Architectural Record, 138, 139
The Architectural Review
    Broadcasting House, 25–26, 36
    Lawn Road Flats, 40
architecture
    American corporate style, 95, 165
    American modernism, 118–19, 120–22, 165, 166, 194
    Bauhaus movement, 27, 40
    as book/communication, 3–4, 89–90, 155, 163–67
    Buck-Morss analysis, 101–8
    as commodity, 196–99

    critiques, 165–67
    curtain wall, 97
    emotion and, 59
    hard vs. soft, 15
    Koolhaas analysis, 171–78
    machines for living, 29, 39–41, 121–22
    as media construct, 7, 10–11, 26, 120–21, 142–43, 163, 165, 170–71, 178, 183–84
    skyscrapers, 140, 141, 173–74, 176–77
    technology and, 2, 8–10, 166, 167
    urbanism, 166–67, 174
architecture, transparency in. *See* public sphere vs. private sphere
artificiality vs. reality
    Broadcasting House, 37–39, 49–53
    public access and, 199–200
Arts & Architecture magazine, 120–21
Associated Press building, 8
AT&T Building, 143
The Audible Past (Sterne), 37
autonomy, theory of, 165

Baldry, Chris, 73

Balfour, Lord, 61
Ban, Shigeru, 146
Band Waggon, 39
Barbrook, Richard, 118
Barthes, Roland, 51–52, 95
Batalov, Leonid, 82, 83, 88, 93, 97
Baudrillard, Jean, 117–18, 122
Bauen in Frankreich (Giedion), 27, 29
Bauhaus movement, 27, 40
BBC, 5
  BBC culture, 70, 71, 76
  centralization of, 47, 59, 65–69, 70–74, 76, 200–201
  See also Broadcasting House; Bush House
BBC World Service, 13, 60–62
  centralization of BBC, 47, 59, 65–69, 70–74, 76
  freedom vs. political control, 62, 70, 76
  See also Bush House
BBC Yearbook 1933, 27
Becker, F., 74
Bell Telephone building, 9
Benjamin, Walter, 8, 12, 13, 49, 51, 53–54
  tradition/modernity, 23, 27, 29, 37, 42–43, 100–101, 194
Berlin Wall, 171–72
Billing, P., 195
Bloomberg building, 143
BMW factory (Leipzig), 197
Bourriaud, Nicolas, 195
  branding, 15, 62, 64, 67, 68, 142, 147, 170
  Prada, 192
  public space and, 193–96
Brecht, Bertolt, 43, 44
Breuer, Marcel, 40
Brezhnev, Leonid, 105
Brin, Sergey, 117, 118
British Broadcasting Corporation (BBC). *See* BBC
British Library, 45
Broadcasting House [BBC], 12, 13
  artificial vs. real, 37–39, 49–52, 199–200
  as center, 26, 45, 46–47, 49–50, 184, 201–2
  centralization of BBC, 47, 59, 65–67, 69, 70, 76, 200–201
  exterior descriptions, 19–23, 24–26, 45–49, 129, 187–89

  in fiction, 13, 24–27, 36–39, 43, 52–53, 187, 200
  as historical object, 22–23, 26–29, 47–48
  interior descriptions, 26–28, 31–36, 43–44, 66–67
  public access to, 21–22, 46–49, 186–89, 192, 197, 199–200
  renovation of, 22, 45–50, 59, 65–66, 187–88, 200–201
  sacred/profane and, 19–22, 23
  technology influences, 29–37, 45, 47, 50–54
Bruce Mau Design, 148, 151, 154, 155
Bruno, Giuliana, 93
Buck-Morss, Susan, 14, 101–2
  Ostankino tower and, 101–8
Building the BBC (Jackson), 67, 200
Burdin, Dmitry, 88, 93
Bush House [BBC World Service], 5, 13, 14
  BBC training, 66–67, 70–71
  as center, 59–60, 67–69, 75–76
  centralization of BBC, 47, 59, 65–69, 70–74, 76
  exterior descriptions, 61–63, 64–65
  flexibility/control, 72–74
  freedom/political control, 62, 70, 76
  hierarchy/open space, 65–66, 72–74
  as historical object, 63–64, 65
  history of, 60–61
  interior descriptions, 64–67, 71–74
  meeting areas and interaction, 66–67, 70–71
  public access to, 73–76
  reorganization of language groups, 65, 71–74
  research sources, 60
  South Asian Hub, 65, 71–74
  as symbol of power, 60
  as symbol of values, 60, 61–64, 68–71
  technology influences, 63, 65, 67, 68–69, 72–74
Bush, Irving T., 61
Business Week, 139

Cameron, Andy, 118
Campbell, Robert, 139
Canter, David, 60
Case Study Houses, 120–22
center vs. non-localized publics. *See* place, sense of

Central Business District (CBD) [Beijing], 167, 168, 169, 176–77, 183, 190, 192
centralization vs. decentralization, 2
    Broadcasting House, 45, 47, 59, 65–67, 69, 70, 76
    Bush House, 14, 47, 57, 59, 65–69, 70–74, 76
    CCTV, 12, 16, 170–71
    Googleplex, 15, 119–20, 124, 129, 133
    media and, 22, 94–95, 114
    Ostankino tower, 95–99, 108–9
    of power, 10, 95
    Rockefeller Center views, 8–9
    Silicon Valley, 117–18
    urban planning and, 119
Chang, Jade, 122, 138
Chapman, Nigel, 65, 69
Chelsea Market, 145
Chelsea Piers Sports and Entertainment Complex, 146, 147
Chermayeff, Serge, 13, 27, 31
Chicago Tribune Tower, 5, 6–7, 10, 129
China Central Television (CCTV) building, 5, 12, 13, 15, 16, 186
    as brand/icon, 170–71, 195
    as center, 170, 171, 184, 201–2
    exterior descriptions, 167–68, 170–71, 176–78, 184–85, 190–92
    hierarchy/open space, 12
    history, 176–77, 183–84
    interior descriptions, 167, 168–69, 176, 177, 192, 193
    as metaphor, 172, 175, 176, 177–78, 192
    as monument, 169, 171, 190, 194
    public access to, 168–69, 177, 185–86, 189–93, 197, 199–200
    as symbol of power, 170, 171, 177, 190
    as symbol of values, 163, 167, 168, 170–71, 177–78, 185–86
    technology influences, 167, 171, 178, 189–90, 195
Chinese media, 200, 201–2
City of Bits (Mitchell), 5
CN Tower (Toronto), 106
Coates, Wells, 13, 25, 27, 29, 31, 36–37, 41–42
    Lawn Road Flats, 13, 39–41
    object design, 41–42

Cold War
    architecture and, 119
    media and, 94, 107
Colomina, Beatriz, 10–11, 29, 142, 165, 193–94
commodification of the production process, 49–53, 186, 196–200
Condé Nast building, 143, 152, 153
Conquerors of Space monument, 90, 92, 106
Constructivist movement, 85, 86, 88, 98, 100–101
Corbett, Harvey, 61
Coronation Street, 21, 49
Couldry, Nick
    myth of mediated center, 1–2, 3, 10, 75, 76
    sacred/profane, 21, 49
Crary, Jonathan, 90
culture industry, 201–2
cybernetics
    Google culture, 113, 118–20
    machine for living and, 40, 121–22, 133
    patterns of space, 10, 97, 119, 120, 121, 165

Daily Beast, 153
Davidson, Julius Ralph, 121
Davidson, Justin, 143, 146, 147, 157
Dayan, Daniel., 2
Death at Broadcasting House (Gielgud and Marvell), 13, 24–25, 36–39, 43, 52–53, 187
decentralization, communication theory, 115–16
"decorated shed" buildings, 8, 147
DeGarno, Ted, 148, 149
Degtereva, Elena, 108
Delder, Renée, 195
Deleuze, Gilles, 73, 98, 197–98
Delirious New York (Koolhaas), 172–73
de Santillana, Giorgio, 119
Desert Island Disc, 49–50
Deutsch, Karl, 119
Dia Art Foundation, 145
The Dialectics of Seeing (Buck-Morss), 101
Diller, Barry, 143–44
    IAC, 15, 137–38, 143–45, 152, 157, 158
    IAC building, 145–48, 151, 154, 155
    distributed computing, 128
Domosh, Mona, 140, 143

Downing, John, 102
"duck" buildings, 147
Duffy, F., 72
Durkheim, Émile, 21, 23
Dyke, Greg, 22, 45

Eames, Charles and Ray, 120
eBay, 128
Egton House, 65, 72, 188
Egyptian pyramids, 22
Eiffel Tower, 85, 88, 95, 106
Eliade, Mircea, 19–20, 23–24, 44, 50
Ellwood, Craig, 120
emergence, communication theory, 115–16
Entenza, John, 121
Exodus, or the Voluntary Prisoners of Architecture, 171, 172
"Experience and Poverty" (Benjamin), 42
Experience Economy (Pine and Gilmore), 195
experiencescapes, 195

fetishes, buildings as, 101
Fiat Factory, 196
fiction vs. reality
   Broadcasting House, 13, 24–27, 36–39, 43, 49–50, 52–53, 186–89, 200
   CCTV, 185–86, 189–93
   media, 184, 186, 199–200
figure vs. ground, 199
flexibility vs. control, 72–74
Forbidden City, 170, 192
Ford Factory, 196
Foreign and Commonwealth Office (UK), 62, 69, 76
fossils, buildings as, 101
Foucault, Michel, 26, 197–98
Frampton, Kenneth, 30
freedom vs. political control
   Bush House, 62, 70, 76
   Ostankino tower, 94–96
frits, 138
Frohne, Ursula, 198
Fun Palace, 195
"Furniture Today and Furniture Tomorrow" (Coates), 39

Gagarin, Yuri, 90
Galloway, A., 156
Gehry, Frank, 15, 137–38, 143, 147, 148–49, 151, 154–55, 156, 157
   Bilbao, 194
   Condé Nast building, 152
General Motors, headquarters, 9
generic cities, 164, 167, 173–74
Generic City (Koolhaas), 173
George E. Ream Company, 119
Georgetown Group, 145
Giedion, Sigfried, 45
   Eiffel Tower, 88
   on Le Corbusier, 12, 13
   Rockefeller Center, 8–9
   tradition/modernity, 27, 29, 54
Gielgud, Val, 24
Gill, Eric, 20, 22
Gilmore, J. H., 195
Glancey, John, 61
Glatt, Linnea, 197
Gmail, 132
Goldberger, Paul, 138, 143, 157
Goldhagen, S. W., 156
Goldsmith, V. H., 26, 31, 37
Google, 15, 113, 114–17
   algorithm, 116–17, 123, 128–29, 132–33
   corporate culture, 117–18, 122–25, 127–29
Google DNA project, 132
Googleplex, 13, 15, 123
   as city, 123, 124
   exterior descriptions, 114, 119–20, 124–25, 129
   hierarchy/open space, 123
   history of, 113, 117
   interior descriptions, 114, 122, 124, 125–27, 129–33
   as metaphor, 113–14, 123–25, 128–29
   as symbol of values, 117,118–22 124, 125–33
Googleware, 128
GOSTELERADIO, 81, 103
Gropius, Walter, 6, 40
Guardian, 62
Guattari, Felix, 98

INDEX | 213

Halid, Zaha, 197
Hall, P., 157–58
Hearst Corporation building, 139, 141, 143
Helenle and Corbett A.I.A., 61
Henn Architekten, 197
hierarchy vs. open space
   Bush House, 65–66, 72–74
   CCTV, 12
   Googleplex, 123
   IAC building, 152–56
   Ostankino tower, 95–96
High Line railway park, 146
Hines, Mark, 48
Hockenberry, John, 149–50, 154, 155–56
Hoffman, Malvina, 61
"How U.S. Cities Can Prepare for Atomic War" (Wiener et al.), 119
Hugo, Victor, 3–4, 12, 89
The Hunchback of Notre Dame (Hugo), 3–4, 12, 89
Hu, Zhengrong, 200, 201
Huyssen, Andreas, 196

IBM building, 9
Infobahn, 5
information theory, 120
informational culture, 114–18, 133
informatization, communication theory, 115, 116, 132–33
Innis, Harold, 11, 12, 22, 139, 158
Intelsat system, 94
InterActiveCorp (IAC), 143–45, 147–48
InterActiveCorp (IAC) building, 13, 15–16, 141
   as branding, 147, 154, 155, 157–58
   exterior descriptions, 137–39, 142, 146–49, 155, 157–58
   hierarchy/open space, 152–56
   history, 137, 143, 145–47, 149
   interior descriptions, 148, 149–56, 157–58
   as metaphor, 138–39, 143, 146–48, 152
   as symbol of values, 142–43, 151, 154–58
   technology influences, 155, 157–58
   as unifying, 144, 154, 158
interior vs. exterior, 2–3, 10, 12, 16, 184
   Broadcasting House, 26–27, 45–50, 65–66

   building materials and, 2, 42, 85–86, 88, 119, 124, 137, 148–49, 194
   Bush House, 64–67, 71–74
   CCTV, 176, 177
   Coates and, 40–41
   Googleplex, 15, 124, 129–33
   IAC building, 15, 139, 150–52, 155–58
   Koolhaas and, 172–73
   light and, 8, 46–47, 89, 97, 98, 151–52
   National Library of France, 175
   Ostankino tower, 88, 95–96
   Seebrügge Sea Tunnel, 175
International Magazine Building, 141
Internet
   Russian TV and, 108
   See also Google; InterActiveCorp (IAC)
Intersputnik system, 94
interstitial space, 45
Interval Leisure Group, 144
Iovine, Julie, 147, 151
ISOKON (Isometric Unit Construction), 39–40
"I Want Media," 142
Izenour, S., 139, 147

Jackson, N., 67
Jameson, Fredric, 16, 175, 178
Jencks, Charles, 194
Johnson, Philip, 143
Johnson, Shannon, 145, 148, 149, 153, 155

Kaca, Ann-Britt, 105
Kaprow, Alan, 195
Katz, Elihu., 2
Kepes, Gyorgy, 89, 97, 199
Khrushchev, Nikita, 86, 97, 100, 105
Kipling, Rudyard, 22
The Kitchen, 145
Klingmann, Anna, 59
Koenig, Pierre, 120
Koolhaas, Rem
   architecture and, 164, 166–67, 171–76
   CCTV, 12, 13, 15, 16, 163, 171, 178, 183, 186
   public space, 192

Land Securities Trillium, 200–201
Langham Place, 188–89
Lash, Scott., 195, 201
Latour, Bruno, 124
Lawn Road Flats (London), 13, 39–41
Learning from Las Vegas (Venturi et al.), 147
Le Corbusier (Charles-Édouard Jeanneret-Gris), 29, 40, 42, 121–22, 165, 173
  interior/exterior, 10, 12, 175, 199
  Pravda building, 8
  Ville radieuse, 174
Lever House, 143
Life magazine, 119
London Calling, 75
London School of Economics, 62
Loos, Adolf, 6, 10, 42, 165
Lury, C., 195, 201

MacCormac Jamieson Prichard Architects (MJP), 45, 186, 201
MacCormac, Sir Richard, 13, 45, 50, 53, 64
  Broadcasting House renovation, 65–66, 186, 200
Manhattanism, 164, 173
marketing. *See* branding
Martin, Reinhold, 9–10, 95, 97, 118–19, 143, 146–47, 154–55, 156, 165
Marvell, H., 24
Marx, Karl, 196
Match.com, 143, 147, 148
Maufe, Edward, 27
McCann Systems, 157
McGrath, Raymond, 27, 31, 40
McLuhan, Marshall, 8, 14
  panoramas, 88–90, 93, 95, 97, 107
McNair, Brian, 102, 103
The Mechanical Bride (McLuhan), 8
media
  as centralizing, 22, 102–4
  Chinese, 200, 201–2
  Cold War and, 94, 107
  as global village, 94, 97, 101, 107–8, 171, 200–202
  houses as, 121
  organization/production of information, 116–17, 127, 131, 144–45, 153, 155

  as panorama, 88–89, 93, 94
  print vs. TV, 89–90
  social, 201
media buildings, 200–202
  access to, 2–3, 21–22, 46–49, 73–76, 81, 83–84, 89, 90–93, 95–97, 99, 104, 106, 168–69, 177, 185–93, 197–200, 203n.4
  as billboards, 7–8, 147–49, 157–58
  as brands, 15, 62, 64, 67
  as centers, 2, 10, 21–22, 49–50, 59–60, 68, 75–76, 143, 164, 170, 183, 201–2
  as history, 5–7, 14–15, 22–23, 63–64
  as modern, 30, 157–58
  as monuments, 90–93, 129–33, 139–43, 169, 171
  in New York, 139–43, 157
  security and, 75–76
  as social media, 201
  as symbols of values, 7–8, 9–11, 14, 15, 16, 60, 140–42, 157
Media Events (Dayan and Katz), 2
media-ocracy, 102–3
Media Park (Beijing), 169, 183, 191
mediated center, myth of, 1–2, 3, 10, 75, 76
media transmission towers
  as observation platforms, 84, 85, 89–90, 93
  Russian, 85–86, 105
  as symbols of power, 102, 104–5
  as symbols of values, 86, 93
  WFGT, 106–7, 108–9
Metal Shutter Houses, 146
Metropolis magazine, 149
Metropolitan Magazine, 122
Meyrowitz, Joshua, 4
Microsoft, 128
Miluti, Joseph, 90, 93
Mitchell, William J., 5, 10
Moholy-Nagy, Lázló, 40
Monument to the Third International, 85–86, 93, 98
Moscow metro, 101
Myer, Val, 29, 48, 187
Mytton, Graham, 70

National Library of France, 174, 175
NBC building, 8

Neutra, Richard, 120
New York Times, 144, 154
New York Times building, 15, 129, 139, 140–41, 143, 157
New York Tribune building, 140, 141
New York World building, 140, 141
Nikitin, Nikolai, 88, 107
1984 (Orwell), 43
Nocera, Joe, 144
Nokia, 68
No Sense of Place (Meyrowitz), 4
Nouvel, Jean, 146
Novgorodtsev, Seva, 75

O'Dell, T., 195
Oettermann, Stephen, 84, 93, 96
Office for Metropolitan Architecture (OMA), 12, 16, 163, 165, 167–68, 173, 176, 178, 183, 186, 192, 194, 195, 200
The Organizational Complex (Martin), 9–10
organizational complexes, 84, 95, 97, 118–19
organization/production of information, 116–17, 127, 131, 144–45, 153, 155
Orwell, George, 43, 200
Ostankino Park, 90–92, 106
Ostankino TV tower/complex, 13, 14
    exterior descriptions, 81, 82, 87, 88, 90–93, 97–99, 105, 129
    future of, 106, 108–10
    hierarchy/open space, 95–96
    as historical object, 101–10
    history of, 81, 84, 86, 88, 94–95, 98, 99–105
    interior descriptions, 83–84, 87, 88, 89, 93, 95–96
    as monument, 90–93, 106–7
    as organizational complex, 84, 95, 97
    political control of media, 94–96
    privatization of, 102–3
    public access to, 81, 83–84, 89, 90–93, 95–97, 99, 104, 106, 203n.4
    restoration of, 103–9
    as symbol of power, 102, 104–5, 108–10
    as symbol of values, 84–85, 86, 88, 93–99, 107–8
    technology influences, 90–94, 98–99, 101
Ouroussoff, Nicolai, 154, 157

Our World, 94

Page, Larry, 117, 118, 132
panopticons, 96–97, 198
panoramas, 81, 84, 89, 97
    mobility and, 93, 96
    TV images as, 88–90
Park Row, 141, 157, 158
Parks, Lisa, 94
Das Passagen-Werk (Benjamin), 8, 27, 42
Pearson, Clifford, 138, 146, 151
Peters, John Durham, 20, 52
Piano, Renzo, 15, 139
Pine, J. B., 195
The Place of Media Power (Couldry), 21
place, sense of
    Broadcasting House, 26, 45, 46–47, 49–50
    Bush House, 60, 75–76
    media and, 1–2, 90
    Ostankino tower, 90
Pop Art, 167
Post, George Brown, 140
power
    centralization/decentralization of, 10, 95
    in information culture, 114–15, 116–17
power, symbols of, 102, 104–5
    Bush House, 60
    CCTV, 170, 171, 177, 190
    Ostankino tower, 102, 104–5, 108–10
Pravda building, 7–8, 85
Price, Cedric, 195
Privacy and Publicity (Colomina), 10, 29
public access
    Broadcasting House, 21–22, 46–49, 186–89, 192, 197, 199–200
    Bush House, 73–76
    CCTV, 168–69, 177, 185–86, 189–93, 197, 199–200
    Ostankino tower, 81, 83–84, 89, 90–93, 95–97, 99, 104, 106, 203n.4
public sphere vs. private sphere, 1, 3, 10, 16, 184
    access to media buildings, 2–3, 21–22, 46–49, 75–76, 81, 185–86, 197–99
    branding and, 193–96
    Broadcasting House, 13, 16, 24–25, 29, 39,

186–89, 192, 197
Bush House, 73–76
CCTV, 16, 168–69, 177, 183, 185, 189–93, 197
commodification of production, 196–99
electronic technology and, 4, 9–10, 73–74
Googleplex, 127–28
National Library of France, 174, 175
Ostankino tower, 81, 83–84, 89, 90–93, 95–97, 99, 104, 106, 203n.4
Putin, Vladimir, 14, 103–4, 105, 108
RCA building, 8

Real, Michael, 1
Reith, Sir John, 20, 22, 48
"Response to Tradition" (Coates), 25–26
Richards, J. M., 26
Robertson, Howard, 30
Rockefeller Center, 8–9, 141, 146, 158
Rose, Joseph, 145
Rosenberg, Harold, 195
Ross, A., 139, 154, 158
Rothenbuhler, Eric, 52
Roth-Ey, Kristin, 94–95
Rowe, C., 194, 199
ruins, building as, 101, 102
Russell, James, 152
Russian oligarchs, 102, 109
Russian Television and Radio Broadcasting Network (RTRN), 95, 105
Rutskoy, Aleksandr, 102

Saarinen, Eero, 9, 120
Saarinen, Eliel, 6
sacred vs. profane space, 19–24, 44, 49–50
Sandvoss, C., 75
Sassen, Saskia, 5, 195
Scheerbart, Paul, 42, 43
Scheeren, Ole, 12, 163, 183, 186
Scott Brown, D., 139, 147
Seagram Building, 143, 155
Seaton, John, 69–70
Seebrügge Sea Tunnel, 175, 176
self-organization, communication theory, 115–16
Shannon, C., 15, 115
Shukhov radio tower, 85, 86

Shukhov, Vladimir, 85
Siegelbaum, Lewis H., 86, 88
signal-to-noise ratio, communication theory, 115–16
Silicon Graphics, 113, 130
Silicon Valley, 117–19
Silver King Communications, 143
Silver, Sara, 141
Singer, Michael, 197
Skidmore, Owings & Merrill, 9
Sklyar, Gennady, 105
skyscrapers, 140, 141, 173–74, 176–77
Slutzky, R., 194, 199
social media, 201
soft control, communication theory, 115–16, 124
Soja, Edward, 166
Solid Waste Management Facility (Phoenix), 197, 198
Sony Building, 143
Soriano, Raphael, 120
space-based vs. time-based media, 11–12, 22
Space Pavilion, 90
SpaceShipOne, 130–31
Space, Time and Architecture (Giedion), 8–9
spatial media studies, 4–5, 164–65
Speaking into the Air (Peters), 20
Stalin, Joseph, 86, 101
Starrett-Leigh Building, 146
Sterne, Jonathan, 31, 37
Stewart, Jason, 148, 154
Stewart, Matthew, 73
Stiegler, Bernard, 13, 51, 53
STUDIOS architecture, 149, 155

Tatlin, Vladimir, 85, 93, 98
Taylor, Frederick W., 196
Taylor, Mark C., 152
Television Cultural Center (TVCC), 169, 191
Terranova, Tiziana, 115, 116, 124
Thompson, Mark, 22
Tien'an Men Square, 170
time-binding media, 11–12, 22
Times Square, 8, 129, 152
Time Warner Center, 139, 141, 143
tradition vs. modernity, 41–43
Broadcasting House, 22–23, 26–29, 47–48

Lawn Road Flats, 39–41
tradition vs. technology, 3–5
    Broadcasting House, 26–27, 29–37, 50–54
    Lawn Road Flats, 39–41
Transparent Factory (Dresden), 197
transparent public spaces. *See* public access
Tusa, John, 62

Urban, Joseph, 141

van der Rohe, Mies, 143
Vanity Fair, 142
Venturi, Robert, 139, 147, 167
Vesnin, Leonid, Victor, and Alexander, 7–8, 85
viewing platforms, 81, 84, 89, 97
    mobility and, 93, 96
    TV images as, 88–90
Villa Garches, 199
Vilnius TV tower, 105
Volkswagen factory (Dresden), 197
von Furstenberg, Diane, 146

Waits, Tom, 24
Walker, A., 60
Wallace, Aurora, 140–41, 142
Wall Street Journal, 145, 152
Walt Disney Concert Hall, 149
Warren, Dorothy, 27
Washington Post, 145
Weaver, W., 15, 115
Welch, Mary, 59
Wellesley, Lord Gerald, 27
Whiteread, Rachel, 43–44
Whiting, Sara, 192
Wiener, Norbert, 15, 97, 115, 118, 119, 124
Wigley, Mark, 165
Wilkinson, Clive, 113, 121–22, 123, 124, 130
Williams, Raymond, 42
wish images, buildings as, 101, 102
Wolff, Michael, 142
Woman's Hour, 49, 51
Woolworth Building, 143
"The Work of Art in the Age of Mechanical Reproduction" (Benjamin), 23, 37, 42, 53–54, 194
World Federation of Great Towers (WFGT), 106–7, 108–9

World Trade Organization (WTO), 200

Yahoo, 128
Yeltsin, Boris, 14, 102–3, 109

Žižek, Slavoj, 16

www.ingramcontent.com/pod-product-compliance
Ingram Content Group UK Ltd.
Pitfield, Milton Keynes, MK11 3LW, UK
UKHW022122230426
12048UKWH00011BA/659